Plato Etc.

V

Plato Etc.

The Problems of Philosophy and Their Resolution

ROY BHASKAR

VERSO

London · New York

First published by Verso 1994
© Roy Bhaskar 1994
All rights reserved

Verso

UK: 6 Meard Street, London W1V 3HR
USA: 29 West 35th Street, New York, NY 10001-2291

Verso is the imprint of New Left Books

ISBN 0-86091-499-2
ISBN 0-86091-649-9 (pbk)

British Library Cataloguing in Publication Data
A catalogue record for this book is available from the British Library

Library of Congress Cataloging-in-Publication Data
Bhaskar, Roy, 1944–
Plato etc. : the problems of philosophy and their resolution /
Roy Bhaskar.
p.   cm.
Includes bibliographical references and index.
ISBN 0-86091-499-2 : £34.95 ($59.95). — ISBN 0-86091-649-9 (pbk.)
£13.95 ($18.95)
1. Philosophy.   2. Critical realism.   I. Title.   II. Title: Plato etc.
B5134.B483P57   1994
100 — dc20
94-21159
CIP

Typeset by MHL Typesetting Ltd, Coventry
Printed and bound in Great Britain by
Biddles Ltd, Guildford and King's Lynn

TO
MICHAEL AND CAROL
THOMAS AND OLIVER
JESSIE, ANNIE AND ROSIE

Contents

Come in, be bold: there are gods here too.

ATTRIBUTED TO HERACLITUS, *c.* 490 BC

Dorothy, Blanche, Rose and Sophia are all present.

ROSE: . . . Did I ever tell you the story about Herde
          Shornbohrst? . . . Well most of you remember he was
          St Olaf's most famous shepherd. Well, Herde used to
          say, you can have a hundred sheep and if one goes
          astray, that's the one you go look for. Especially if it's
          the best-looking one.   [*Rose exits*

DOROTHY: Rose has got to find some new role models.

The Golden Girls, 'Comedy of Errors', 1991
Touchstone Pictures and Television

Preface

Whitehead famously remarked that (western) philosophy was a series of footnotes on Plato. This book is a commentary on and critique of those footnotes. His illustrious collaborator on *Principia Mathematica* (1910–13), Bertrand Russell, wrote a famous book called *The Problems of Philosophy*. This seemed to crystallize the idea that the problems of philosophy were unresolvable. Worse was the growing assumption that philosophy merely produced, in Bradley's words apropos of metaphysics, bad reasons for what we believe on instinct. This book is an attempt to explain why philosophy is on the wrong track, and how it got there; why irrealism is dominant, or, to put it another way, why philosophy is (increasingly) out of kilter with reality, or incapable of saying much credible on human (and environmental) problems; why it finds it so difficult to accommodate to the facts of epistemic relativity without giving up on judgemental rationality; why it at once so often falls foul of the authorities, yet is repeatedly accused by radicals (including myself) of being an accomplice of the powers that be; why its history is, despite itself, worth studying (if only because, as Freud claimed, we repeat what we cannot recollect); of how its problems can, contrary to received opinion, both be rationally resolved and offer diagnostic clues to the nature of social, political, economic, cultural, ethical and scientific reality or realities — realities which are both intrinsically geo-historical (rhythmically tensed) and the site of power struggles; and why philosophy falls prey to paradox (meaning literally 'beyond belief') and becomes complicit with categorial error — of which paradox is merely a surface form.

Today, philosophy, for the most part, only reflects the superficial sheen of reality (there is no depth), normalizes the status quo ante (there was history, but, like ideology, it is no more), sequesters existential questions and legitimates the spread of more of the shallow same, treats relations as external and contingent (dis-connecting, as it screens, contradictions and conflicts), and per-petuates the combination of a physicalistic reductionism and dualistic disembodiment (reification and voluntarism). At the same time there is a profound dualism between discourse and agency; emotivism appears as an ideology for masters, personalism as one for slaves and decisionism as one for the masters of slaves who are themselves slaves of masters; the ideologies of alienation, commodification, reification and fetishism reign supreme in a world characterized by gross and growing inequalities between peoples intra- and internationally.

This book is no quick or easy fix. It is a tour through the history of philosophy, the theory of knowledge and philosophy of science, the philosophy of logic and language, of space, time and causality, of society, ethics, politics and aesthetics, through dialectic and the sociology and philosophy of philosophy, to the position which I have recently articulated as 'dialectical critical realism'. The fact that I maintain there is such a thing as philosophical truth is sometimes held against me. But it is not sufficient for the objectors to express a difference in opinion. It is encumbent upon them to show where my arguments are unsound. Another point often advanced against me is that I employ neologisms. But a new abstract terminology, with a multiplicity of points of entry into it, is often a prerequisite for intellectual progress. Pre-Socratic philosophy and late scholastic science are two examples of what can happen in its absence.

Plato Etc. (originally entitled 'Philosophy and the Dialectic of Emancipation') is the second member of the quartet constituted by *Dialectic; Plato Etc.; Hume, Kant, Hegel, Marx*; and *Dialectical Social Theory*. The net project of *Dialectic* and *Plato Etc.* is to attempt an anti-Parmenidean revolution, reversing 2500 years of philosophical thought, in which negativity (absence and change), ontology, structure, diversity and agency come to the fore. The Appendix forms a bridge to *Philosophical Ideologies*, to be published by Harvester Wheatsheaf in 1995 in conjunction with revised third editions of *A Realist Theory of Science* and *The Possibility of Naturalism*; and the last two chapters prefigure a much longer *Critical History of Western Philosophy*.

It is time to express my debts. First, to the growing worldwide interdisciplinary network of critical realists and those interested in it for criticism, stimulation and encouragement. A valuable point of convergence here has been the Annual Conferences on Realism and the Human Sciences and a special thanks must go to the organizers of those conferences over the years. Next I must thank Colin Robinson and the team he orchestrates so well at Verso for their efficiency and friendliness and the prompt and smooth publication of this book. Then I must once more express my profound gratitude to Sue Kelly for secretarial assistance of immeasurable value. Also to Cyril Ducker, Victoria Jaye and Liz Long for excellent work of cognate character. I am again indebted to Justin Dyer for the quality of his copy-editing. Next, I owe an immense debt of gratitude to Linacre College, Oxford, and the City University, London. Finally, I must record my appreciation of the support of many friends, from whom I can only specifically mention here Bill Bowring, Andrew Collier, Julie Jeffery, Rajani Kanth, Androulla Karaviotis, Judit Kiss, Mariann Kiss, Tony Lawson, John Lovering, Jo MacNeill, William Outhwaite, Kate Soper, Linda Thornhill and, above all, Hilary Wainwright.

ROY BHASKAR
January 1994

=1=

Is Philosophy Worth It?

The safest general characterization of the European philosophical tradition is that it consists in a series of footnotes to Plato

WHITEHEAD (1929)

§ 1 The Life-and-Death Struggle

Western philosophy did not begin with Plato. Moreover, in the ancient Greek world there were probably thinkers of equal philosophical genius — the dialectician Heraclitus, the mathematician Pythagoras, the atomist Democritus and the stoic Chrysippus. But we know them only in fragments and by second hand; whereas Plato's dialogues have come down to us intact, as have the most important works of those of his prodigious pupil and critic, Aristotle, thanks, in the latter's case, to their preservation in the Islamic world. Together they initiated a recognizable practice — of philosophy.

In this chapter I want to explain why philosophy matters. In due course I shall come on to Socrates, Plato's teacher, and Plato. But I start with a much more recent figure, Hegel. For Hegel, like Socrates, philosophy was literally a matter of life and death. He wrote about it as such in probably his greatest work, *The Phenomenology of Mind*, completed on the eve of Napoleon's victory in the battle of Jena (1806). We shall see how, at the very least, his chapter on 'Self-Consciousness' casts light on contemporaneously existing attitudes to discursively moralized power relations in society.

There are three decisive influences underpinning the story unfolded in Hegel's chapter. The first was the sundered world at the dawn of modernity. Hegel's generation yearned for the restoration of a Greek-like, as they imagined, expressive unity, but one which, especially in the context of German socio-economic-political back-wardness, would not sacrifice what they took to be the gains of the Enlightenment, especially differentiation and freedom. 'Have courage to use your own reason', Kant had enjoined. But Kant's own philosophy was dichotomous in the extreme: subject was opposed to

1

object, form to content, duty to desire, theory to reason. Hegel's main philosophical motive in the *Phenomenology* was to overcome these oppositions, and in particular in the chapter on 'Self-Consciousness' to show how sentient socialized self-awareness seeks to remove the external character of the world. It first attempts to do this alone by grasping it in desire, but in so doing it remains dependent on it. It then seeks its satisfaction in another self-consciousness, and this takes me to the third formative influence on the chapter. For years in the 1790s, ruminating on Christianity, Hegel had experienced a self-diagnosed 'hypochondria', recapitulating the fate of Jesus in his early unpublished writings, alienated from his peers and the community in which he lived, suffering the fate of the 'Beautiful Soul'. In the *Phenomenology* Hegel was out to overcome this. It broke with all philosophical conventions (his more famous friend Schelling was not even mentioned by name), yet claimed in the end to attain absolute truth. This was Hegel's own life-and-death struggle. And throughout his career he seems to have felt that risking one's life was a necessary condition for attaining true self-consciousness, and hence humanity.

The two self-consciousnesses want at once recognition from and negation of the other. They fight, but the winner cannot achieve recognition from a corpse and so enslaves rather than kills the loser. The master, it seems, has freedom and recognition; while the slave experiences only work and discipline. But the slave, by objectifying, recognizes himself in the object of his labour and so actually succeeds better than the idle master in removing the externality of the world. We now pass to a series of attitudes to reality, which can be extended to include the persistence of the master—slave relationship or any structure or relation of domination, exploitation, subjugation or control such as between men and women, classes, nations or individuals. I shall call these *generalized master-slave-type relations*, power$_2$ relations — with the subscript differentiating it from power in the sense of the transformative capacity inherent in action as such (power$_1$). The first attitude Hegel considers is that of the *Stoic*, who purports to be indifferent to the reality of the world. Marcus Aurelius, the emperor, and his slave, Epictetus, are on a par. But although the Stoic is engaged in pure thought (*Denken*), he remains dependent for the contents of the conceptualized forms he produces on the outside world; that is to say, he remains heteronomous rather than autonomous. What the Stoic would ignore, the *Sceptic* attempts to deny. Yet however much the Sceptic denies the reality of the world in theory, this is not his stance in practice. He leaves the seminar room by the door, not by the second-floor window. Hegel now makes explicit the *theory/practice inconsistency* implicit in scepticism in the figure of the 'Unhappy Consciousness', who seeks refuge in other-worldly asceticism or solace in the projective duplication of another world, an after-life or beyond (*Jenseits*) where, for instance, happiness will be in accord with virtue (as Kant had believed).

A feminist might question much in the chapter's topography. Why should we assume that agonistic struggle rather than mutual trust or nurturing care is our basic existential or mode of being in the world? And is not the last, in the context of the *primary polyadization* involved in childcare and the individuation of a self, a necessary condition of the first? Hegel gives no explanation for the appearance of the second self-consciousness. And the idea that we are social and mutually inter-dependent *ab initio* chimes in with the critique of the mono-logicality, or tacit individualism, of the post-Cartesian philosophy of consciousness essayed by the contemporary writer Jürgen Habermas.[1] Yet, even granting these objections, it is not difficult to find the attitudes Hegel describes as of continuing relevance. The Stoic affects in-difference to the reality of the difference intrinsic to the power$_2$ relation in which she is held. The Sceptic even denies that it exists. The Unhappy Consciousness either (a) accepts the master's ideology and/or (b) compensates in a fantasy world of, for example, sport, soap or nostalgia.

Can we continue this updated version of Hegel's chapter? What of the agent's attitude to herself? On the first line, it is but a short hop (a) to treating herself as a mere thing — reification; on the second (b), to effectively disembodying herself or her attitudes, regarding them as pure spirit. This — or something like it — is in fact what happens, according to Karl Marx, under capitalism, commodification and fetishism (indissolubly linked) respectively. But it also portends the most common attitudes to the 'mind–body' problem (to be discussed in Chapter 5) — physicalistic reductionism and dualistic disembodi-ment. This connects to the question of whether we are machines driven by causes or creatures acting on reasons. And that relates to the issue that dominated the reflections of Hegel's predecessor, Kant. How could Kant accept, as his intelligence impelled him to, Newton's seemingly deterministic conclusions and remain sincerely committed to Pietist morality on which, as he put it, 'every being that cannot act otherwise than under the Idea of freedom, is therefore from a practical point of view, really free'. The conundrum of free-will and determinism.

Kant's solution, first published in *The Critique of Pure Reason* (1781), was to accept both; but to locate them in different worlds. Determinism reigns in the world as apprehended by sense-experience and categorized by the intellect, the 'phenomenal' world described by physical laws; free-will (*Willkür*) is sovereign in the 'noumenal' realm under which we must act. This solution has been immensely influential. In the twentieth century, the physicist Pierre Duhem, the linguistic philosopher F. Waisemann and the contemporary pragmatist Richard Rorty are all committed to forms of it (although nowadays it is more heavily mediated by an emphasis on the language frames in, or aspects — e.g. third and first person respectively — from, which we must view things). Moreover, it continues to underpin, albeit in more or less diffracted forms, the opposition between the leading tendencies in the social sciences — positivistic hypernaturalism (especially of a reductionist bent) and anti-naturalistic hyper-hermeneutics or discourse theory. It has, however, one enormous defect: it makes embodied intentional causal agency impossible. Noumenally, however free we conceive ourselves to be, we are in fact unable (as far as we can know) to affect the course of events that would otherwise have prevailed. And with this, morality and the attribution of responsibility, scientific experimentation (which entails interference and control) and day-to-day life alike become impossible . . . . The shipwreck of a theory.

But was Kant right to believe that Newtonian physics implied determinism? The form of determinism he accepted was the regularity determinism implicit in David Hume's (1711–76) theory of causal laws. (It was Hume who, Kant averred, had awoken him from his 'dogmatic slumbers'.) Hume had denied the necessity we impute to causal laws was anything other than a projection of mind, the legacy of constant conjunctions of perceptions, accumulated in our experience. This left a gaping problem: the problem of induction. For no number of conjunctions could gainsay the supposition that apples *might* start rising like balloons rather than fall to the earth. So long as the grounds for a universal principle are restricted to its instances, a sceptic can always deny it. It is also worth pointing out that the problem of induction that Hume himself isolated, and to which, in sceptical frame of mind, he saw no remedy but 'carelessness and inattention', opens the door to belief in the existence of miracles, and thence to the dogmas of religion, that it was one of the express intentions of his *A Treatise of Human Nature* to shut.

Now Kant had thought that if he could establish the principle that every cause must have an effect, inductive scepticism could be ruled out. But the trouble with this is that for any description of a finite system there are in general an infinite number of descriptions consistent with it. (Compare the fate of the turkey who has been fed for 364 days . . . .) Aristotle's (384–322 BC) theory of knowledge also relied crucially on induction. But in his case the missing element that converted an empirical regularity into something universal-and-necessarily-certain was furnished by *nous* or intellectual intuition rather than 'synthetic a priori' principles of mind. For Plato (427–347 BC) defining 'knowledge' as of 'what is' had distinguished it (*epistēmē*) firmly from mere belief (*doxa*). Knowledge had to be of what was universal and necessary. And he had brought out this distinction most vividly in his contrast between an unchanging world of Forms or Ideas, aligned under the Form of the Good, and the transient sensate material world of flux. Why, Plato had asked, 'is a man a man?' Because he participates in the form or, one feels like saying for him, essence of man. But why, Aristotle had charged, 'is the Form of man a man (albeit an ideal one)?' Surely, on Plato's theory, only because it participated in a Form of the Form — in effect, a *Third Man* with which we are mired into a vicious regress, as the later Plato himself appreciated.

For the prima facie more materialistically inclined Aristotle ('if the eye were an animal, then sight would be its soul', he had declared) the Forms were a myth. Knowledge was of this world, which was admittedly ultimately sustained by the self-thinking thought of God. And it was attained largely by induction supplemented by *nous* or intellectual intuition. Together they led to knowledge conforming to the rationalist credentials laid down by Plato and subject to the deductive syllogistic reasoning brilliantly codified by Aristotle in his logic. But what exactly was intellectual intuition? A modern interpretation might hold it to be something like a Popperian 'conjecture'.[2] However, for Aristotle, it involved a procedure whereby an identity was achieved between the essence actualized in the object of knowledge and that actualized in the mind of the knower, which acted as matter to the form impressed. Having established explanatory principles, the necessity of particular matters of fact could then be demonstrated by deduction in a valid syllogism; and the upshot of any process of knowledge was a form expressing the essence of a thing susceptible to non-equivocal statement in a real definition (the genesis of the science of taxonomy). But without the concept of the *multi-tiered stratification of being*, or ontological depth, which would have supplied Hume's ground for necessary connection, it was clear neither how Aristotelian essences differed from Platonic Forms nor how they evaded Humean inductive scepticism. Rational justification was lacking in both vertical and horizontal directions. What was required were grounds for the universal *distinct* from the universal concerned and *other* than its instances. Philosophy was thus stuck — on what I am going to characterize as the *Platonic/Aristotelian fault-line*.

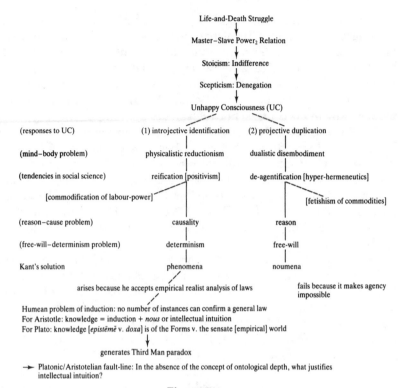

Figure 1.1

We have come a long way since the Life-and-Death Struggle, so let me illustrate the connections in Figure 1.1. Note that Kant's dichotomous solution of the problem of free-will and determinism (in the third antinomy) only arises because he accepts Hume's *empirical realist* analysis of laws, viz. as constant conjunctions of events — where empirical realism is the doctrine that the world is constituted by the objects of actual (and, sometimes, possible) experiences. The impasse in which the retrospective story I have been sketching ends — or begins — can be seen, from the *critical realist* standpoint from which this book is written, as that of 'what justifies the attribution of necessity and universality, when they are, to law-like statements in science?' We will return to these characters and problems anon, including the flaws and shortfalls of Hegel's resolution of the dialectic of self-consciousness. (It is just worth remarking that Hegel's transition into self-consciousness from consciousness is as empirical realist as they come.) But now we must focus on Plato and Aristotle, as founding definers of our contingent, inherited philosophical tradition.

§ 2 The Problematicity of Philosophy

Plato's career passed through three distinct phases. In the first Socratic period, the hero of which was normally Socrates (whom we only know through Plato's writings), Plato's concern was — through dialogue — the search for the real definitions or truth of things and qualities like courage, goodness, etc. These investigations almost always ended in failure; but they allow us to pinpoint two enduring features of the philosophical tradition:

(α) its concern with giving a *rational* account or *logos* of the nature of things, as opposed to one accepted, say, purely on the basis of authority (Hegelian 'positivity') or faith or force or caprice or tradition or convention;

(β) its concern with the *perplexity* of phenomena, with paradox and the *problematicity* of being.

Let us take a simple example from Plato's early period, Meno's paradox, which seems to show the impossibility of knowledge: 'a man cannot inquire either about that which he knows, or about that he does not know: for assuming he knows he has no need to inquire; nor can he inquire about that which he does not know, for he does not know about that which he has to inquire.' What this paradox highlights is (a) that an inquiry never starts from scratch, it always has presuppositions, mostly pre-existing beliefs or knowledge — we are always, to use the Heideggerian term, *'thrown'* into a context of beliefs; but (b) that equally it never arbitrarily halts, it always potentially leads to a further inquiry — thus suppose we have discovered the causes of x, we can always consider the causes of those causes. Knowledge-acquisition, to use my (not Plato's) terms, is a *pre-existing ongoing social* affair. To Plato, by contrast, such paradoxes suggested *anamnēsis* or recollection of knowledge acquired in a previous life (a viciously circular argument — for how was such knowledge thus established?), indicating the immortality of the soul.

In his middle period, Plato comes out with a positive theory of his own, the two-worlds theory that we have already witnessed. It is worth going into why this theory breaks down in a little more detail. Plato tries to explain an instance of blueness in terms of its participation in the Form 'blue' and this leads him into a vicious regress. More to the point, it does not take us very far. A modern scientist would explain a blue hue in terms of its reflecting light or wavelength of 4400Å units, exemplifying *ontological depth* and introducing us to a new circle of concepts not initially implicit in that of the quality or idea blue. The theory of the forms breaks down because it lacks progressive import.

Plato himself in his third period realized this and initiated the practice of the close analysis of fundamental activities like predication and negation. The great Eleatic monist Parmenides had said (paradoxically) that we could not speak of that which is not. But clearly we must be able to reject propositions in science. Very roughly, Plato's analysis is that if you say 'x is y' and I say 'x is not y', then I am saying x is other than or *different* from y. But there is a problem in Plato's explanation. What happens if the same substance, x, becomes or ceases to be y while remaining in every other particular, or in its essential attributes, x? If I say 'Sophie was dying her hair at time t_j', am I not referring to a *process* of substantial change which cannot be captured by the formal difference between the statement that her hair was grey at t_i and is now brown at t_k? And is not every statement an *act* which changes the world in some way? These difficulties, though Aristotle did not question the Platonic analysis of negation and change in terms of difference, exemplify the *aporetic* method of Aristotle. Aristotle was a superb logician and a stupendous biologist, as well as being one of the three or four greatest philosophers. What is the aporetic method? Aristotle's typical philosophical approach was to start from common or received opinions (*endoxa*), work through the *aporiai* or puzzles they generated, to a settled or balanced or consensual account of the topic or subject matter concerned. This was Aristotelian dialectic. 'Let us first go through the views others hold; for the proofs of one theory are difficulties for the contrary theory. Besides, those who have first heard the arguments on the other side will be more likely to have confidence in what we are going to say. We shall be less open to the charge of trying to win our case by default.'[3] What Aristotle is recommending here is something very close to the method of *immanent critique*. If you assert x on grounds a and I assert the contrary y on grounds b, where b do not constitute a refutation of a, and perhaps even have no possible bearing on a, then we are making no progress. Immanent critique is indeed *the* characteristic method of criticism and advance in all spheres of life; and it may be generalized to include theory/practice inconsistency (cf. Hegel's portrayal of the practice of the Sceptic) and practice/practice inconsistencies in virtue of the belief-expressive or quasi-propositional, conceptualized, character of practice.

When it came to substantive science, Aristotle's procedure was to supplement induction with intellectual intuition to form the starting-points or *archai* of the deductive reasoning he expounded in his *Prior Analytics*. His philosophy of science is expounded in his *Posterior Analytics*. We reason *inductively* to general laws and then we *deduce* their lower-order consequents, less general laws or particular facts. This was the essence of the accepted account of science until the 1970s! It is the backbone of what one commentator has aptly called the 'arch of knowledge' tradition.[4] We will consider *its* aporiai in the next chapter. For the moment I want to stick with what we are now in a position to say about philosophy.

First, it is a disciplinary matrix with a lineage that can be traced back to Socrates, Plato and Aristotle. Second, it is constitutively dialogical. Third, it is inherently aporetic. Fourth, it is ideally, or at least has been, characterized by an orientation to rationality (as distinct from authority or tradition). It is a requirement intrinsic to rationality that it be accountable, and so self-reflexive. Fifth, it is typically concerned with the explication of what are held to be the most fundamental principles or categories in being generally, some particular domain of being or a form of social life.

Let us focus on the third feature: its *problematicity*. When do problems arise? Typically, when we are *stuck*; when we do not know how to go on. Problems *matter*; when we need to go on — when we are faced with the imperative to act (the *'axiological imperative'*). Problems pose *dilemmas*. But, as we have seen in the case of Meno's paradox, dilemmas have *presuppositions*. Now it is characteristic of twentieth-century philosophy to regard its problems as *unresolvable*. For instance, Bertrand Russell said in 1923: 'if you are willing to believe that nothing exists except what you directly experience, no other person can prove you wrong, and probably no valid arguments against your view exist.'[5] Unlike Russell, I believe, as the subtitle of the book indicates, that the problems of philosophy are (rationally) resolvable. I see the problems of philosophy as supervenient on life, mediated in particular by science and more broadly society. For conventional philosophers, on the other hand, the problems of philosophy are sui generis and compartmentalized within their disciplinary matrix.

In these disciplinary matrices a figure called the *'sceptic'* plays a seminal role. The sceptic will question some supposition, well grounded or not. In the latter case the sceptic may ask what reason we have for supposing that water will not freeze rather than boil when it is heated from tomorrow ('Goodman's paradox'). The rational response to scepticism here is to say that anything that froze when it was heated would not be water, because we know that the electronic configuration of water is such that it must tend to boil when it is heated. This response redescribes the sceptic's presuppositions, which include the presumption that we are restricted in our knowledge of boiling water to the observation of instances of it. Instead, it invokes a deeper level of structure as the grounds for our rationally justifiable knowledge. It redescribes the sceptic's problem-field, and in so doing it redescribes the sceptic's theoretical presupposition, that causal laws are empirical regularities or constant conjunctions of events. Scepticism, then, presupposes a *theory problem-field*, and, because I am arguing in this chapter that philosophy makes a difference to life, a '*theory problem-field solution set*' (TPF(SS)).

A cynic might say that it is not surprising that philosophy — the love of wisdom — should be out of joint with reality considering the world we live in (of irrationality and injustice). But what happens when a false philosophical theory is applied? To sustain itself, 'There Is No Alternative' to invoking some supporting defensive mechanism or compromise in what I am going to call a 'Tina formation' (acronymously). In particular, false philosophical theories will constitute internally inconsistent ensembles in a schema representable as:

$$[S] \rightarrow [T_I \ldots T_N] \rightarrow [TF],$$

where 'S' stands for scepticism and 'TF' for 'Tina formation'. This chimes in with the fact that philosophy, as inherently dialogical, will not just have one, but a competing range of theories; that its *constitutive antagonisms*, empiricism v. rationalism, materialism v. idealism, etc. keep it going. If philosophical problems are such because they are about or embody puzzles about the most basic categories of being and doing, they will tend to be mediated by *substantive analogies*, which they in turn will inform. As such, philosophical problems may be, or comprise *diagnostic clues* to, real extra-philosophical problems. Moreover, we must not fall into the trap of thinking that, because academic scepticism tends to be '*unserious*', scepticism as such is always misplaced. As the propaedeutic to immanent critique, scepticism is essential to progress. Hence the *Janus-faced* character of philosophy, fluctuating between reason and rationalization, enlightenment and mystification, present and past. But I shall be arguing that within this duality, (especially but not only) contemporary philosophy is temporarily lapsed, lagged on to antiquated analogies and regressively nostalgic.

It is time to be a little bit more systematic about problems. *Axiological indeterminacy* is a consequence of being in a problematic situation. How does one set about resolving a problem? One can toss a coin, decide on whim or wishful thinking, or ignore it, but these hardly count as rational procedures. An obvious response is to seek to acquire, within the time and resources at one's disposal, more information about the matter to hand. This can be conceived as one of the ways of *redescribing the alternatives, de-problematizing the situation*. Consider, for instance, Zeno's paradoxes of motion, purporting to show that because at any moment of time a thing in motion can only be at one place, motion is impossible. This presupposes a punctualist view of time and an aggregative view of transitions. A scientific account of motion *begins* with the phenomenon of change. Or consider the problem of free-will and determinism, which will be dealt with in greater depth later. I have already argued that Kant's solution to it is necessitated by his acceptance (in the Second Analogy) of an empirical realist account of causal laws. At the heart of the problem is the reduction of the necessary and the possible to the actual. But if entities such as people are endowed with structures and the possible is regarded as constitutive of the real, then it makes perfect sense to say all of the following:

1. that A, possessing more causal powers than B, and subject to the same constraints on a class of acts (ϕ), is freer to do what she chooses than B;
2. that A, in virtue of her intrinsic structure, can choose what to do under the prevailing circumstances; and
3. that her choice of time t_k could not have been predicted before she decided at time t_j, let alone from some set of antecedent conditions at time t_i; that is, before she caused what she actually did, ϕ_w.

This is an example of a philosophical problem based on (inter alia) the false assumption of *actualism*, viz. that the real is constituted by the actual, to which I will return in Chapter 2. The methodological point to stress here is that *problems possess presuppositions*.

In this book I am going to use a four-dimensional analysis for classifying and resolving the problems of philosophy, which I have deployed elsewhere.[6] The key critical category at 1M (first moment) is non-identity, at 2E (second edge) negativity, at 3L (third level) totality and at 4D (fourth dimension) agency. 1M problems typically turn on

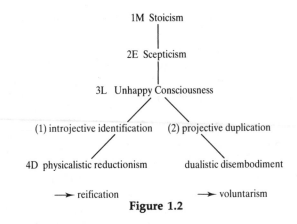

Figure 1.2

homology or infinite regress and are resolved by reference to concepts such as stratification and levels. Examples have already been given in the case of the Third Man and Goodman's paradoxes. 2E problems characteristically pivot on positivity or opposition and are repaired by resort to negative or mediating concepts. 3L problems involve detotalization of some kind and are repaired by an appropriate retotalization. 4D problems pertain to agency and in one form in which we have already examined them we have seen them to involve the quite false dichotomy of reification or disembodiment. Let us apply this taxonomy to the attitudes to power₂ relationships that we gleaned from Hegel's chapter on 'Self-Consciousness'. The Stoic purports indifference to non-identity (the master−slave relationship may be regarded as the very paradigm of non-identity); the Sceptic denies reality (the theory/practice inconsistency or performative contradiction involved pinpoints an absence in the theory of the Sceptic's practice); the Unhappy Consciousness is split, passing over to one and/or both of two species of de-agentification (in either case effecting a detotalization of or alienation from herself), as illustrated in Figure 1.2. In virtue of the activity-dependence of society to be explored in Chapter 5, we might add a fifth component (5C) to this typology, pinpointing the opposed errors of reification and voluntarism in respect of social structure, individualism and collectivism in respect of society, and over- and under-naturalization in respect of social science, the first of each pair of which is tendentially encouraged by reification at 4D and the second by disembodiment. At this juncture it is worth pointing out that opposed category mistakes, especially when they derive from a common ground (such as at 4D the lack of a concept of embodied intentional causal agency), are very often mutually reinforcing. Thus it is characteristic of philosophers who hold a reificatory reductionist materialism in the 'extrinsic aspect' of causality to dualistically disembody themselves in the 'intrinsic aspect' of their own intentional agency, e.g. speech action.[†]

We have discussed the aporetic character of philosophy in this section, but now, before we commence our systematic investigations, I want further to stress why philosophy matters and show how certain philosophical positions undermine or 'deconstruct' themselves (a particular form of immanent critique).

§ 3 Further Illustrations

No scientific theory, tradition or research programme of any scope or explanatory power has ever been free of anomalies. According to the rules of deductive logic, they should all have been falsified. But this is not what happens in practice. In reality, scientists circulate in and out of the spheres of formal reasoning, in a dialectic of non-analytical (dialectical) and analytical reasoning. Thomas Kuhn, Imre Lakatos and Paul Feyerabend are among the relatively recent writers who have brought out that the canons of deductive logic do not play the role that tradition, whether in its orthodox inductivist or heterodox fallibilist forms, has pre-ordained for it. Whence arises the idea of the yielding omnipotent jurisdiction of logic? Let us listen to Ludwig Wittgenstein, one of the greatest twentieth-century philosophers:

> We have the idea of a super-mechanism when we talk of logical necessity, e.g. physics tried as an ideal to reduce things to mechanisms or something hitting something else. We say that people condemn a man to death and then we say that the Law condemns him to death. 'Although the Jury can pardon him, the Law can't' ... the idea of something super-strict, something stricter than any Judge can be, super-rigidity ... cf. a lever-fulcrum, the idea of a super-hardness. 'The geometrical lever is harder than any lever can be. It can't bend.' Here you have a case of logical necessity. 'Logic is a mechanism made of infinitely hard material. Logic can't bend' ... This is the way we arrive at a super-something.[9]

Let us return to Plato's distinction between *epistēmē* and *doxa*. We *know* that metals conduct electricity in the sense that we can provide a scientific explanation for it, in virtue of their possession of free

---

[†]   Thus the contemporary philosopher Richard Rorty combines in *Philosophy and the Mirror of Nature*[7] advocacy of both a reductionist materialism and free conversation or 'hermeneutics' as a dissolution of philosophical problems.[8]

electrons; whereas, at the very best, we only have *belief* as to whether astrology is true[†] — we do not understand the generative mechanisms at work whereby celestial position could affect human traits at birth. In the *Republic* Plato illustrates the distinction between the different cognitive realms by a number of superb analogies. Start with a line AB and divide it unequally at C. Then divide AC and CB in the same ratio at D and E respectively, as in Figure 1.3, so that BC:CA = BE:EC = CD:DA. BC stands for the world of sense and CA for the realm of forms. BE designates copies or reflections of material objects EC. CD stands for mathematics as a bridge to the realm of Forms.

This example also illustrates something about the role of analogies. If knowledge were an axiom system, or, contra Plato, a stable hierarchy of forms, it couldn't grow. But we know that it does. And it grows by the constant exploitation of the past and the outside: analogies (the wave theories of light and sound), metaphors (force, contradiction), metonymies, in which the part stands in for the whole. Indeed Nietzsche (1844–1900) went so far as to characterize truth as 'a mobile army of metaphors'. (He would have done better to say that its discovery *depends* upon such an army.) This he regarded as a 'truth' (sic) one had to *forget* to cope with life, amongst the conditions for which were 'errors'. Now I can know this, or my reformulation of it, as a philosophical truth at one level and at the same time discuss scientific, ethical or ordinary truths at another, lower-order level. Paradoxically, Nietzsche was being too literal about truth, accepting the classical metaphysical concept of it as fixed and unchangeable, and coupling this with a depthless account of the real multi-tiered stratification of the human personality and human thought. Moreover, underlying this was the actualist ontology, on which I have already cast critical aspersions. We do not have to forget the truth about truth in order to hammer a nail, any more than we have to forget the fact that we are mortals and will die.

Jacques Derrida is one of the most famous living philosophers. In *Of Grammatology* (1967) he shows how Rousseau's *writing* on writing and speech, in which he constantly prioritizes speech, deconstructs or

A _____ D _____ C _____ E ___ B

Figure 1.3

[†] Because, for instance, of the contra-evidence provided by the different trajectories of persons born at the same place and time.

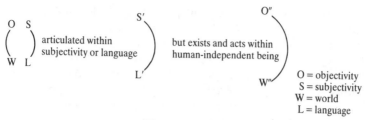

$$O\ S$$
$$\left(\quad\right)$$ articulated within
$$W\ L$$ subjectivity or language

$$S'$$

$$L'$$

but exists and acts within
human-independent being

$$O''$$

$$W''$$

O = objectivity
S = subjectivity
W = world
L = language

Figure 1.4

subverts itself. In effect Rousseau is guilty of theory/practice inconsistency or *performative contradiction*. But Derrida himself then notoriously declares 'there is nothing outside the text'. At first blush, this seems monstrous and performatively contradictory. After all, his text is materially inscribed and causally conditioned writing (in the media of pen, computer or microcassette), replicated, published and discussed by jet-flying, video-watching, hamburger-eating, defecating human beings. One might treat Derrida's assertion as an injunction to understand reality as if one were reading a text, in the way one reads the time off the clock; or as drawing attention to the thorough-going linguistic permeation of our mediations with reality; or as declaring that in cognitive or other human activities the duality of world and language can only be articulated in language.

One might also relate it to what Martin Heidegger, like Wittgenstein, one of the great twentieth-century philosophers, wrote in *Being and Time* (1927), namely that the 'scandal of philosophy' was not that proofs as to the reality of the ('external') world had yet to be accepted but that '*such proofs were expected and attempted again and again*'.[10] Being, for Heidegger, was always mediated by human being (*Dasein*). But adopt for a moment a stance of *detachment*. We know that our world came into existence long before human beings and that it, or the cosmos, which is after all being, will survive our species, human being. Moreover, we know — it is a condition of the possibility of science — that the laws of nature, to which, for instance, footballs are subject, exist and operate quite independently of our activities; just as we cannot alter the speed of light or the specific gravity of alcohol. The duality of world and language is situated within an over-reaching material objectivity, as Figure 1.4 attempts to represent. Of course I am *writing* this, but in this book I am going to show that the world is more and other than this totality of discursively articulated facts; and that philosophy must address, with existential urgency, the conditions or possibility of that totality too.

Quine, Davidson, Putnam and Rorty are all leading contemporary philosophers who would sympathize with Heidegger's diagnosis of the scandal. They would accept, of course, that there is a causally efficacious world 'out there' but deny that it is possible to say anything useful about it philosophically; they accept the strictures against ontology — the study of being — that Hume and Kant, as we shall see, deployed. But it is easy to construct a prima facie case for ontology — through the notion of *referential detachment*. This is the detachment of the act by which we refer to something from that to which it refers, or of reference from referent. Discourse must be *about* something other than itself, at the very least potentially, for us to be able to refer at all. (Even if it is about itself it must be objectified as a real social entity for us or anyone else to refer to it again — e.g. for the purposes of the clarification of its meaning or the adjudication of its truth.) In the same way, desire must be *for* something other than itself (that is to say, to use Brentano's phrase, it must have an 'intentional object' to which it is internally related) for it to count as desire — even if the desire be for the state of desire. Again, actions must be *with* something other than themselves (ingredients, tools, words) for the agent to be said to perform an act (cooking a meal, constructing a kitchen, saying 'well done!'). Consistently carried through, this principle issues in a critique of *foundationalism* — of the quest for incorrigibility or an unhypothetical starting-point that, until very recently, has obsessed philosophers in their pursuit of rationality since Plato's day on. The epigraph from Whitehead at the head of this chapter is no exaggeration. Philosophy has been a series of metacritical comments on comments of Plato (where a metacritique isolates an absence or inconsistency) or a refined restatement of Platonic positions or presuppositions. And in the next chapter I shall show that contemporary self-referential paradoxes have the same source as the Platonic self-predicative (e.g. 'Third Man') paradoxes. It was Hegel, with whom we started this chapter, who said that 'when philosophy paints its grey on grey, then has a shape of life grown old'. It is time for a new beginning.

Philosophical irrealism (non-realism) of a sort which I will define more precisely as we go along is the chief philosophical target of this book. We shall see how it is endemically aporetic. And in due course we shall see how it derives ultimately from an ancient Greek figure predating Plato, the monist Parmenides, born in the sixth century BC. Furthermore, in the Appendix we shall be tracing its ideological effects. *Philosophy matters because it is causally efficacious*, and bad philosophy is, so I shall argue, *regressively* so. In the course of this book we shall be treading a path through the theory of knowledge, the philosophies of language, space and time, and social science and ethics to the sociology of philosophy and its history. But I start with the philosophy of science and the rational resolution and critical diagnosis of the theory problem-field solution set of the arch of knowledge tradition that Aristotle, in his lecture notes that have come down to us as the *Posterior Analytics*, bequeathed us.

2

Explanation and the Laws
of Nature

Purple haze is in my brain.
Lately things don't seem the same.
HENDRIX

§ 1 Scientific Explanation

In the course of this chapter I shall show how one can rationally
resolve a fair number of the textbook problems of philosophy. But my
aim is also constructive: to provide a sketch of an adequate account of
science. In considering a complex subject matter such as 'explanation
and the laws of nature' it is often a sound idea to approach it with a
number of sets of coordinates in mind. Thus there are the following:

[1] *The arch of knowledge tradition*, with its *upward* and *downward*
limbs formed by induction (U^*_i), retroduction (U^*_r), introduced into
modern discussion by the American pragmatist C.S. Peirce, or
conjectured hypothesis (U^*_c), particularly associated with Karl
Popper, and deduction (D) respectively. This is to be found in
antiquity, in the 'analytic-synthetic method' of the medieval Padua
school, as the method of resolution and composition in seventeenth-
century Port Royal logic as well as in contemporary philosophy of
science.
[2] The dominant twentieth-century form of this, *positivism*,
characterized by a *monistic* theory of scientific development and a
deductivist theory of scientific structure. Although positivism itself has
an ancient ancestry,[1] it was in its essentials fully developed by Hume.
Its most well-known form in the twentieth century was as *logical
positivism* forged by an alliance of the epistemology of Hume and
Mach (who wrote that natural laws were nothing but 'the mimetic
reproduction of facts in thought, the object of which is to replace and

18

save the trouble of new experience'[2]) and the powerful new logical techniques of Frege, Russell and Wittgenstein. It was with criticism of logical positivism that the arch of knowledge tradition began to crumble.

[3] The Humean theory underpinning *deductivism*, which can be formulated most succinctly in two principles:

P_1 the principle of *empirical-invariance* that laws *are* (P_{1e}), or at least *depend upon* (P_{1k}), empirical regularities (*empirical realism*) or constant conjunctions of events, states of affairs and the like (*actualism*); and

P_2 the principle of *instance-confirmation* (or -falsification) that laws are confirmed or falsified by their instances.

The underlying Humean theory of causal laws can be interpreted as a theory of meaning or of justification and as claiming more weakly that the events be specified under their known or only under some other possible set of descriptions. It entails the thesis of *regularity determinism*, viz. that for every x there is a set of events $y_1 \ldots y_n$ such that they are regularly conjoined under some set of descriptions. This is different from the principle of *ubiquity determinism* which stipulates merely that every event must have a real cause — that is, that there must be causes for changes and differences, which is one formulation of the principle of *sufficient reason*.

[4] The dispute between *empiricists* and *rationalists* as to whether laws are induced from sense-experience or deduced a priori, that is, from pure thought alone, without recourse to experience. If one is an actualist then these, or (as with Kant) some combination of them, will seem to exhaust the alternatives. This is an effect that I shall identify as the '*primal squeeze*' exerted on the Platonic/Aristotelian fault-line.

[5] The issue over P_1 is to whether laws are merely empirical regularities (P_{1e}), as *classical empiricists* maintain, or whether they depend also upon some contribution of the individual or socialized mind (P_{1a}), as *transcendental idealists* contend, or whether they are neither sufficient (contra P_{1e}) nor necessary (contra P_{1k}) for the attribution of laws, as I, as a *transcendental realist*, shall be advocating.

[6] The question as to whether explanation involves reference to laws, *nomotheticism*, or whether it is essentially a contextualized social affair in which puzzlement is resolved, *contextualism*, or whether it paradigmatically or at least potentially consists in elements of both, *realism*.

The canonical deductivist model of explanation, with an ancestry in Aristotle, Descartes and J.S. Mill but popularly known nowadays as the Popper—Hempel or deductive-nomological (henceforth D-N)

$$C_1 \dots C_k$$

$$\underline{L_1 \dots L_r}$$

$$\underline{E}$$

Figure 2.1

model of explanation, is that to explain an event, etc. is to deduce it from a set of initial conditions and universal laws as in Figure 2.1, where $C_1 \dots C_k$ are statements of particular facts and $L_1 \dots L_r$ of general laws, together comprising the *explanans*, and E is the phenomenon to be explained, the *explanandum*. This model implies the symmetry of explanation and prediction, in that were one to be in possession of the knowledge required to explain an event prior to the event's occurrence, one would thereby have been able to predict it; and it also implies the parity of explanation, prediction and falsification, in that a failed prediction falsifies. It readily encourages an instrumentalist view of science and reason: *savoir pour prévoir*. And it may easily be extended to cover statistical explanation, the explanation of lower-order by higher-order laws or theories, and of theories, and even whole sciences, by more basic ones to which they may then be said to have been 'reduced'. Rigorously articulated, it implies the other fundament of positivism, a monistic theory of scientific development.

Let us look at some of the problems with it. To say that this acid turns litmus paper red or that this metal conducts electricity because all do is hardly explanatory. It merely redescribes the phenomena in generalizing it. This is to leave aside the question as to how we know the generalization is true, relevant and sufficient. Transcendental idealists and contextualists emphasize that what is required for a genuine explanation is the introduction into the explanatory context of new concepts and ideas, not already (explicitly or implicitly) contained in the explanandum, such as *models* picturing plausible generative mechanisms for the production of the phenomena concerned. Thus when Kepler added the organizing idea of an ellipse to the recognized facts of planetary motion, he read it into the data, or 'superinduced' it, by an act of creative insight which was at once novel and explanatory. The kinetic theory is explanatory of the gas laws and their instances inasmuch as gas molecules are imagined to be in certain respects (the positive analogy) like billiard balls bouncing off each other and exchanging their momentum by impact (while the respects in which they are unlike billiard balls are ignored). This then forms part of the source of a model (a paramorph) of the way in which their possession of free electrons, behaving analogously to gas molecules, explains the electrical conductivity of metals. Realists go further than 'model theorists' such as W.H. Whewell in the nineteenth and N.R. Campbell in the early twentieth century by allowing that, under certain conditions, these explanatory concepts or models can come to be known to denote newly identified deeper, more basic, inclusive or encompassing levels of reality. (This happens quite empirically — either directly, by normally prosthetically aided perception; or indirectly, by the perceptual identification of their causal effects.) On this *vertical* existential realism, science is seen as a continuous and reiterated *process* in motion from manifest phenomena, via creative modelling by what the French philosopher Gaston Bachelard called 'scientific loans' and experimentation (on which more in a moment), to their generative structures, which now become the new phenomena to be explained.

At this juncture I must digress for some strictures against epistemology and some sideswipes at contextualism and transcendental idealism. Nothing has been so obfuscating as the assimilation of all kinds of knowledge (or belief) to a single type. The differences between knowledges within the various sciences (and especially between the social and the natural sciences), between theoretical and applied explanations, between scientific and lay knowledges (with the former requiring an arduous socialization process of its own), between practical and discursive and tacit and explicit knowledges have become blurred or obscured. Thus 'Ilona pushed the door open' constitutes a perfectly good explanation as to why the door is ajar — one which, moreover, satisfies the deducibility, although not the covering law, requirement of the D-N model. Contextualists are vulnerable to the objection that there are many other ways to resolve puzzlement than the provision of an adequate explanation; and that in science and everyday life it is as worthy to identify a relevant puzzle as to resolve one. Transcendental idealists, for their part, would tie knowledge too closely to the familiar and the past (failing to recognize the extent to which in science we often need enormously to stretch our imagination). Moreover, in omitting to situate the raising of existential questions, they miss the most dynamic knowledge-extending part of science.

The D-N model is rife with other absurdities. It cannot sustain the distinction between a necessary and an accidental sequence of events. Thus there may be a perfect correlation between the consumption of mangoes in Manchester and the Japanese birthrate but there is no *connection* between them. A rash may be a good *symptom*, but it is not the *cause*, of measles. Exploratory activities, such as bird-watching, clinical diagnosis, prospecting for oil, risk-bearing investment, confute the alleged symmetry between explanation and prediction, as do probabilistic explanation, explanation by selection and random mutation, emergence or totality, and geographical and idiographic explanation, together with prediction by inductive computation, extrapolation or trend. Moreover, an explanatory reduction in science seldom leaves conceptual schemes intact and, more generally, almost all explanations have a secondary retrospective corrective moment at the level of the description of the explanandum in the course of and/ or subsequent to the identification of the explanans. In such cases the covering law, but not the deducibility, requirement of the D-N model may be satisfied.

If one is a vertical realist, it is natural to go on to ask: If explanatory structures *exist* independently of their human identification, do they not *act* so? That is to extend one's realism to *causality*, in what one could think of as a *horizontal* direction. (In fact vertical realism presupposes horizontal realism both ontologically, insofar as things are constituted by their causal powers, and epistemologically, in that they are identified by their direct or indirect causal effects.) This is the move that transcendental realists make. The question they pose is: Is P_1, the principle of empirical invariance, which transcendental idealists as well as classical empiricists accept, in fact true? The answer is: no. For empirical regularities are in general only forthcoming under experimentally, or otherwise locally (e.g. astronomically spatio-temporally) *closed* contexts. It is only therein that the actualist formula 'whenever x, then y' applies. Conversely, the significance of experimental activity is precisely that, in *disrupting* the course of nature (including any conjunctions) that would otherwise have prevailed, we gain access to explanatory structures, generative mechanisms and laws which continue to operate, but *transfactually* (transphenomenally, transsituationally, translocally), outside the experimental contexts in which they are identified. If one still wishes to maintain the Humean theory that laws are constant conjunctions (a position I have dubbed 'strong actualism'[3]), then one will have to concede that there are no laws known to science. If, on the other hand, one holds them to be empirical but restricts them to closed systems ('weak actualism'), then one is left without a rationale either for experimental activity or for the practical applied diagnostic and exploratory work of science. That is to say, laws can be universal *or* empirical (or more broadly, actual) but not both.

For transcendental realism, by contrast, the point of experimental activity is to identify the relatively enduring structures of nature and their characteristic ways of acting. Such structures may be classified into *natural kinds,* possessing causal powers, which, when triggered or released, act, as generative mechanisms, with *natural necessity* and *universality* (within their range) so as to codetermine the manifest phenomena of the world, which occur for the most part in open systems: that is, where constant conjunctions do not pertain. The law of gravity operates whether you are stationary or in free fall. It is just that in the former case it is counterbalanced by contrary structures and forces. The logical form of a law of nature is given by the concept of a transfactually efficacious *tendency,* which may be possessed without being exercised, exercised without being actualized, and actualized without being empirically identified by human beings.

We are now in a position to see that the whole arch of knowledge tradition, that is to say, over two millennia of philosophy, pre-supposes actualism, and hence closure, in three dimensions — the absence of differentiation (open system simpliciter), of depth and of an open future. And we can appreciate how the problem of induction arises: namely because (P_2) there is no reason *other than* instances (such as is provided in science by knowledge of its atomic structure) why iron should *tend* to rust. The English philosopher C.D. Broad pronounced the problem of induction the scandal of philosophy at about the time (in 1926) that Heidegger was diagnosing it as consisting in the attempt to prove the reality of the external world. They are not so far apart. What grounds induction, retroduction and falsification in science is *ontological stratification.* This is a condition of the possibility of science in general. This is entailed by the argument, from experimental activity, which demonstrates that science presupposes existentially independent and transfactually efficacious laws such that $D_r > D_a > D_e$ where D_r = the domain of the real, D_a = the domain of the actual and D_e = the domain of the empirical. Science may be justified, when it is, by its causal efficacy and explanatory power. But a moment's reflection will show that existential independence and transfactual efficacy, and hence ontological stratification, is a condition of the possibility of the most mundane activities from making a pot of coffee to passing a football (both of which presuppose a structured, law-governed, not just empirical, world). That said, its corollary must be drawn out. Induction is *not justified* at the level of the empirical or the actual. The surface course of nature is very far from uniform. There are other contexts in which induction is not justified. In the terminology introduced in Chapter 1.2, at 2E, for a changing cosmos to be possible, sometimes one and the same thing must be changing its causal powers, a truth which becomes more obvious the closer we get to the 4D realms of geo-historically changing agency. Similarly at 3L, for an at least potentially

totalizing cosmos to be possible, some things must be constituted by
another entity's causal powers, so that it is not the case in Bishop
Butler's famous phrase that 'everything is what it is and not another
thing'. This example serves to show (a) that philosophical problems
can be real (there are real 2E occurrences of the problem of induction)
and (b) that they may possess a plurality of sources.

Popper claims to have bypassed the problem of induction[4] in his
fallibilist methodology of conjectures and refutations. But it is only if a
putatively refuting counter-instance is replicable in principle — that is
to say, is put in transfactual or *normic* logically universal form — that it
is rational to regard it as refuting the conjecture in question.
Moreover, to switch perspectives to the epistemological side of the
coin, a refutation constitutes, or at least depends upon, a claim to
positive knowledge, which to confute a conjecture must be something
more than conjectural — or conventional, because 'convention' is
fallible too. To learn from our mistakes we must at the very least *know*
that they are mistakes.

It is now possible to sketch the lineaments of a rational account of
(1) theoretical and (2) applied explanatory science.

1. We start at what Kuhn has called 'normal science',[5] involving the
consistent Description of a base level at what I shall characterize as
the *Humean* level of knowledge of natural necessity. Much of this
work consists in the clarification and resolution of routine anomalies.
It is important to stress that there has never been a successful stretch
in science without such aporiai, which, according to the basic
Popperian model, means that they ought to be straight away
discarded rather than persevered with. Then comes the period of
scientific revolution when such anomalies proliferate, abound and
coagulate — this is the Popperian moment proper, which corresponds
to Kuhnian 'revolutionary' science. This typically consists in
transitions within, as Lakatos has stressed,[6] competing research
programmes in which paradigmatically a plurality of theories are, or
should be, as Feyerabend has emphasized,[7] considered. The content
of these theories, which are designed at once to illuminate the
phenomena of the base level, S_i, and to resolve the anomalies in our
knowledge of it, exploit all manner of metaphors and analogies,
drawn for the most part from pre-existing knowledges[8] in the
construction of plausible models of generative mechanisms and
causal structures explanatory of S_i. This is the time of Retroduction
$R_1 \ldots R_n$ of possible causes of S_i corresponding to the transcendental
idealist or *Kantian* level of knowledge of natural necessity, in which
competing theories of underlying structure invite us to imagine or
schematize the world as being so. Rigorous tests, wherever possible,

under experimentally closed conditions, lead to the Elimination of inadequate theories. This process goes hand-in-hand with the construction of sense-extending equipment and other knowledge-garnering devices until the operative generative structure is Identified at a deeper and/or more inclusive level, S_j. What characterizes this moment? Scientists are prepared to *referentially detach* S_j, or some (transfactually efficacious) phenomena at it, as the real reason R_i for, or, as I shall also say, the *alethic truth* of, S_i or a set of phenomena at it. At this moment of identification three kinds of activity may well be *simultaneously* commenced (which allows me to qualify the temporal periodicity of my initial description of the model). Two are aspects of the practice of normal science: (a) the retrospective Correction of the description of the base explanandum level of the structure, which allows me to style my model the *DREI(C)* model of theoretical scientific explanation, together with the resolution of outstanding anomalies or new anomalies created for it; (b) the detailed description of the properties of S_j, formally initiating a new round of scientific development. At the same time (c) members of the next generation or cohort or avant-garde of the day, acting perhaps only on the basis of intuition, may embark on the search for the real reason R_k at an even deeper or more englobing level of structure S_k for newly identified

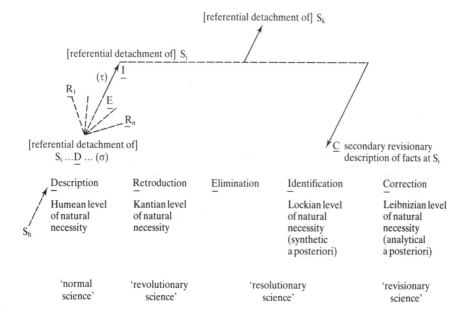

Description	Retroduction	Elimination	Identification	Correction
Humean level of natural necessity	Kantian level of natural necessity		Lockian level of natural necessity (synthetic a posteriori)	Leibnizian level of natural necessity (analytical a posteriori)
'normal science'	'revolutionary science'		'resolutionary science'	'revisionary science'

Figure 2.2

phenomena at S_j. This model is depicted in Figure 2.2, where I have marked the period of anomaly σ and of revolution τ.[†]

Five features of the discovery of S_j in this model of scientific explanation should be noted. First, we have the satisfaction of the most stringent possible or Lockian criteria of natural necessity, manifest in the *deducibility* from the description of explanatory structure at S_j of the tendencies operative at S_i, codetermining results there. Second, we now have the best possible (viz. deductive) grounds for attributing truth (as well as necessity) to these phenomena. Thus we have optimal grounding for believing that 'water is blue is true' (and not just a local accident or subjective delusion) when we are in possession of the scientific explanation for it. Thus we can write

'water is blue' is true if (optimal grounding) we are in a position to causally explain it (T_1)

or

'water is blue' is true if (next best grounding) we have good grounds for believing there is a scientific explanation for it (T_2).

This contrasts favourably with the triviality of

'water is blue' is true if water is blue (T_3).

[†] In *Dialectic* Chapter 3.2 I characterized alethic truth as (a) ontological, corresponding to the moment of referential detachment, and as (b) the truth of (or dialectical ground or reason for) things, states of affairs (phenomena, including structures) generally, as distinct from propositions. (b) presupposes (a) but not vice versa. Thus in Figure 2.2 referential detachment as S_i is not shown thereby to constitute the alethic truth of a lower-order level. But referential detachment of S_j licenses the assumption that it is the alethic truth of S_i, and similarly for S_k in respect of S_j. I would prefer to restrict the concept of alethic truth to (b), thus making ontological truth, established by referential detachment, without alethic truth possible. This makes alethia a form of the wider concept of ontological truth. That said, it is clear that in science, characterized by the reiterated movement from manifest phenomena to explanatory structure, one will be dealing in general with an actual or potential *alethic ellipse* in which optimally grounding reason at S_x explains optimally grounded reason at S_{x-1} and so on recursively. See Figure 2.3.

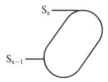

S_x

S_{x-1}

Figure 2.3

Third, the avant-garde, en route for S_k, may well decide to make, at the *Leibnizian* level of natural necessity, possession of the structure S_j definitional of the substance of or kind in question. This has the consequences of making it analytic (a posteriori) that it possesses the properties it does, and, because all knowledge is fallible, that that analytic truth at time T_x may come to be falsified at time T_y. Fourth, there is a dialectic of taxonomic and nomothetic knowledge, of existential and normic knowledge, in the explanatory dialectic I have sketched. Knowledge of natural necessities stimulates knowledge of natural kinds which stimulates knowledge of their ways of acting, which, invoking the generalized concepts of reference and referent which I shall justify in Chapter 3, leads to an extended concept of existence (embracing causality) and a fortiori of classification, such that transfactually active tendencies may themselves be grouped into natural kinds (of causal laws). Finally, alongside this dialectic there is a Hegelian/Gödelian epistemological dialectic, in which the discovery of an inconsistency leads to greater completeness, which, for epistemic and/or ontic reasons, may lead to a further inconsistency, stimulating greater completeness and so on recursively in a dialectic without conceivable end.[†]

2. In general, applied scientific explanation is a much messier, less unilinear and more context-specific affair for reasons I will go into anon. But insofar as the explanation is of a phenomenon such as a typical open-systemic event, codetermined by a multiplicity of mechanisms, which has the character of a conjuncture, the explanation will depend upon the following steps:

(a) Resolution of the event into its components.
(b) Redescription of these components in a theoretically significant way so that theoretically established laws can be brought to bear on them.
(c) Retroduction via such laws to possible antecedent causes.

As there will be in general a disjunctive plurality as well as a conjunctive multiplicity of (possible) causes in open systems, the next step will consist in the

(d) Elimination of alternatives.

[†] I have described this epistemological dialectic in *Dialectic*, Chapter 1.9. It may be called Gödelian insofar as Kurt Gödel showed very roughly that no formal system can be shown to be both consistent and complete. Extra-formal systems are usually, and I have argued necessarily, neither.

This process may continue until

(e) Positive *I*dentification of the generative causes at work in the production of the conjuncture is forthcoming (if it is).

And thence here again, as in the theoretical case, there will usually occur

(f) Secondary recessive Corrective work in the description of the explanandum conjuncture.

This is the *RRREI(C)* model of applied scientific explanation. But in a multi-angular, pluriversal world of emergent entities subject to dual and multiple control, comprised of the phenomena of processual, holistic and intentional as well as structural transfactual causality, applied explanations will be not only complicated but also dependent on judgement as to the appropriate degree on the scale of abstraction — concretion, scope and perspective.

§ 2 The Generalization of the Problem of Induction

The problem of induction, in its original Humean form, is the problem of what warrant we have for believing that the course of nature will not change. We have already seen that this supposition must be considerably nuanced. For instance, in its actualist Humean form the answer is: none, for, on the contrary, we have very good grounds for supposing that it will change. On the other hand, on the transcendental realist ontology, the stratification of nature provides — within limits which I will come to shortly — each science with its own internal inductive warrant. If there is a real reason, located in the nature of the stuff, and independent of the disposition concerned, such as its molecular or atomic structure, then water *must* tend to boil when it is heated. It is inconsistent with this reason (explanation) that it should tend to freeze, blow a raspberry or turn into a toad. But it remains true that in an open world any particular prediction may be defeated. (As every chemistry student knows only too well.) So transcendental realism allows us to sustain the universality, or, better, transfactuality, of laws in the light of the complexity and differentiation of our world, so as to enable us, for example, to infer tendencies in extra-experimental contexts, so resolving Poincaré's problem which is, as he put it, that 'on the one hand, [laws] are truths founded on experiment and approximately verified so far as concerns isolated systems. On the other hand, they are postulates applicable to the totality of the universe and regarded as rigorously true.'[9] It is thus natural to generalize the problem of induction, involving influence from the past to the future, to that of 'transduction', inference from closed to open systems.[10]

Now note that it is not because it is part of the nominal or customary definition of water that water tends to boil when it is heated that we would be justified in rejecting the appellation 'water' to any sample of a stuff that did not tend to do so. But rather because we can deduce from a description of its electronic configuration, which may constitute (at the Leibnizian level) its *real* definition, together with other relevant scientific facts, the tendency in question. But supposing a sample did not do so, the following possibilities arise:

(a) that the fact describing the tendency is false;
(b) that our explanation of it is false;
(c) that the substance was incorrectly identified; or
(d) that the substance had changed.

Now given only that (b) is false, i.e. that our explanation of it is true, which must be the case when we in turn know the reason for it (the R_k of R_j), i.e. the alethic truth of it, inductive scepticism as it is posed as an aporia for philosophy, i.e. cases (a), (c) and (d), can be ruled out. As we know its alethic truth, (a) is eliminated. (c) is irrelevant. If the substance is not in fact water but a strip of aluminium, then its failure to boil is irrelevant to the truth of the tendency at stake. Similarly if, as in case (d), it had turned into Piccadilly Circus. Now if in fact there are real problems of individuation in the 3L context of totality and if, as I have argued elsewhere, ultimata, including emergent continuants, must be characterized by their dispositional identity with their changing causal powers at 2E, then we are in fact situated in a world within philosophical metacritically identifiable limits within which there may be real occurrences of the problem of induction. But in this section, and chapter generally, I am concerned with the resolution of the problems of philosophy (in 1M terms) as they are customarily posed in which an ontology of closed systems and atomistic events is a condition of intelligibility of the problem of induction as an aporia for philosophy.

Closely associated with the problem of induction are the problems of distinguishing a necessary from an accidental sequence of events, of subjunctive conditionals and of Goodman's and Hempel's paradoxes. All these turn on the absence of a real (non-conventional) reason, located in the nature of things, for predicates to be associated in the way they are. In virtue of his genetic constitution, if Socrates is a human being, he must die. To each of the aporiai in the inductive theory problem-field there is a transductive counterpart. To the distinction between the necessary and the accidental, there corresponds the distinction between the real and the actual. To the problem of subjunctive conditionals — if the grounds to laws are restricted to their instances, why should I believe that this pig will not fly? — we have the problem of normic ones — why should I believe that gravity is operating on that pig as it wallows in its pen? To the paradoxes of confirmation — e.g. Hempel's paradox as to why my belief that ravens are black is not further confirmed by its logically contrapositive instance, the sighting of a white shoe[†] — there are paradoxes of falsification — laws and theories are straightaway falsified in open systems if we give them an actualist interpretation. To the problem of justifying the use of hypotheses in theory construction (the 'theoretician's dilemma'), there is the problem of falsifying a ceteris paribus clause in theory application (the 'engineer's excuse').

But the problem of induction can be generalized further than transduction to what, following Peter Manicas, I am going to call 'transdiction'.[11] This covers *retroduction*, inference to posited explanatory structures, generative mechanisms and transfactually efficacious laws, and *retrodiction*, inference *via* these to possible antecedent causes. Each is justified by ontological stratification and the possibility of grounding by alethic truth, which is the condition of the possibility of science and everyday life alike. Let me call this problem group the 'transdictive problem complex'. We will examine its further extension. But let me make clear the twofold character of my objection to the whole group:

(a) in each case, there exists a rational realist response to the transdictive problem; while

(b) failure to take it necessitates, in the terms of Chapter 1.2, a Tina compromise formation with axiological necessity (that is, causally impinging reality). Such a regressive response must be accepted on the basis of faith (fideism), authority (positivity), social conformity (conventionalism), caprice, fate ('*fortūna*') or what Nietzsche called the will-to-power (essentially voluntarism). The result is an internally inconsistent ensemble (theory

---

[†] The answer is, of course, because it is irrelevant to it — there is *no* conceivable connection between the colour of shoes and ravens.

problem-field solution set), theory/practice inconsistency, detotalization or split, categorial absurdity, axiological indeterminacy and ideological pliability.

Let us consider some of the extensions of the transdictive complex. I have already noted the duality of the principles and aporiai of instance-confirmation and instance-falsification. Then there is what has been called the indeterminacy of explanation. This stems from the fact that for any finite system there will be an infinite number of descriptions compatible with it. But once we have identified the higher-order explanans and referentially detached it, unless there are positive grounds for introducing, say, a place-time-dependent predicate (as space and time may sometimes be, as we shall see in Chapter 4, causes), there is no justification for adding an arbitrary or irrelevant one, so there remains nothing indeterminate about the explanation. Note that when the explanans of an explanandum is itself alethically explained, then there can be no further practical doubt about it. Hence my emphasis on multi-tiered stratification. A full consideration of 'ultimate explanations' will have to be postponed until Chapter 4, but we shall see that they necessitate no breach in transcendental realist principles.

There are a whole series of analogies, metaphoric and metonymic displacements of the core problem of induction. First, while Wittgenstein's 'private language argument' can be seen as a weak form of weak actualism, Winch's use of the late Wittgenstein in a metonymic displacement of positivism results in 'rule-uniform-itarianism'.[12] Second, the Hobbesian problem of order, at the very least as thematized in sociological theory, is a homeomorph of the Humean problem of induction. Third, there is no reason why it cannot be illuminatingly generalized to cover the explanation of non-cognitive components of action, e.g. compulsively neurotic responses to situations; or to bring out the socio-psychological presuppositions of regressive or ego-dysntonic routines, or the structure of what Bourdieu has called a 'habitus'. Fourth, to return to more recogniz-ably philosophical contexts, Feyerabend's 'Dadaist' prescription to science, 'anything goes', can be understood as a metaphoric epistemological displacement (in epistemology's 'intrinsic', inten-tional or normic aspect) of Hume's ontological verdict: 'anything can happen.'

Next, scepticism about particular knowledge can be incorporated into a transdictive net by recognizing that it is in principle susceptible to a potentially infinite number of interpretations or translations and/or verifications (from a further potential infinity of angles, perspectives, aspects); that it is liable to grounding in universal form; and that, on Humean or actualist theory, it itself is an instance of, or at least presupposes a generalization of, the logical form 'whenever x, then y'. Solipsism has been an endemic problem-field since Descartes inwardized and subjectivized rationalist criteria of knowledge. The *ego-present-centric* standpoint readily lends itself to scepticism about the existence of an external world, of other minds, of my body, my past states and thus of myself and hence of any thought at all, including doubt (so that Cartesian doubt is no exception), and so about anything and hence about everything. There are three ways to counter the solipsistic problem-field. On the first we start from the fact of primary and sempiternal polyadization and conceive them as embedded in a material context of necessary connections — so we move step-wise from intra-subjectivity to inter-subjectivity to sociality to material causally-spatio-temporally distanciated and efficacious objectivity. The second is to see individuation within an intra-subjective (polyadic) context as itself an instance of necessary (dis)connection. The third is to see intentionality as dependent upon pre-existent social structure and as only (a) meaningful or (b) efficacious as such, so that the ego-present-centric standpoint has itself to be causally explained. These three approaches can be used to complement each other.

The paradoxes of material implication are a reductio ad absurdum. In their most basic form they are that a false proposition materially implies everything and a true proposition is materially implied by anything. Here the absence not just of necessary connection but even of simple relevance is palpable.[†] The fact that I am not now reading *The Times* is irrelevant to the weather in Timbuktu. Moreover, on the logic of the truth table, the only case when a conditional is false — the case when the antecedent is true and the consequent false — is precisely the logical form of a normic statement describing a transfactually efficacious tendency, that is, the logical form of all the laws known to science. This should be the final nail in the coffin of deductivism.

To the problem of induction in respect of nomothetic knowledge there corresponds the problem of universals in respect of taxonomic knowledge. The realist response is the same. If there is something, such as the possession of a common atomic or electronic structure, which graphite, black carbon and diamonds possess in common, then chemists are justified in classifying them together. On the other hand,

---

[†] As 'relevance logicians' such as Belnap and Anderson[13] have not been slow to point out.

if there is nothing of any scientific significance that sailing boats, bicycles and helicopters possess in common then here a resemblance, rather than a realist, theory works best. The positions are indeed exactly parallel. *Structurata*, to deploy Andrew Collier's useful term,[14] are seen as *simple* (corresponding to the closed system case) or *compounded* (the open case) instances of *structures*, endowed with causal powers and classified into *kinds*, a classification which is ultimately justified by its explanatory power — that is, to cast light on the enduring generative mechanisms of nature. Thus resemblance presupposes realist theory, and just as 'ordinary' events, in open systems, turn out to be metaphysically 'conjunctures', ordinary things turn out to be, perhaps uniquely, 'laminated'[15] compounds.

Turning on the same theory problem-field solution set are the Platonic self-predicative paradoxes. Thus we saw in the previous chapter how Plato tries to account for some instance of blueness in terms of its participation in the Form 'blue' — instead of, for example (and, given the science of his day, this would of course have been impossible), its reflecting light of a certain wavelength, thereby invoking a deeper or more encompassing level of structure. A certain pattern in these aporiai is now becoming evident. What happens in the case of the actualist explanation by deductive subsumption and the Platonic self-predicative paradoxes is that the putative explanans is merely saying the same thing or repeating the explanadum. This is true — now in a horizontal, rather than vertical, direction — of the accumulation of instances in induction. In both cases we have homology or infinite or endless regress. Homology is one of the contraries of 'heterology', that one which means the same as itself. The ontological presuppositions of homology are an undifferentiated (closed) and unstratified (depthless) ontology. It is closure which underpins the horizontal homology of the problem of induction, depthlessness, the vertical homology of the self-predicative paradoxes.

The other side of closure is the incapacity to explain the ordinary singulars or particulars of the world. This is already evident in Plato's concern about 'lowly' forms, such as 'mud', but becomes fully manifest in the Aristotelian aporiai of matter and accident. If we can know only what is universal-and-necessarily certain, viz. what is actual, how can we know accidents, such as the length of my toe-nails? How, indeed, on reflection, can we know anything at all, because the particular instances which we are to subsume under the universal generalization have to be individuated and differentiated as instances, which means there should be a unique form or essence for each one of them. Hegel was faced with an analogue of the Aristotelian aporia of accident. He claimed to be able to deduce or to develop the overall contours of nature and spirit from the unfolding of the absolute idea. A certain Professor Krug challenged him to deduce the existence of his pen. And with Hegel's inevitable acceptance of the necessity for contingency the absoluteness of his idealism was lost. It transpires that the world is replete with demi-actualities, irrational existents which his system cannot explain, including the future which is essentially contained within the present, the demi-present. Leibniz's principle of the identity of indiscernibles is informed by actualism. Two separate individuals may be empirically or actually indiscernible, but really distinct, different in their internal structures. The principle of the indiscernibility of identicals is equally suspect. General knowledge would be impossible if there could not be two or more tokens of the same type. Two hydrogen atoms, identical in structure, may manifest themselves very differently under different actual or empirical circumstances. Suppose spatio-temporal location is built into the definition of identity. I have already suggested that in a changing and intra-active cosmos we need to think the co-incidence of identity and change and identity and difference. Contextual action, holistic causality, what I will call rhythmic process, not to mention variable action at a distance or the intentional and intensional phenomena of the social world, all refute this alleged principle.

It is actualism that informs the twentieth-century self-referential paradoxes too. Suppose you are lost in Crete and you ask a Cretan the way and in the course of his directions he ventures the observation that all Cretans are liars. Both his directions and his observation may be true. Tendentially Cretans may be liars, but in this particular open systemic case his statement may be actually true. The distinction between the levels of the real and the actual offers a clue to the unravelling of the other self-referential and self-theoretic paradoxes, which turn again on the distinction between the structure and the instance, where the structure may be a totality characterized by an emergent principle. A book is a totality and it is characteristic of prefaces for the author to absolve his referees or colleagues of any responsibility for 'the mistakes that remain'. There is nothing paradoxical about the phrase in quotation marks. An author may be quite sure that her book will be revealed to contain errors but quite unable to say now what they are, as she is certain that, in virtue of her genetic constitution, she will die (a life is an emergent totality), although unable to say when or how. Take the set-theoretic paradoxes. These stem from treating totalities as aggregates. Insofar as a set is or represents a totality, it must be supplied with an emergent principle of structure. Conversely a member of a set must be supplied with a corresponding principle of differentiation. Unless this is done, the situation is ungrounded. A person is not an instance of herself. She *is* herself. The set T* of all sets T which are not an instance of themselves (viz. set T) is clearly not an instance of itself — it is itself, namely set T*. What about Grelling's paradox? Is 'heterological' heterological? Insofar as it posits an identity relation, it itself exemplies homology and is ungrounded. Insofar as it posits a non-identity relation between the two tokens of heterology, the set-characterizing instance must be supplied with an emergent principle of structure and the instant-designating instance with a principle of differentiation. They are then not the same and the paradox is dissolved. Let us consider again Nietzschean forgetting. If a person is stratified, she can remember the truth about truth (supposing it is, which I have already questioned and will pursue in the next chapter) in a meta-reflexively totalizing situation at level W, while assessing the truths of scientific statements in her daily practice as a researcher at level φ. Similarly reflection on the arguments of Chapter 1.3 above will show that we do not have to resort to Heideggerian erasure of being (b̶e̶i̶n̶g̶).

I shall later show how regarding people as material entities with emergent powers resolves the mind–body problem and allows us to sustain, through the notion of intentional causality, the concept of reasons as causes. Through the related figure of constellationality we can sustain a conception of society as contained within, as an emergent product of, nature which over-reaches it, though patently society is capable of reacting back on the materials out of which it is formed. In this section I have been considering mainly aporiai. But philosophical problem-fields are not only aporetic but constitutively antagonistic: empiricism v. rationalism, the Friends of the Forms (or the Gods) v. the Friends of the Earth (or the Giants). It is easy to appreciate how the arch of knowledge tradition renders these two characterizations not only compatible but mutually reinforcing. Thus the inductive limb will encourage emphasis on common sense, experience and particulars and tend to reductionism and materialism, and the deductive limb will encourage emphasis on metaphysics, reason and universals and tend to dualism and idealism. The primal squeeze on the Platonic/ Aristotelian fault-line (concerning which we can at least say that both Plato and Aristotle had correct intuitions — pure science is, as

Plato thought, a non-quotidian affair[†] but it is explicitly constitutive of, as Aristotle believed, our everyday world[‡]), resulting in the dual 'positivistic' and 'speculative' illusions, depends precisely on the actualist elimination of the mediating terms of *empirically controlled scientific theory* describing the *natural* (non-logical) *necessity* of *natural kinds* in the explanation of the transfactual phenomena of the sensate and non-sensate world. Aristotelian *nous*, Christian faith, Cartesian certainty, Humean custom, the Kantian synthetic a priori, Fichtean intellectual intuition, Hegelian hyperintuition, the Nietzschean will-to-power, Wittgenstein's language games, Popperian conventionalism, Strawsonian dissolution or Rortian changing the subject are just some of the false attempts to fill the missing terms squeezed out at that primal fault-line.

§ 3 The Collapse of the Arch and the Consequences of Actualism

The philosophical theory of knowledge — or epistemology — is concerned with the nature, varieties, origins, objects and limits of knowledge. Among the questions that it has been concerned with are (1) is knowledge possible?; (2) if so, are its objects real or ideal?; (3) is it source, experience or reason?; and (4) are its objects unitary? The philosophy of science encompasses questions about science in general; particular groups of sciences (e.g. the social sciences); and about the concepts or implications of individual sciences (e.g. of relativity theory for our ideas of space and time). Generally realism in philosophy asserts the existence of some disputed kind of entity (e.g. universals [predicative realism], material objects [perceptual realism], moral facts [moral realism]). Thus one can be a realist about causal laws and an irrealist about unicorns. In the first part of this section I want to show how scientific realism, more especially transcendental or critical realism, arose as one among a variety of responses to the collapse of the arch of knowledge tradition. As I have already intimated, this is a relatively recent affair. It takes off from criticism of the logical positivism of the Vienna Circle of the 1920s and 1930s, which married the epistemological empiricism and rationalism of

---

[†] So much so that the historian of science Koyré could describe post-Renaissance and especially seventeenth-century physics as a triumphant revindication of Platonism over Aristotelianism.

[‡] It would not be totally misplaced to regard Plato as the theorist of Aristotelian practice.

Mach, Pearson and Duhem, on which entities such as atoms were widely thought to be, in Alexander Bain's words, merely 'representative fictions', with the logical innovations of Frege, Russell and Wittgenstein to form the backbone of the dominant view of science in the mid twentieth century. Its principal members were M. Schlick, R. Carnap, O. Neurath, F. Waismann and H. Reichenbach. C. Hempel, E. Nagel and A.J. Ayer were intellectually close to it, while Ludwig Wittgenstein and Karl Popper were on its periphery. Linguisticism and formalism were characteristic of the Circle.

The positivist vision of science pivoted on a *monistic* theory of scientific development and a *deductivist* theory of scientific structure. The former came under attack from five main sources. The first was in effect a product of the main internal difficulty in logical positivism. The Vienna Circle employed the traditional epistemological analytical/ empirical dichotomy in the form of a criterion of meaningfulness (initially formulated by Schlick as 'the meaning of a proposition is the method of its verification') and a criterion of demarcation of scientific from non-scientific discourse. But the verifiability principle was neither analytic nor synthetic (empirical) and so should be nonsense. Moreover, neither historical propositions (and so statistical evidence) nor universal laws (because of the problem of induction) could be conclusively verified. There is no space here to consider the variety of the responses to this,[16] but this aporia began the process of undermining the idea of fixed foundations of knowledge and paved the way for W.V.O. Quine's decisive attacks on the analytical/ empirical and theory/fact distinctions and arguments for a holistic view of knowledge[†] as in effect 'a field of force whose boundary conditions are experience'. Drawing on this, Mary Hesse and other 'model theorists' argued: (a) that scientific language should be conceived as a dynamic system constantly growing by the metaphorical extension of pre-existing (natural and scientific) languages, and (b) that observational predicates were not isomorphs of (physical, sensual or instrumental) objects, but were clusters or 'knots' attaching the semantic network to the object-world in a theory-dependent and mutable way. Second, this was powerfully reinforced by Wittgenstein's critique of his early philosophy, and in particular the possibility of a private language, which fatally undermined the sociological individualism implicit in the model; and

---

[†] Thus every scientific result is (a) a test of a multiplicity of hypotheses (any one of which may be saved), (b) in principle consistent with a (generally infinite) plurality of further sets of hypotheses, and (c) subject to subsequent revision or redescription in the history of science.

Wittgensteinians, such as Hanson, Toulmin and Sellars, latched on, like the model theorists, to the non-atomistic and changeable character of the 'facts' in science. Facts were social products not to be confused with things, states-of-affairs and the like. This linked up with rejection of the idea of immediate knowledge (most usually of reified facts interpreted as raw data) and the critique engaged by Chomsky of autonomized ('empty') minds. Third, closely connected with this, it became apparent, on the one hand, that key terms such as 'experience' were under-analysed and used equivocally, e.g. by the failure to distinguish social practice and experimentally controlled inquiry, and, on the other, that underpinning the atomism (and autonomization of mind) and reductionism was the *reification* of facts and their conjunctions, and that the positivist model lacked the concept of scientific praxis as *work*. Now work is paradigmatically transformative activity; so here was an a priori argument for change. The background to the fourth source is given by the scientific earthquakes of relativity theory and quantum mechanics which shattered the classical world-view. This stimulated Popper and Popperians such as Lakatos and Feyerabend in their conviction that it was falsifiability, not, as the logical positivists had supposed, verifiability, that was the hallmark of science, and that it was precisely revolutionary breakthroughs such as those associated with Galileo or Einstein in which its epistemological significance lay. From France, Bachelard and his school argued a similar position. Finally, Kuhn and other historians and sociologists of science drew scrupulous attention to the real social processes involved in the reproduction and transformation of scientific knowledge in what I have called the *'transitive'* (epistemological/social) dimension of science.

We have already done much of the spadework for appreciating the attack on the deductivist theory of scientific theory. It initially came under fire from Michael Scriven, Mary Hesse and Rom Harré for the lack of *sufficiency* of Humean criteria for causality and laws, Popperian-Hempelian criteria for explanation and Nagel's (deductivist) criterion for the reduction of one science to another more basic one. Rom Harré in particular drew attention to the role of (especially paramorphic or many-sourced) models in raising *existential* questions in what critical realism calls the *'intransitive'* (or ontological) dimension of science. The vertical existential of theoretical realism (in the terminology of §1) thus indicated was further motivated by the linguistic arguments of Kripke and Putnam that the use of natural kind terms, such as 'gold' and 'water', presupposed that the substances had real essences, although not necessarily known to us. I generalized this line of critique to incorporate the lack of *necessity* (cf. §1 [5]) of Humean/Hempelian criteria arguing for a horizontal, causal or transfactual realism to complement the vertical or existential one already indicated. It is of some significance that the attack against deductivism was both initiated and carried through by writers with a strong interest in the human sciences where what William Outhwaite has called the 'law-explanation orthodoxy'[17] was never even remotely plausible.[18] Moreover, the attack on the symmetry of explanation and prediction chimed in with the Frankfurt School's critique of purely instrumental reason.

Two other developments are worth recalling. Peter Strawson, especially in *Individuals* (1959) and *The Bounds of Sense* (1966), had initiated a turn to transcendental arguments. It was now possible to argue that the umbilical cord between transcendental arguments and transcendental idealism (roughly the doctrine that we can know the world insofar as we can construct it) could be, and had to be, cut. Transcendental arguments are merely a species of the retroductive-analogical arguments discussed in §1 distinguished by the fact that their premises and conclusion embody some categorial necessity, i.e. for a mode or domain of being. Second, I argued, as I shall resume in more detail in the next chapter, against the post-Kantian prejudice against ontology, enshrined in the doctrine which I have called the epistemic fallacy, that statements about being must always be analysed or explicated in terms of statements about our knowledge of being. Underlying this, we shall see, is a deep-seated anthropo-centrism in philosophy. Without a new ontology — the ontology of (dialecticized) transcendental realism — the philosophy of science, and epistemology, has been unable to reconcile the facts of epistemic change with either (α) ontological realism or (β) judgemental rationality. Instead it has followed a transmutation path from positivism through the conventionalism of (in different respects) Kuhn, Bachelard and Popper, via the pragmatism of Rorty, the constructivism of Feyerabend to the post-structuralist superidealism of a Baudrillard (for whom the Gulf War of 1991 was a 'media event').

Arguments for scientific realism may be divided into three broad groups:

(a) Transcendental arguments of the type I deployed in §1 to develop transcendental realist accounts of causal laws and scientific explanation, which inevitably function as transcendental refutations of irrealist positions and metacritically allow the exposure of their effects. (A metacritique$_1$ is a critique which demonstrates some categorially significant absence. A metacritique$_2$ additionally explains the [necessity for the] absence. It thus necessarily involves the sociology of philosophy and science.)

(b) Reductiones ad absurdum of irrealist positions, such as the puzzles and aporiai we discussed and resolved in §2, which necessarily develop in practice into internally inconsistent Tina formations and, as such, are suitable objects of metacritique$_2$.

(c) Inductive arguments from the directionality, history or successes (or failures) of science. Thus Putnam and Boyd used to argue that the cumulative character of scientific development, and, in particular, one could interpose the growth in its existential knowledge (on the generalized concept of existence introduced above), strongly indicates that theories are (fallible) attempts to describe real states and structures as they succeed and/or accrete on one another in providing deeper and/or more complete accounts of a theory-independent reality.[19]

Let us by way of summary of this part of this section return to the coordinates from which we started the chapter.

[1] Ontological stratification and the possibility of alethic truth ground induction, retroduction and falsification in science, when they are in fact justified. Although deduction plays a role in the dialectic of science, e.g. at the Lockian level of natural necessity in the derivation of tendencies, or at the eliminative moment in the derivation of consequences for the experimental test of theories, as an *actualist* account of the nature of knowledge and/or the world it is fatally flawed.

[2] Although there is an extant neo-positivist current, both the monistic theory of scientific development and the deductivist theory of scientific structure must be rejected. I shall show in Chapter 3 how epistemic relativity is consistent with judgemental rationalism.

[3] Both the principles of empirical invariance and instance-confirmation (or -falsification) have been refuted, as has the Humean theory of causal laws. I turn to the critique of (regularity) determinism in a moment.

[4] Neither empiricism nor rationalism nor their Kantian combination or attempted synthesis will work. This covers [5]. And in Chapter 3 I will show how transcendental realism can combine transfactual nomotheticism in the intransitive dimension and the insight of contextualism that science is a social process.

Peter Winch once contrasted the 'under-labourer' and 'master-scientist' conceptions of philosophy. The arch of knowledge tradition tried to combine both. The sceptic in theory (cf. the upward limb) must be a dogmatist in practice (cf. the downward limb). In self-conscious practice the actualist scientist generates reductionist, prefigured by Comte, and complexifying, prefigured by J.S. Mill, regresses in his or her search for a more atomistic and/or complete state description. The models of scientific explanation I have sketched are not meant to be exhaustive. Much historical, or biographical, explanation takes the form of what I have elsewhere called 'continuous series' and in Chapter 4 I shall considerably qualify my account of applied explanation by considerations of the concrete universal in the criss-cross, mish-mash world in which we live subject to a multiplicity of levels, orders and angles of determination and perspective.

I now turn to consider the status and implications of the chief villain of the plot of this chapter, actualism, before concluding by resuming my critique of determinism. In its most general sense actualism is the reduction of the necessary and possible, equally constitutive of the domain of the real, to the actual. But if the actual is regarded as known, then it becomes a generalized subject—object identity theory, as in the D-N model of explanation. This implies, as we have seen in this chapter, the reduction of structures and generative mechanisms to (constant conjunctions of) events or states of affairs, and, as I will show in the next chapter, of change to difference and difference to generality. These phenomena, apprehended in identity theory, may be regarded as empirically ascertained, in which case the identity theory is empirical realism (as in Hume or Kant), or conceptually deduced, in which event it constitutes a conceptual realism (as in Leibniz or Hegel). (These do not exhaust the possibilities.) Identity theory may be held in a sceptical manner or adopted with a dogmatic or complacent stance. The universality of the regularity has traditionally, from the time of Aristotle, been regarded as necessarily certain. And it entails, as I have already intimated, as corollaries the absence not only of differentiation and depth, but also of an open universe, which I shall call blockism (after those who believe in what is known as a block universe, entailing the postulation of a simultaneous conjunctive totality of all events — a position I discuss in Chapter 4).

Now actualism is inherently dilemmatic, since this reduction of the real to the actual (and thence to the empirical or conceptual) cannot be consistently carried out. This is readily witnessed in open systems, where actualism can only be saved by the forfeit of knowledge (i.e. philosophical theory sustained by the sacrifice of science) or, as in the case of the Hegelian demi-actual, by according the non-actual a lower ontological status as an irrational existent. To drive the point home, consider Humean or Kantian empirical realism: the actual cannot be both universal and empirical — universality can be retained but then empirical regularity must be jettisoned; or empirical regularity can be retained but then universality collapses. In actualism, the actual is necessarily divided against itself: the world is *detotalized* and split. This is a 3L consequence of a 1M category mistake. At the heart of actualism is the absent concept of the non-actual real, just as we shall see at the heart of monovalence is the void left by the absent concept of the non-positive or non-present real at 2E and at 3L that left by ontological extensionalism of the absent concept of the internally real and at 4D that which flows from the absence of the notion of embodied intentional causality. The *anti-Parmenidean reinstatement of negativity* and the *anti-Kantian revindication of ontology*[†] are, we shall see, the pivotal keys to the rational resolution of the problems of philosophy. As aporiai or in immanent critique they typically but not necessarily appear in oppositional (e.g. antinomial, dilemmatic, etc.) form. In metacritique$_1$ this opposition will be seen to be grounded in a common absence which generates the splits concerned; while in metacritique$_2$ both the presence that screens the absence and its intra- and extra-philosophical causes will be isolated and explained — as totalities unified by absence but never self-identical — in terms of their 1M−4D/5C grounds and consequences.

In general, $D_r > D_a > D_s$, whether D_s is conceptual or empirical. But if $D_r = D_a = D_s$, as it is posited in identity theories, such as empirical or conceptual realism, then both epistemic and ontic change become impossible, resulting in a static '*fixism*', which is an inevitable irrealist corollary of actualist blockism. This is a 2E consequence. So long as there is a divide or separation between subject and object (of consciousness or apprehension), there is no true identity and the object can only be metaphorically said to be empirical or conceptual. So actualism entails an achieved identity and the concept of alterity or sheer determinate other-being is lost. There is *no* non-identity or difference — a 1M consequence. Strictly carried through, this must result first in a reductionism, then in a monism, which, insofar as it is anthropormorphized (as the concepts of empirical and conceptual realism entail), must be (a perhaps panentheistic) solipsism and an idealism. This is the ultimate fount of philosophy's characteristic idealism.

[†] It was Plato who rationalized Parmenides' repudiation of negativity and who prepared the ground for the transition from Descartes to Kant by already subordinating ontology to epistemology.

EXPLANATION AND THE LAWS OF NATURE

Let us step back a little and assume a social world. Then the identity achieved in empirical or conceptual realism must be at the price of the reification of facts or the hypostatization (substantialization) of ideas. Both presuppose the *fetishism* of closed systems. This is the 4D implication of actualism. Once more the false dichotomy of the reductionist reification or dualistic disembodiment of agency looms. Note that the humanization of nature implicit in the concept of empirical and conceptual realism goes hand in hand with the naturalization or mechanization of science (in empirical realism) or its formalism (in conceptual realism).

One could pursue these consequences further, tracing the way in which the epistemic fallacy implicit in identity theory, of which actualism is a generalized form, leads all the way from what Adorno called 'identity-thinking' through fixism to an ontology of stasis, which, insofar as the social world is characterized by what I called in Chapter 1 generalized master–slave-type relations, functions as an ideology of repression. More generally, reification, hypostatization and fetishism act as ideologies eternalizing the status quo, which, in a neat circle, is what actualism in the philosophy of science does to experimentally, and thus humanly, generated sequences of events. And one could trace the Tina compromises and escape (metaphysical λ) clauses and routes which actualist theories deploy and *their* effects.[20]

Determinism, as normally understood, is the thesis that for everything that happens there are conditions such that, given them, nothing else could have happened. In the form of *regularity determinism* it appears, as we have seen, as the thesis that for every event x there is a set of events $y_1 \ldots y_n$ such that they are regularly conjoined under some set of conditions. It is of course a consequence of actualism. But we have enough material now to suggest that reflection on the conditions under which deterministic outcomes are possible (from which determinism as a metaphysical thesis derives its plausibility) shows that, apart from experimentally established and a few locally naturally occurring closed systems, laws set limits, impose constraints or more generally operate as tendencies codetermining outcomes rather than providing uniquely fixed results. In particular they have a normic, transfactual, non-actual and non-empirical character. Moreover, they are consistent with situations of dual and multiple control, multiple and plural determination, contextual and joint action, emergent, totality, holistic and processual causality and intentional human agency (e.g. in experimental activity!). From the perspective I have been developing in this chapter, laws are neither contingent (the upward limb) nor actual (the downward limb) but necessary and real; as properties of mechanisms, not conjunctions of events. The only sense in which science presupposes determinism is the non-Humean non-Laplacean sense of ubiquity determinism, that is, the ubiquity of real (but it cannot be assumed necessarily intelligible) causes for events, i.e. changes in states of affairs and differences in them. (And hence the possibility of stratified explanations.)

Regularity determinism, which is how 'determinism' is normally taken, can then be seen to rest on a naïve actualist ontology of laws, and in particular on the error of supposing that because an event was caused to happen, i.e. produced, it was bound to happen before it was caused. This confounds ontological determinism with epistemological predetermination. Nor are relations of natural generation logically transitive. Thus it is not true that because S_1 produced S_2 and S_2 produced S_3 that S_1 produced S_3 — if, for instance, S_2 possessed emergent powers with respect to S_1 or the system in which S_3 is formed is open or if the processes involved are stochastic. It has been appreciated for some time that quantum mechanics, where it appears impossible to simultaneously determine the position and the momentum of elementary particles, casts doubt on the supposed scientific suzerainty of regularity determinism. The development of catastrophe and chaos theory has dealt another blow to it, insofar as they illustrate that non-linear dynamic systems (of which the world monetary system and the ecosphere form pertinent real-world examples) can yield highly irregular (chaotic and unpredictable) results.

The relative rarity of deterministic outcomes and the complexity of agents has implications for the issue of free-will. The dominant position has tended to be the 'compatibilist' one that free-will presupposes determinism. But in the second half of the twentieth century, under the influence of Ryle, Austin, the later Wittgenstein, Strawson and Hampshire, the common-sense view that determinism places our normal concepts of agency, chance and responsibility in jeopardy has gained ground. Yet this has usually been reconciled with the continued commitment to determinism at the physical level in the doctrine that the two sets of concepts operate at different logical levels or language strata. But once questions of referentiality are posed this is a very difficult position to sustain. (For it seems to leave the human strata 'unreal'.) However, as I have argued in Chapter 1, once actualism is jettisoned and people are regarded as structured entities with causal powers irreducible to their exercise or their physiological basis, a naturalistic revindication of the causality of reasons and the potential applicability of the term 'free' to agents, their actions and situations is opened up. This is a topic to which I shall return, and which will occupy us considerably in later chapters in the book. But now I can turn to consider how, rejecting identity theory, we can use words meaningfully to refer to the world and, inter alia, state truths about it.

================================ 3 ================================

Reference, Truth and Meaning

The linguistic philosophy, which cares only about language, and not about the world, is like the boy who preferred the clock without the pendulum because, although it no longer told the time, it went more easily than before and at a more exhilarating pace.

RUSSELL (1969)

Philosophy is a battle against the bewitchment of our intelligence by means of language.

WITTGENSTEIN (1953)

§ 1 The Linguistic Turn and the Inexorability of Realism

It could be argued that had Kant made the distinction between transcendental arguments and transcendental idealism, he could have deployed a transcendental argument to establish the knowability of the transcendental subject who synthesized or categorized the phenomenal world and thus avoided blocking off the transcendental subject and the understanding-in-itself *and* the transcendental object and the world-in-itself from the experiencing human ego. However, such a move would have unlocked the floodgates. There would have been no reason to deny the applicability of the categories to things-in-themselves, or to deny that we have (partial, fallible) knowledge of being not just phenomena. Kant's opposition to ontology per se would have collapsed and, in the vein of contemporary critical realism, he could have allowed that we had geo-historically relativized and domain-specific synthetic a priori knowledge of the world, establishing, for instance, by transcendental argument from experimental and applied scientific activity that the world must be structured, differentiated and changeable (and changing). As it is, he did not make this move; but declared an embargo on ontology as such, not just in the styles practised by Leibniz or Locke, but quite generally, so that Hegel could bemoan the spectacle of a people 'without metaphysics'.

46

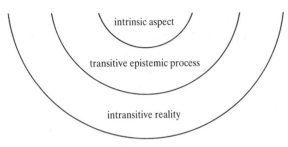

Figure 3.1

The first step in revindicating ontology is to appreciate that (α) *philosophical ontology* need not be dogmatic and transcendent, but may be conditional and immanent, taking as its subject matter not a world apart from that investigated by the sciences and other disciplines (a Platonic or Leibnizian noumenal realm), but just that world considered from the point of view of what can be established about it from conditional a priori or transcendental argument. One must then, of course, distinguish philosophical ontology, as so understood, from (β) *specific scientific ontologies*, that is, the entities posited or presupposed by some particular scientific theory or *epistemic* inquiry. I shall call such entities *ontics*; they may be positive (onts) or negative (de-onts), as I shall explain in the next section. Intermediate concepts of ontology are possible, e.g. designating orders of abstraction or particular configurations, but (α) and (β) are the concepts I shall be concerned with in this book. Ontology corresponds to what I have called the intransitive dimension and contrasts with, but also *contains*, epistemology or what I have called the transitive dimension, which must be conceived as including in principle the whole material and cultural structure of (past or present agent-dependent) society. Within this transitive process, its *extrinsic* or causal aspect contrasts with but again also contains, constellationally, the *intrinsic* or intentional, normative stream of action, so that, as I shall show in Chapter 5, reasons are, but do not exhaust, causes. Constellationality is a figure of containment of one term distinguished from an over-reaching term, from which the over-reached term may be diachronically or synchronically emergent. The relationship between intrinsic aspect, transitive process and intransitive reality is illustrated in Figure 3.1. I will be arguing for the constellational containment of (the possibility of) judgemental rationality in the intrinsic aspect within epistemic relativity in the transitive dimension within ontological realism in the intransitive dimension.

Now any theory of knowledge presupposes an ontology specifying what the world must be like for knowledge, under the descriptions given it by the theory, to be possible. Thus the Humean theory of causal laws presupposes, in J.S. Mill's words, that 'what happens once will, under a sufficient degree of similarity of circumstance, happen again',[1] i.e. that there are constant conjunctions, or parallel cases, in nature. From this standpoint, the *epistemic fallacy* — that is, the post-Humean and Kantian dogma that statements about being can always be analysed in terms of statements about our knowledge of being; that it is sufficient, in Wittgenstein's words, to 'treat only of the network, not what the network describes', or, in Ryle's, that 'ontologizing is out', or, in Quine's, that 'to be is to be the value of a variable' — is a multi-consequential disaster. In the first case, it merely glosses the generation of an *implicit* ontology — in the dominant twentieth-century Humean case, of atomistic events and closed systems — and a fortiori of an *implicit realism*; here, empirical realism. Thus, as I have already suggested in Chapter 1, it is easy to show, for example, that despite Rorty's failure to be explicit about ontology, he implicitly commits himself to an empirical realist physicalistic reductionist determinism in respect of the extrinsic aspect of agency and a de-agentifying disembodying 'hermeneutics' in respect of its intrinsic aspect, thus duplicating Kant's mistake in the third antinomy.[2] To say that he is merely talking about two languages does not let him off the hook. For either the second 'intentional' language refers, in which event we have intervention in the domain and falsification of the first; or it does not, in which case it is a myth and the charge of dualistic disembodiment stands — and he is committed, like Kant, to the double of empirical and transcendent realism. It is customary of irrealist philosophers from Quine to Rorty to admit to what might be called, in a curious echo of the final proposition of the early Wittgenstein's *Tractatus* (1922) — 'what we cannot speak about we must pass over in silence' — an *ineffable realism*, to the effect that there are of course forces and impacts 'out there', but they leave their nature untheorized. The result of this exercise is that, because philosophy abhors an ontological vacuum, irrealist philosophies merely tacitly secrete the (normally inherited) ontology their epistemology presupposes. The question is not *whether* to be a realist, but *what sort of realist* to be — a transcendental (or critical) realist, or an empirical, conceptual, intuitional, voluntaristic (Nietzschean) and/or a transcendent realist. Scepticism or agnosticism about realism or professed neutralism between realism and idealism always already presupposes some solution set, a realist function of some specific kind.

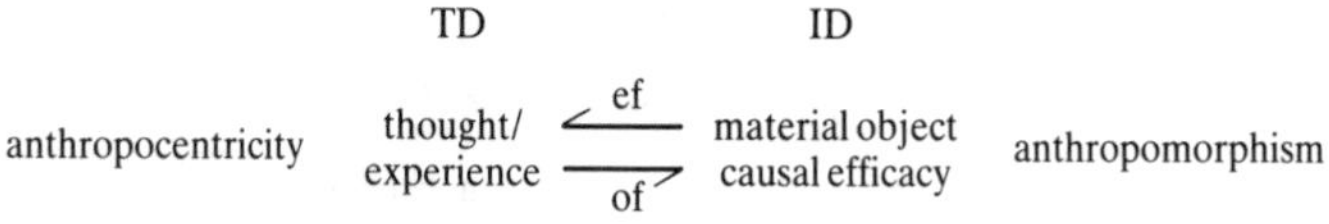

TD   ID

anthropocentricity   thought/ $\xleftarrow{ef}$ material object   anthropomorphism
                      experience $\xrightarrow[of]{}$ causal efficacy

TD = transitive dimension
ID = intransitive dimension
ef = epistemic fallacy
of = ontic fallacy

Figure 3.2 The Anthroporealist Exchanges

Second, the epistemic fallacy conceals a deep-seated anthropocentric bias in contemporary irrealist philosophy, underlying which is what we may denominate as the *anthropic fallacy* — the analysis of being in terms of (some or other attribute of) human being. Third, and closely connected to this, it co-exists with the esoteric naturalization of knowledge — e.g., in the Humean case, through the reification of facts and their conjunctions, underpinned by the fetishism of closed systems: that is to say, with, in effect, the compulsive determination of our knowledge of being by being itself — in the reciprocating, equilibrating *ontic fallacy*. Here the result of the categorial error of the definition of being in terms of some attribute of human beings, e.g. sense-experience or reason, is immediately manifest in the duplicity (and consequent ideological plasticity) of (subject–object [epistemic–ontic]) identity theory. For anthropocentric identity theory presupposes an anthropomorphic realist dual, the result of the combination of which may be equivocity over the independent existence of things and the dogmatic anthropomorphic reification of socially produced facts, as depicted in Figure 3.2. Both because (a) an achieved identity/duplicity theory is impossible (because the world exists independently and acts transfactually) and because (b) of the internal aporiai (e.g. of the transdictive complex), such a theory complex generates, as its necessary complement, a transcendent realism which must be tacitly or explicitly invoked (e.g. fideistically) in response to transdictive aporiai. This complex constitutes the *irrealist ensemble*. Even with a transcendent reinforcement, the resulting internally inconsistent system, of which we have already had a foretaste in witnessing the actualist splitting of the concept of the actual, will require, in the face of the axiological necessities it violates, a *defensive shield* incorporating a metaphysical λ clause or safety-net. The resulting Tina compromise formation looks as in Figure 3.3. There will be several levels of presupposition, and orders of effects. Particular identity theory necessitates actualism,

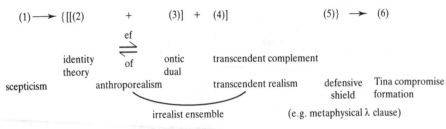

Figure 3.3

generalized identity theory. If atomistic, it will result in ontological extensionalism (and encourage nominalism); if reductionist, in reification. Actualism will presuppose fetishism and, in general, fixism. The complex will be theory/practice inconsistent and liable to immanent critique (and metacritical analysis). Alterity, change, totality and agency will all be scouted (at 1M−4D). The contingency of existential questions will be sequestered and the conceptual, epistemic and social status quo dogmatically reinforced. Such are the effects of the denegation of ontology.

Finally, transposed to the social world and set in a hermeneutical or otherwise linguistified register, the collapse of the intransitive dimension takes the form of the *linguistic fallacy*, viz. the analysis of being in terms of our discourse about being. Indeed this is the form which the epistemic fallacy has most characteristically assumed in the twentieth century, to which I will shortly come. It might be thought that Heidegger escapes my charge of anthropism. But for the early Heidegger, being was essentially mediated by *Dasein* or human being, and for the later Heidegger it was disclosed by its human traces or effects.

Reacting against the prevailing idealism, Russell and Moore initiated the linguistic century, *formal* as epitomized by the Wittgenstein of the *Tractatus* and the Vienna Circle, *informal* as epitomized by the Wittgenstein of the *Investigations* and Oxfordian linguistic philosophers in the manner of Ryle and Austin. The former were animated with a desire to regiment language into a monistic scientific cast, recognizably continuous with the tradition of 'British empiricism'; the latter reacted against this with an emphasis on the plurality of language games and on 'common sense', which Russell dubbed the metaphysics of the Stone Age and Gramsci the practical wisdom of the ruling class. Both tendencies were anti-ontological, a-geo-historical and a-social. The later Wittgenstein saw language as materially inscribed in social practices, though he was careful to caution that philosophy 'may no way interfere with the actual use of language; it can in the end only describe it. For it cannot give it any foundation either. It leaves everthing as it is.' Or, as Wisdom put it, 'philosophy begins and ends in platitude'. But Bakhtin/Voloshinov in Russia and Bachelard and Canguilhem in France were already conceiving 'language games' as in internal and external tension and paying attention to the emergence of new concepts, soon to be joined in the Anglo-Saxon world by Kuhn and Feyerabend, who drew attention to the actuality of meaning change, and even incommensurability.

However, the collapse of the intransitive dimension and the failure to sustain the potential causality of reason led to confusion here. Thus Kuhn came out with formulations such as 'though the world does not change with a change of paradigm, the scientist afterward works in a different world'.[3] Disambiguating between the intransitive object world and the transitive scientific social worlds would have obviated the need for recourse to such paradoxical formulations. Moreover, Kuhn withheld the possibility of making comparative evaluative judgements between theories, despite enunciating in a number of places criteria for telling which theory is 'later'. However, if T_1 can explain more significant phenomena in terms of its descriptions than theory T_2 can do in terms of its descriptions of the same or overlapping theory-independent world,[†] then there is a rational criterion for choosing T_1 over T_2 whether or not it is 'newer', and even if they are 'incommensurable'. In this way transcendental realism can sustain judgemental rationality within the intrinsic aspect within epistemic relativity in the transitive dimension within ontological realism in the intransitive dimension, and a possible sense can be given to the claims of the rational development of the sciences in space-time. But it is probable that claims about incommensurability were in any case exaggerated — diachronically, semantic continuity is never completely lost as the logic of scientific discovery draws on past and exterior sources of meaning in the analogical-retroductive moment in the dialectic of dialectical and analytical reasoning I described in Chapter 2. In this dialectic, discourse continually circulates in and out of the sphere of formal reasoning, in which meanings and truth values remain stable (or fixed in their indeterminacy). The apprehension of the relativity of knowledge did, however, generate a transmutation route — in the absence of explicitly thematized ontology — in the epistemology and the philosophy of science. Thus, making use of the figures portrayed in

---

[†] In social science the object world, although still existentially intransitive, is only relatively independent causally.[4]

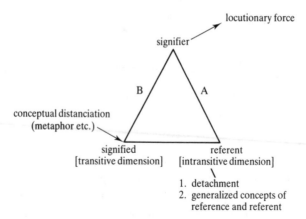

Figure 3.4 The Semiotic Triangle

Chapter 1, we can contrast the stoic indifference of the conventionalist Kuhn to reality (at 1M) as it passed over to the outright scepticism of Rorty with his theory/practice inconsistency (at 2E) to the Unhappy Consciousness (at 3L) in the constructivism, anarchism, superidealism of a Feyerabend or the insouciant play of a Derrida, who can declare there is nothing outside the text. Meanwhile the twentieth-century obsession with language showed no signs of abating. The century which saw the birth of scientific linguistics with Saussure, and its development, most notably by Chomsky, witnessed the evolution of Oxford linguistic philosophy into the speech action theory of Searle and the theory of communicative action of Habermas and the development of the structural anthropology of Lévi-Strauss into the post-structuralism of Derrida, Foucault and Lacan in antinomic fashion. The antinomy is rationally resolved by understanding the duality of immediate (action) and mediate (genealogical) knowledge, and the complementarity of hermeneutics oriented to mutual understanding in communicative interaction and semiotics concerned with the conditions of the possibility of the production of any meaning at all.

To think our way clearly here we have to display the semiotic triangle (see Figure 3.4). Whereas nominalist extensionalism (Quine, Davidson) has postulated an unmediated relation along axis A, eliding questions of meaning-change, post-structuralism has elided the referent in its preoccupation, in concepts such as the trace structure of the sign, with axis B. I want to re-emphasize the importance of the nature of referential detachment. This is the detachment of the act of reference from that to which it refers. This establishes at one and the same time the existential intransivity of a being and the possibility of another reference to it, which is a condition of any intelligible discourse at all. But just ask any modern Cratylus[†] who enunciates scepticism or neutralism over reality to repeat, or clarify the meaning of, it. To do so they must regard their initial statement or its content as an objectified socially real entity. In the end irrealism as stated, taken consistently, must collapse into solipsism; real solipsism, or at least ancient (serious) scepticism. Otherwise to clarify its ideological function we must study irrealism as rhetoric.

We have already seen the role that referential detachment plays in the guise of alethic truth in the rational resolution of 1M problems of philosophy — those that turn on relations of non-identity, such as ontological stratification. In a moment I will turn to look at the role that the generalized concept of reference and referent, and a fortiori existence, plays in establishing the case for 2E negativity as a propaedeutic to resolving those problems that turn on it, or its absence, but before I do this I want to reiterate that the argument for referential detachment is the argument for ontology; and to note the persistent effects of the post-Humean and-Kantian denegation (denial in theory, affirmation in practice) of ontology.

Contemporary analytic philosophy begins with the figure of Gottlob Frege (1848–1923), a great logician, philosopher of mathematics and of language. Perhaps his most enduring contribution to philosophy was a clear distinction between sense and reference. Analysing the structure of subject–predicate sentences, he argued that each of subject, predicate and sentence had both a sense and a reference. The sense of a subject such as 'this apple' was a (complex of) description(s) while its reference was the object to which it referred. (I distinguish the speech act of reference from the referent designated.) The sense of a predicate such as 'is green' is a concept and its reference a function; while the sense of the sentence 'this apple is green' is a thought and its reference is nothing other than its truth-value. So Frege had a generalized concept of reference and was an ontological realist, albeit one who, insofar as he was committed to bivalence (a position against which I have argued elsewhere), could discriminate only two states of reality. He would have done better to say not that the reference of a sentence was its truth-value, but rather

---

[†] Cratylus was a Sophist and contemporary of Socrates, who, there is some evidence to suggest, may have had some early but lasting influence on Plato. Exaggerating some features of Heraclitus' system, which we will look at in Chapter 9, he trumped the Heraclitian dictum that you cannot step into the same river twice (because it is continually changing) by saying that you could not step into it even once. According to Aristotle, he eventually avoided speech altogether, merely pointing. How he thought that avoided the dilemma we do not know. For, by his silence, he was saying something; just as in pointing he was indicating a relative persistent.

that the referent of a sentence may or may not be detachable (a fact which we may get right or wrong), and that in the former case it has the ontological value 'true'.

As it was, the crypto-realist intuitions of Frege form the basis of truth-table semantics and, married to Machian epistemology in the early Wittgenstein's logical atomism and the logical positivism of the Vienna Circle which the *Tractatus* heavily influenced, it became submerged under a scientistic epistemology committed to the epistemic fallacy. The taboo on ontology has its effects on realistically inclined philosophers today. Thus Bernard Williams conjures in his *Descartes*[5] with the notion of an 'absolute conception of reality' but still conceives this as a conception which would account progressively for ever more inclusive competing representations of reality. In other words he thinks the intransitive dimension as somehow detransitivizing itself, rather than from a standpoint of transcendental detachment of what exists independently (absolutely or relatively) of any representation of it (which if, when and where they occur are then constellationally contained within being, i.e. the intransitive dimension). Similarly, Saul Kripke in *Naming and Necessity*[6] uses the concept of a rigid designator uniquely tying an object to an original act of baptism as a surrogate or proxy for the absent concept of same being, irrespective of any act of naming or historical chain of connections at all. Here again there is a radical epistemologism lurking, the failure to detransitivize reality. A related shortfall is at work in Thomas Nagel's *The View From Nowhere*, in which the author, striving for impartiality, argues that the aim of objective knowledge is 'naturally described in terms that, taken literally, are unintelligible: we must get outside ourselves, and view the world from nowhere within it'.[7] Of course we cannot do this, but there is nothing to stop us, if we distinguish, after Strawson,[8] transcendental arguments from transcendental idealism (as I argued at the beginning of this section Kant should have), from establishing how the world must be for certain human activities to be possible and then (in what I have called 'transcendental detachment') detaching our conclusions from our premises, just as scientists and logicians do, and so establishing ontological propositions sui generis.

§ 2 The Critique of Ontological Monovalence and the Problems of Philosophy

By 'ontological monovalence' I mean a purely positive account of reality. I aim in this section to argue for ontological bivalence — or rather polyvalence, including 'non-valence' — and to show that ontological monovalence is fatally flawed. Although ontological monovalence — like, indeed, the epistemic fallacy — harks back to Parmenides,[†] it was canonized by a triple transposition of Plato's:

(α) the analysis of statements about non-being into false statements;
(β) the analysis of change in terms of difference;
(γ) the presupposition of the satisfaction of reference.

(α)–(γ), which already exist to screen the 'epistemological' contingency of existential questions, are subsequently backed up by

(δ) the assumption that difference can be analysed in purely positive terms.

The crucial concept I will employ in arguing against ontological monovalence is that of real negation or *absence*. And I want to affirm all of the following:

(a) that we can refer to absence, or, to use the Platonic terms, non-being;
(b) that absence (non-being) exists;
(c) that absence has ontological priority over presence within zero-level being, i.e. a world containing positive existence; and
(d) that absence (non-being) has ontological priority simpliciter.

First some terminological clarification is called for. Negation has a bipolarity, designating a process/product ambiguity. If absence is, as I am going to demonstrate here, at the heart of existence, absenting is, I will show in the next chapter, the hub of space, time and causality (which I will there unify with existence). In fact absence has a fourfold polysemy: it can denote product (simple absence, with which I shall

---

[†] Parmenides (born in 515 BC) wrote a famous poem declaring that it was impossible to say 'it is not'. By forbidding negation, Parmenides ruled out absence and change, and alterity, diversity and multiplicity alike. His poem is also a performative contradiction. A world without negation is conceivable only as an all-pervasive token monism without structure and infinite in character and extent. As for the Parmenidean monist, he must first fall into Cratylan silence (a curious reversal for the Heraclitian caricature) and thence into solipsism. These positions are both practically self-refuting and so liable to immanent critique and vulnerable to metacritical analysis and explanation.

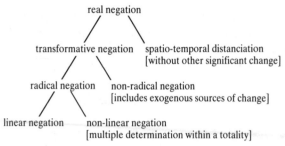

Figure 3.5 Concepts of Negation

be mainly, but not exclusively, concerned here), process (simple absenting), process-in-product and product-in-process (the former represented by the constitutive presence of the past or exterior, the latter by iteration or ongoing social activity). Next, different concepts of real negation or absence must be distinguished. *Real negation* is consistent with spatio-temporal distanciation without trans-formation; *transformative negation* is consistent with exogenous sources of change; and *radical negation* is consistent with multiple determination within a totality — which if it is single-sourced may be called *linear negation*. This is illustrated in the tree diagram Figure 3.5. The causal 'absenting' sense of real negation is better brought out by the concept of negativity, which also designates the other main sense of negativity with which I shall be concerned in this book: ill-being. There are of course many other senses of 'to negate', including to 'deny', 'oppose', 'contradict', 'exclude', 'marginalize', 'criticize', 'condemn', 'erase', 'undo', which have some bearing on my primary senses, which will be thematized in due course. For our purposes here the one theorem, to be explicated in the next chapter, essential for this is that *to cause is to negate or to absent*; normally — indeed paradigmatically — *in space-time*.

How might one set about a transcendental deduction of the concept of real negation or absence in, say, science? By noting the spaces (absences) in the text of a research report, its reliance on data not present in it, on pre-understanding of its context, including its spatio-temporal geo-history. Or by noting the absence of extraneous intervention or countervailing causes that the epistemic access to an underlying and normally absent (to consciousness, from actuality) generative mechanism that an experiment is designed to afford. Or by noting the reliance in scientific retroductive modelling of metaphors and analogies drawn from the past (the wave theory of light) or other disciplines (Dalton's training as a meteorologist or Darwin's interest in Malthus will exemplify the cross-fertilization of creative science and philosophy†).

Now reference is quite neutral between absence and presence. I can refer to the hole in my sock, the empty cupboard, the missed plane, the failed monsoon, the unkept date, just as I can create a fiction or reject a proposition. There are thus three distinct senses of 'non-being'. It is the first ontological one in which I am interested, although by the development of a theory of levels (or 'types') it constellationally incorporates the other two. The intransitive object of specific epistemic inquiries may then be present, in which case I shall call the ontic an 'ont', or absent, in which case I will call the ontic a 'de-ont'. Thus we have ontology > ontics > onts. If de-onts are necessary for being, as the transcendental deduction of the previous paragraph indicates that they are, then they are equally necessary for our apprehension of being.

But are they indeed necessary for being? The classical corpuscularian/mechanical world-view was characterized by a conception of the externality of causation, transmitted by a contiguous contact on atomic rigid fundamental entities without internal structure or complexity set in the context of absolutist concepts of space and time, with novelty, variety and transformation in nature regarded as metaphysically secondary qualities. It is worth recalling that Newton always regarded gravity as a temporary stop-gap and that the Michelson—Morley experiment which retrospectively vindicated Einstein was designed to demonstrate the existence and properties of the ether — a continuous substance which transmitted the motion of light. Action by contiguous contact betwen atoms is conceptually incoherent.[9] Matter is necessarily intrinsically 'loose' and extrinsically 'clustered'. In short, absence is constitutively necessary for presence; but the converse is not the case. There *could* have been nothing rather than something; but there could not be something without nothing. Absence, then, has absolute and relative physical priority over presence.

Despite the proliferation of non-existential proofs in science — of caloric, phlogiston, the ether, Vulcan, and many more according to our generalized concept of reference and existence, in which there are no a priori limits on what one can refer to, and hence on what can be said to exist — the Popperian dogma that non-existential proofs are impossible in science is still the received wisdom. But fallibilism itself

---

† Some examples: Plato's obsession with mathematics, Aristotle's brilliant biology, Aquinas's ecclesiastical motivation, Cartesian physics, Leibnizian polymathematism, Kantian astronomy, Hegelian historiography, Russellian logic.

depends upon ontological bivalence, and the whole point of argument is to identify and eliminate mistakes. (Later I shall argue that the identification and elimination of absences, which function as constraints, is essential to ethics and ought to be so for politics.) Even more simply, intentionally to say 'I do' at a wedding is to absent an absence. Not to admit absence to our ontology — in that very inadmission — is to commit *performative contradiction*, to be guility of theory/practice inconsistency. Alterity, the central motif at 1M, or otherness can be seen as absence by a simple perspectival switch — absence from the point of self-identity; totality, the crucial figure at 3L, depends on the absenting of the absence of relevant distinctions and connections, and of detotalizations and splits; and agency, the pivot at 4D, is just absentive absenting, viz. embodied intentional causal agency — or, more simply put, getting rid of (absenting) an absence or presence. In a curious engrossment and desubjectivization of the solipsism which, we saw in Chapter 3.1, irrealism entails, only an all-pervasive token monism (such as a Parmenidean monism or something like the panentheism of which Hegel is sometimes accused, but without Hegelian constellational differention) is the only conceivable ontologically monovalent world.

I should like to argue for ontological polyvalence and not just bivalence for two types of reasons. First, ontologically, because of the existence of borderline situations (when we need to speak of the co-incidence of identity and difference or that of identity and change) and of the existence (or the possibility of the existence) of certain types of fundamental entities or ultimata, which I shall treat in Chapter 4, characterized by a systematic ontological ambiguity. Second, epistemologically, because some questions of presence or absence, more generally existential questions, are undecidable for us now. Here we need to be ready with a non-valent response, identifying precisely our explicandum, as a propaedeutic perhaps to the Socratic response of 'problematizing the question' in a search for a fuller, richer, deeper and/or more relevant set of descriptions of what appears as an inherently dilemmatic situation — to which the best response is to redescribe, or, in the practical domain, otherwise alter the alternatives.

Why does the Platonic analysis of negation (and change) in terms of difference fail? First, to say that Sweetie the bull is not in his field does not *mean* the same as to say that he has got into the cowshed; just as to say that I have lost my voice doesn't mean the same as to say that I won't be speaking at the Colloquium. Second, our whole spatio-temporal locating system, and hence the possibility of any referential act, depends upon a material system characterized by exclusion relations of change as well as difference. None of this means that the concept of difference, or sheer other-being, is not as important to our ontology as the concept of change; or that time — classically conceived as the dimension of change — has ontological priority over space — classically conceived as the dimension of difference (later I will argue that this is far too simplistic); or that we do not need the notion of differentiating changes as much as changing differentiations.

What implications does the critique of ontological monovalence have for the problems of philosophy? We must first differentiate (a) specifically 2E problems of philosophy, viz. those that turn on the absence of the relevant categories of negativity, from (b) the implications of negativity and categories of negativity such as oppositionality, and the dialectic (of which negativity is the linchpin) for the problems of philosophy in general. Let us consider (b) first. Critical realist dialectic is specified by the terms of non-identity (1M), negativity (2E), totality (3L) and transformative praxis or agency (4D). Now, as already noted, it is characteristic of philosophical problem-fields to be internally riven, constitutively split into opposing factions, such as materialism and idealism, or empiricism and rationalism. A *dialectical* explanation of the opposition would seek its grounds in a common mistake; and a metacritically$_2$ dialectical explanation would seek to explain that mistake in its social context. Thus we have seen how the opposition between empiricism, characteristically subject to the positivistic illusion, and rationalism, undergirded by the converse speculative illusion, is grounded in the *absence* of the mediating terms of empirically controlled scientific theory, in the transitive dimension, seeking to identify deeper or fuller layers of ontological stratification (a fault which Kant tried to repair in the medium of philosophy and without the concept of ontology, and so a fortiori lacking the concepts of natural necessity or ontological stratification[†]). Similarly the opposition between materialism and idealism, as applied to human agency, appears in the form of a split between physicalistic reductionism (reification) and spiritualistic dualism (effective disembodiment), to both of which philosophers of the first persuasion tend to need to be committed (to sustain their own discursive agency). The roots of this split lie in the *absence* (again) of the concept of embodied *intentional causal agency*; and more generally of an emergent powers materialism. Indeed, before this book is through, we shall see how the problems of

---

[†]   Although in his very later works he was much concerned with finding mediating levels between noumenal and phenomenal realms.[10]

philosophy typically stem from the anthropocentric epistemic fallacy (at 1M), spawning identity theory and actualism, ontological mono-valence (at 2E) blocking change, and what I shall call rhythmic causality (for now, roughly spatio-temporal process) and contradiction, ontological extensionalism (at 3L) cutting the ground from under categories of totality, including crucial mediating notions such as mediation itself, constellationality, duality (with or without a hiatus), and the emergent powers materialism that is necessary to sustain the concept of the causality of reasons (at 4D), and (anti-humanist, de-agentifying) reification and/or disembodiment (includ-ing voluntarism with respect to social structure, the past, the exterior and intra-dependent totalities). These generate various illicit fusions, eliminating essential distinctions (cf. especially at 1M), and illicit fissions, eliminating essential connections (cf. especially at 3L).[†] The central absence is the concept of absence, and its derivatives from geo-historicity to contradiction, opposition and critique. Metacritically$_2$ the 1M−4D network, pivoting on 2E lack, offers us important diagnostic clues to the nature of the social realities in which the aporiai of philosophy, resolved, diagnosed, unified and metacritically$_1$ (viz. *omissively*) critiqued, will be explained.

Elsewhere I have dubbed ontological monovalence, the epistemic fallacy and primal squeeze (on the Platonic/Aristotelian fault-line) the unholy trinity of irrealism. They are related as follows. The epistemic fallacy generates actualism, the generalized form of subject−object identity theory, whether it is regarded as achieved (e.g. in Aristotle) or not (as in Plato). Now a completely achieved identity theory is as untenable, if only because of the dilemmas of actualism observed in Chapter 2.3, as a completely unachieved one is useless, so referring back to the schema of Figure 3.3 we have the theorem of the interdependence of anthroporealism and transcendent realism, of weak and strong actualism and of immanent and transcendent accounts of reality. On this, and the figure it illustrates, the tacit complicity of dialectical antagonists grounded in a common mistake, I will comment further later. Back to the unholy trinity. As ontological monovalence, taken literally, entails the exclusion of alterity, otherness, it implies, as primeval monism, the identity of thought and being, whether this takes the form of the epistemic fallacy or the ontic fallacy. I shall later argue for the historical primacy of the former from Plato, following in fact Parmenides. But in any event we have

---

[†] If there were a single key to clarity in philosophy, it would be the ability to think the constellational unity (embracing the difference) of distinctions and connections — itself a figure of what I shall call the dialectics of co-inclusion.

the ordering: ontological monovalence → epistemic fallacy → primal squeeze.

I turn now from the antinomial/dilemmatic/oppositional forms of philosophical problems, to those aporiai which depend essentially upon the absence of concepts of negativity or its derivatives. These may range from: (a) 2E occurrences of essentially 1M problems, when, for instance (i) ontologically, situations of inductive scepticism occur and we have to attribute to one and the same being, or continuant, changing causal powers, as in the problem of 'personal identity', when an infant matures, a prodigy's powers wane or a wasting disease gradually takes its toll,[†] or (ii) epistemologically, in a scientific revolution, when one has to stand Tyndall's criterion, viz. 'ask yourself whether your imagination can accept it', on its head and ask oneself whether one can continue to accept one's imagination. This leads us naturally into (b), viz. those aporiai which stem from the absence of an appropriate 2E concept. Thus it is not difficult to see that a monovalent ontology can accommodate neither epistemic nor ontological change; nor, a fortiori, sustain the difference between them. Thus, on Humean assumptions, what is the difference between the change in a course of nature and a breakdown in intellectual conformity? The inadmissibility of change is the source of the crisis that the actuality of social and epistemic relativism — particularly in the political and scientific earthquakes of 1905 and 1917 — induced when they seeped into foundationalist philosophy and is the proximate cause of the judgemental irrationalism, including voluntaristic superidealisms and dogmatically reactionary fundamentalisms, that dot our social landscape. Or let us take as an example of the result of the absence of the concept of contradictions within a multiply determined totality, such as an individual human's subjectivity, the problem of *akrasia* — or 'weakness of the will'. This arises because we do not think of the springs of action in a multi-componential arena, in which sensibility may be at loggerheads with cognition (and itself), routine or habit in opposition to decision or will, etc. Particularly important here are the repression of spatio-temporalities from philosophical consciousness, which generates the aporiai of time-consciousness (and by a short route the problem of memory) for punctualism, or the Aristotelian aporia of future contingents for blockism; or those stemming from the disembedding

---

[†] Here we have real 2E occurrences of the problem of induction, when one and the same entity's causal powers change. If geo-historical entities, such as social individuals or the cosmos, are processes-in-products (in process), then we have to think them under the aspect of their identity with their continually changing causal powers.

of the concepts of space, time, place and tense from each other; or those which turn on the absence of the concept of the emergence of contradictory tendencies, which makes it difficult for a linguistified age to think the concept of hermeneutic struggles over generalized master–slave-type relations or discursively moralized power$_2$ relations; or of the emergence of new forms of being or concepts (e.g. in science) in the face of the doubly dogmatic reinforcement of the status quo that 1M identity theory locked with 2E monovalence exercise, screening its geo-historicity and contingency alike.

§ 3 Truth, Judgement and Consistency

Truth seems to be at once (a) the easiest and (b) the most complex of concepts. We can derive the fourfold characteristics of *judgements* as such (and not just truth judgements) from (a). Saying 'true' to a proposition is

   (i) to give one's assent to it, from which redundancy and performative theories derive their plausibility, corresponding to which we have

   [1] the *expressively veracious* aspect of judgements;

   (ii) to accept a claim about the world, roughly to the effect that this is indeed the way things are, whence correspondence theories since Aristotle's time have derived their power, corresponding to which we have

   [2] the *descriptive* aspect of judgements;

   (iii) a claim, which in principle needs to be grounded, which points in the direction of coherence theories, corresponding to which we have

   [3] the *evidential* aspect of judgements;

   (iv) which is also a claim that carries the normative force 'trust me — act on the basis of it', corresponding to which we have

   [4] the *imperatival-fiduciary* aspect of judgements.

To the four-dimensionality of the judgement form I will return. For the moment it is sufficient to appreciate that it is in virtue of its world-reporting meaning that truth-talk satisfies a transcendental-axiological need, acting as a steering mechanism for language-users to find their way about the world. But first let me focus on some of the aporiai stemming from the complexity of truth.

Outside the Marxist camp, the most influential correspondence theories in this century have been Wittgenstein's picture theory, Tarski's semantic theory and Popper's theory of verisimilitude. The basic objection to them is that there seems no Archemedian standpoint from which a comparison of the putatively corresponding terms can be made. This is further strengthened once we, epistemologically, reject autonomized immediate knowledge and the reification of facts endemic to identity theory, of which the ontic side of correspondence theory is merely the anthropomorphic form. That said, it has to be recognized that there is an inherent epistemic – ontic duality or bipolarity which cannot be completely gainsaid in a fully adequate truth theory. Coherence theories seem most plausible as an account of the criteriology of truth (which one would in any event expect to be as variable as the contexts in which truth claims are made) rather than their meaning. Moreover, whether in mainstream or Hegelian (on which truth is the conformity of an object to its notion, ultimately the whole) form, they seem to presuppose a correspondence-theoretic account of correctness (although it could be argued that if one treated the world parahermeneutically, like a text, coherence would be the best account of correspondence). Deweyian pragmatism is vulnerable to the objection that a proposition may be warrantedly assertable but false; while Nietzschean perspectivism, on which truth is a 'mobile army of metaphors', seems ultimately self-erasing. Redundancy theory, initially formulated by Ramsey, seems either to smuggle in truth disquotationally or to deny the axiological necessity of the truth predicate, as something we language-users employ as a steering mechanism to get around the world. Performative theories of the type advocated by Strawson and Searle seem more plausible in this respect, but they in turn underplay the extent, stressed by Kripke, to which the use of the truth predicate needs to be grounded. Consensus theories are subject to the objection that a consensual opinion can be false, and, if given an ideal-typical interpretation (as, for example, by Habermas, or earlier Gramsci), that they do not explicate our existing concept of truth. Marxian theories have been torn (although this is not true of Marx himself)[11] between a naïve reflection of the object theory in dialectical materialism and a practical expression of the subject theory in western Marxism.

An adequate theory of truth must take into account the fact that it is a many-layered concept, in which there are four basic components: which I will nominate the *truth tetrapolity*:

(α)   truth as *normative-fiduciary*, truth in the 'trust me — act on it'
      sense. Trust is of course itself a complex concept, as we shall
      see in the next chapter, but we can take its paradigmatic
      locutionary force here to be in inter-subjective communication;

(β)   truth as *adequating*, as 'warrantedly assertable', as epistemo-
      logical, as relative in the transitive dimension;

(γ)   truth as *referential—expressive*, as a bipolar ontic—epistemic
      dual, and in this sense as absolute; and, the sense I have
      already introduced,

(δ)   the truth as *ontological*, no longer tied to language-use per se
      and in this sense objective and in the intransitive dimension,
      typically achievable when referential detachment (see §1)
      occurs; and a special case of which is

(δ') truth as *alethic*, i.e. the truth of or reason for things, people and
      phenomena generally (including in science most importantly
      causal   structures   and   generative   mechanisms),   not
      propositions.

We can best see how this works by articulating a *dialectic of truth* with
reference to Figure 2.2 in Chapter 2.1. A group of scientists are (a)
subjectively empirically certain about the reason S_j for some well-
attested phenomena S_i at T_1. They succeed in convincing their
colleagues about (b) the intersubjective facthood of S_j, so that it
becomes referentially detached, on our generalized concepts of
reference and existence at T_2, as (c) the reason for, or the objective
truth of, S_j, while (d) the new wave of scientists is at the same time
heading the search for the reason S_k for S_j (which will produce the
alethia of S_j in turn). Thus we go from subjective certainty →
subjective facthood → objective truth → alethic truth. Note two
points in particular about the tetrapolity. It is the difference between
(β) and (γ) that accounts for the difference between warranted
assertability and truth. Second objective, referentially detached, truth
at (δ) and (δ') is no longer praxis-dependent, or tied to language-use,
although of course claims to it are. It is sui generis ontological.

   All the aspects of the judgement form are universalizable — albeit in
different ways.

   [1] Expressive veracity: 'if I had to act in these circumstances, this
        is what I would act on.'

   [2] Descriptive: 'in exactly the same circumstances, the same result
        would ensue.'

   [3] Evidential: 'in exactly the same circumstances, the reasons
        would be the same.'

[4] Fiduciary: 'in exactly *your* circumstances, this is the best thing to do.'

[2] and [3] are valid only if a normic interpretation of the 'same circumstances' is given; and when the reasons in [3] specify the alethic truth of [2], i.e. when [2] is optimally grounded and [3] is optimally grounding. [4] licenses in Kantian terms only an assertoric imperative: it is tied to the *concrete singularity* of the addressee. Concrete singularity is one of the four moments of the concrete universal which I shall discuss more fully in the next chapter, but before then it may be specified as follows:

(α) universality corresponding to 1M;
(β) rhythmicity or causally absenting spatio-temporal processuality corresponding to 2E;
(γ) particular mediations corresponding to 3L;
(δ) concrete singularity corresponding to 4D.

The moments of the judgement form are internally related and it expresses, whether in the sphere of theoretical or practical reason, a *theoretico-practical duality* or function. The fiduciary nature of the expressively veracious judgement immediately entails a *dialectic of solidarity* with the addressee of the judgement, while its assertoric aspect implies this will be welcome. We shall explore some of the implications of this in Chapter 7.

I have laid emphasis on the figure of theory/practice inconsistency as a weapon of immanent critique. But what exactly is (1) dialectical or developmental or (2) theory/practice consistency? Developmental consistency, such as exemplified by the connection of ongoing theories in a progressive research programme or in nature by the metamorphosis of a caterpillar into a butterfly, is clearly not the same as analytical or formal consistency. It may be exemplified by the Hegelian 'speculative proposition', which I have also called *subject negation*, which describes an object in the process of formation. Ontologically, it breaks with fixism, and epistemologically with both formalism (rigid definitions) and nominalism (arbitrary definitions) — that is to say, it presupposes semantic 'open texture'. Judgements about developmental consistency are necessarily intrinsic to (the description of) the process concerned.

But what about theory/practice consistency? This concerns consistency in a praxis in a process. It should be (a) practical, (b) oriented to an end-state or process, i.e. directional, and (c) universally accountable, such that it is (i) transfactual, (ii) concrete (i.e. satisfies all the moments of the concrete universal), (iii) actionable (which entails being achievable by the agent concerned, so agent-specific, which is also an implication of the criterion of concrete singularity) and (iv) transformatively directional towards the end-state specified. Actionability also carries the implication that, at the price of theory/ practice inconsistency, the addressor of the expressively veracious assertorically sensitized fiduciary remark should act in solidarity with her addressee. But solidarity is not subsitutionism. It is the agent's self-determination in some respect to which the fiduciary remark is oriented. A prefigurative condition is also an implication of the theory/practice consistency in a praxis in a process. This has two ingredients: first, means – ends consistency insofar as it is possible; second, that the praxis embodies or expresses in some way, and to the extent feasible, the values of the end-state, which of course may itself only be transitional or conceptualized as a process. Theory/ practice inconsistency leads to pathologies of action, from repression through compromise formation to ad hoc grafting, all subjects of interest to Marxists, Nietzscheans and Freudians alike.

Theoretical and practical reasoning exemplify duality-with-a-difference. Theoretical reason is concerned to adjust our beliefs to conform to the world, but by the merest transcendental perspectival switch it may be seen as intentional agency; so that, for instance, an assertoric expressively veracious truth judgement implies a commitment to the dialectic of solidarity and thence, I will argue, to the alethic truth of ethics (moral truth), universal human emancipation. Practical reason is concerned to adjust the world to conform to our will (interests, needs, desires), but this presupposes theoretical reason in the form of (ideally, alethically) grounded belief, that is to say, a theory of transformation or transition. And just as theoretical reason presupposes practical judgement, practical reason may be seen again by the simplest transcendental perspectival switch as belief-expressive, quasi-propositional, indicating or betraying the subject's beliefs about the world. Following Hegel, I will call the unity of theoretical and practical reason *absolute reason*; but insist, contra Hegel, that their unity — or perhaps better coherence — be achieved not in the realm of theory but in that of transformative praxis. There is a two-way dialectic of truth and freedom mediated in practice by phronesis or practical wisdom, the application of which may be called *'dialectical rationality'*.

Causality, Change and Emergence

But it does move.[†]
GALILEO (1632)

Change is constant.
DISRAELI (1867)

§ 1 Space, Time and Causality

Space, time and causality are all 2E categories of negativity. In this chapter I am going to tie them very closely together — chiefly in the notion of a *rhythmic*, which may be defined as a tensed spatializing process consisting in the exercise and/or impact of the causal efficacy of the powers (that is to say, tendencies) of a structure or thing. Such rhythmics may have supervenient causal powers of their own — for space and time are far from causally inert. Rhythmic is a paradigmatic 2E category insofar as it characteristically designates transformative distanciating *absenting process*. Such processes are usually but not necessarily substantial; they may be discontinuous and/or efficacious across a level-specific void. (And so may be said to exist, on the generalized notion of reference I am employing; so that we may talk of the intra-cosmic constellational unity of spatio-temporality, causality and being.) Rhythmics have, like absence, a process/product ambiguity so that they may also be used to denote the spatio-temporal material impact of a thing. Your reading this book is part of just one of the rhythmics in which you are currently engaged. Others may be cooking a meal, having a baby, engaging in a research project, enjoying life, all with characteristically different spatio-temporalities.

[†] Referring to the earth, after his inquisition.

I shall say that things and processes have *spatio-temporalities*. Space-time itself has a fivefold character:

(a) as a *referential grid* for identifying the presence of existents or non-existents (absences, de-onts), employing appropriate demonstrative and recognitive criteria;

(b) as a *measure* or matrix for locating, dating and individuating entities, events, potentials, fields, etc.;

(c) as a set of *prima facie mutual exclusion relations*, turning on difference in extent (space) or change in endurance (time);

(d) as a potentially emergent *property* — either:

    (α) as new relata of an existing system of material things, in which case they may well possess (possibly discrepant) causal powers of their own; and/or

    (β) as relata of a new (emergent) system of material things, a topic I develop in the next section; and

(e) as a (currently macroscopically generally entropic) process or *rhythmic*.

It should be said straight away that there is nothing at all anthropocentric about the reality of space, time, tense, place and process. I shall defend the reality and irreducibility of MacTaggart's A-series (past, present and future) to his B-series (earlier than, simultaneous with, later than); that is, the *reality* of tense and the *irreducibility* of space-time on any world-line both for the transitive observer and the intransitively observed. I shall be opposing, on the one hand, indexicalism and punctualism, generating the idea that only the present here exists, leading to the pole of Cratylan solipsism; and opposing, on the other, blockism and closure, generating the idea that everywhere everywhen simultaneously (co-locationally) exists, leading to its curious inverse, the pole of Parmenidean monism.

Spaces and times intersect and overlap. Consider a welfare queue deafened by the noise of an overhead low-flying supersonic aeroplane in a shut-down hospital site strewn with fashion magazines and with a video portraying a sporting contest in Dubai in a Labour borough in contemporary England governed by an antiquated constitutional system. This example illustrates the way in which overlapping, elongated, truncated, spatio-temporalities may coalesce. But it also illustrates the constitutive dependency of entities (natural as well as social) on their geo-historical processes of formation. (Think of a mountain cliff sedimentally stratified by the layers of different geo-historical epochs. Think of a person like this too.) Corresponding to this case in the domain of 3L totality is systematic constitutive intra-relationality, the way in which a social entity such as a person is existentially *constituted* by — not just dependent upon — their relations with their 'significant others' (from primary polyadization on) and perhaps their occupation, possessions (even, fetishist-ically[?], their clothes and/or their car), such that without these relations they should be essentially different. This throws into sharp relief the inadequacies of our existing concept of personal identity,[1] a legacy of Christian-Cartesian 'soul' and bourgeois-individualist 'man' (sic).[2]

The first (2E) case is an example of a process-in-product (one of the fourfold senses of real negation) and at the same time of the intrinsic presence of the past and outside. There are four modes in which the past and/or outside may be said to be present:

(α) *Existential constitution*, just discussed, which includes mere containment without the implication of essentiality and as a parallel of the presence of the future mediated by the presence of the past (consider pregnancy).

(β) *Existential pre-existence*. We are 'thrown' into a world created by the past, socially by dead labour. Look at the statues in the town square, the education system you have progressed through, the health service which has failed you or doesn't exist, the dwellings in which you live, the books that line your study. Its weight is massive. The futuricity of praxis must draw on it or doom itself to failure.

(γ) *Co-inclusion*, from memory to the existence of a tradition, event, etc. tensed as past with reference to a locating-dating system regarded as explanatorily more basic (or perhaps just merely conventionally accepted) with distanciated or stretched/spread spatio-temporality. The clock strikes twelve but you have been reading for an hour. Within the mode of distanciated time-consciousness (a) different rhythmics may interlope or clash in Joycean fashion, (b) any given rhythmic may seem slower (the last hour of a six-hour train journey) or faster (the characteristic fate of joy). Or spread stretches may condense in a rendez-vous.[3] This is perhaps the place to make the point that the dialectics of co-inclusion not only violates Leibnizian derivations of space and time but, more importantly, renders the Kantian notion of a necessary unity of time-consciousness as phenomenologically suspect as it is (by relativity theory) scientifically antiquated.

(δ) *Lagged, delayed efficacy*, e.g. of the volcano, or the Freudian unconscious, of many of the possible effects of global warming (including the chaos-theoretic triggering of a due new Ice Age) or the spread of AIDS. One might like to think of such phenomena as mediated by transfactual processes, but there is no necessity, especially in emergent domains, for continuous rhythmics.

The concept of spatio-temporality should not lead us to overlook the multiple disembedding of its components. Thus we have:

(a)   the disembedding of space from time, e.g. in a (long-distance) telephone conversation:
(b)   the disembedding of time from space, e.g. in a trans-Atlantic aeroplane flight;
(c)   the disembedding of space from place, e.g. in the investment decisions of a multi-national corporation; and
(d)   the disembedding of time from tense, arguably in the context of abstract homogenized labour-time.

Emergence is also characteristic, for instance, in the conceptual field, first of time from space, and then of time from tense, or, in the case of the virtualization of reality, say in a 'theme park', first of space from place (the pre-existing 'organic locale'), then of time from space and finally of time from tense.

Truths, including alethic truths, may be changing (in which case they may be said to be reflexive), or unchanging (irreflexive). Metacritically we are situated within limits. There must be sufficient constants, such as the speed of light, for scientific activity to be *possible*, but there must equally be sufficient change for scientific *activity*, absentive absenting agency, to take place. More generally, the critique of ontological monovalence shows the *transcendental necessity for reflexive truth*; physics and psychology alike impress upon us the reality of novelty and emergence (including disemergence and decay). When it comes to ultimate entities in a domain or for the cosmos as a whole, a realist interpretation of them is saved by considering them as instantiating the *dispositional identity* of a thing, such as a person with her changing causal powers. Then *to be is to be able to become*. But in a cosmos or entity in motion, some at least of the ultimata must consist in their rhythmic identity with the *exercise* of their changing causal powers. At this point it makes perfect sense to talk of the identity of identity and change, just as in the 3L case of intra-relationality when one entity is existentially constituted by another one might want to talk of the identity (or, perhaps better, co-incidence) of identity and difference.

The irreversibility of space-time is established by the impossibility of backwards causation. Antecedence is essential to causality and is implicit in all transitive action verbs. The postulate of backwards causations is philosophically only plausible on the assumption of the deprocessualization of reality, as is implicit in Humean theory, in which case, as is ironically brought out in the thesis of the parity of explanation and prediction, the order of a constant conjunction of events is irrelevant to the attribution of causality. The transcendental necessity for and irreducibility of the A-series, and a fortiori tense, can be established either by the argument from ontological monovalence of the preceding paragraph or by the argument against backwards causation (which turns essentially on the fact that a power cannot, analytically, be possessed subsequent to, although it may be simultaneous with, its effect). It is of the foremost importance to see that, as in the case of our critique of the Platonic analysis of change in terms of difference, to say that, to take a famous example from Aristotle, a sea-battle, say event E_o, hasn't happened doesn't *mean* the same as to say that it is earlier than some other event, which is quite consistent with its having already occurred.[†] It only *seems* to do so if we are tacitly identifying the second event with our own ego-ethno-anthropocentric now. Consider another example. An event on another world-line E_a lies in the future for its inhabitants, but suppose we could *per impossible* (because of the finite speed of light) observe it now. Does not this show the unreality of tense? No — it only seems to do so again because we are tacitly superimposing the now on our world-line on to the future of E_a's inhabitants, something physics prohibits us from doing. If the first example illustrates ego-/anthropo-centrism, the second illustrates ego-/anthropo-morphism. And this leads me conveniently into my critique of irrealist theories of space, time and tense.

Irrealism about tense inevitably leads to irrealism about causality (which is directional process), whence it is a short step to irrealism about existence and hence space and time too. We retreat to the position called indexicalism, that only the present exists. Squeeze this position on to here and it becomes punctual: the present is reduced to a punctual now here. This is Heidegger's 'vulgar' conception of time. It is beautifully refuted by Virginia Woolf's novel *Orlando*, whose main character perfectly illustrates the dialectics of co-inclusion (base

---

[†] Martin Amis's novel *Time's Arrow*[4] only invokes the *frisson* of backwards causation because (a) the story is told forwards, i.e. it is not set in the context of an ex post continuous series, and (b) the main line is contextualized by the detail of well-known forwards causation, which the gripped reader conveniently suspends or forgets but is entirely necessary for its plausibility.

place: Fortnum and Mason's; base time: 1926), changing sex while living through three centuries and enjoying all manner of experience in his/her *distanciated* embodied existence. If one is a sceptic about the existence of the past, then, as all inference and cognition (even the recognition of two graphemes as tokens of the same type) depends upon memory, one must end in solipsistic silence. The converse fallacy is the blockist closure postulate that all times simultaneously co-exist in an 'anthropomorphically projected' 'God's-eye' view of the world. But if the critique of ontological monovalence is valid, we must accept a necessary open future and totality. For the mere fact of intentional causality, or of emergence, or of a beginning or end in time establishes a critique of actualism (and its consequent, identity theory). The physicist's, no more than the sociologist's, universe is no longer Humean-Laplacean, blockist or closed, and we have no grounds for not accepting the radical contingency of the future, as we trace out differentiated, diverging physical (and converging social?), including epistemic and philosophical, world-lines. When it comes to space and time, philosophy's 'analogical grammar' is stamped by the scientific folklore of the past.

What is the reality of the tenses? The past is real as existentially intransitive and determined, though our knowledge of it is constantly becoming. The future is the (as it approaches, increasingly shaped) possibility of becoming. The present is an indefinite boundary state, of a duration that depends on the event or context which is happening — be it a cup of coffee, the housework, a research programme or a geographical epoch. This means the present is always liable to contain multiple parts in the mode of co-inclusion, perhaps in internal antagonism and disarray. To say that everything always occurs in the present is to make the best possible case for the reality of the tenses, which may, as I have elsewhere suggested, be thought in a (spatio-)temporally indefinite C-series.[5] Here 'P' was true between T_1 and T_i, false between T_i and T_j, and is true again at T_k and is open for the foreseeable future, where 'P' stands for 'is raining in London' illustrates the irreducible reflexivity and reality of tense.

I have floated the topic of emergent spatio-temporalities. It is now time to travel through emergence to the 3L realm of totality and consider its properties and the aporiai that arise there, before I return to the topic of causality, and therefore spatio-temporality, in illustrating what I will call the causal chain which traverses all moments of dialectical critical realism, under the suzerainty of traditionally repressed 2E negativity.

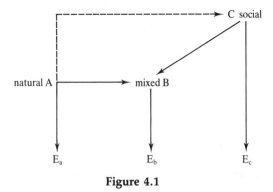

Figure 4.1

§ 2 Emergence and Totality

In the previous section I discussed the phenomena of emergent spatio-temporalities and in Chapter 2.2 I referred to emergent principles of structured totalities. Emergence may be defined as the relationship between two terms such that one diachronically, or perhaps synchronically, arises out of the other, but is capable of reacting back on the first and is in any event causally and taxonomically irreducible to it, as society is to nature or mind to matter. It is thus a figure of constellationality, pivots on the openness of being and the falsity of actualism (for the second term could have been neither induced nor deduced from the first) and incorporates the concept of levels, which, as we have already seen in another context, plays such an important role in avoiding the homology and/ or vicious regress characteristic of 1M problems of philosophy. Figure 4.1 illustrates the cases of natural, social and mediated or mixed determinations, where the dotted line represents relations of continual constraint and conditioning and where one should imagine feedback loops from $EA - EC$ and on to each of A, B and C. In general, the material causes of social phenomena (such as the forms of manifestation of eating, sexuality, ageing, illness or play) can rarely be explained in *wholly* physical or biological terms; while the effects of social causes will normally assume some physical form (a transaction over a counter, the articulation of phonemes in speech, the drilling of a hole in a road), and must in principle be mediated by past or present embodied agency. The term 'mediation' is an important 3L category, a moment of the concrete universal which I shall be discussing, and a way of avoiding the reductionism and dualism and the dichotomy of reductionism versus dualism in what may be tersely described as 'undialectical' thought (see Chapters 6 and 8). In general, if x achieves z via y, then y may be said to mediate their relation. Figure 4.2 is a perspectival switch on Figure 4.1. The form of 'ontological' materialism to which critical realism is committed asserts:

(a) the unilateral ontological dependence of social upon biological and thence physical forms; but

(b) the taxonomic and causal irreducibility of social to biological (and thence physical) forms, defining what may be characterized as a *synchronic emergent powers materialism*.

It does not deny the geo-historical emergence of organic from inorganic matter or of human beings from hominids, but it contends that reference to properties *not* designated by physical theory or biological theory is necessary to explain those physical states which are the result of or are mediated by intentional agency. The human world is an irreducible and causally efficacious dependent mode of matter. This illustrates once more the value in philosophy in thinking the duality, or, more precisely, articulation, of distinctions and connections within a posed dichotomy or opposition, such as society and nature (in the sense of the cosmos as a whole rather than, say, 'countryside') or mind and body. In the case of the mind—body dualism we avoid the extremes of physicalistic reductionist materialism and idealist dualistic disembodiment in the concept of *intentional causality* manifest in embodied agency. The reductionist materialist is vulnerable to the charge of theory/practice inconsistency or performative contradiction for what is his eliminative claim but an intentional self-cancelling act? Idealistic dualism, on the other hand, as we saw in Chapter 1.1 in the case of Kant, as has been repeated in countless forms (discourse theory, non-naturalistic hermeneutics,

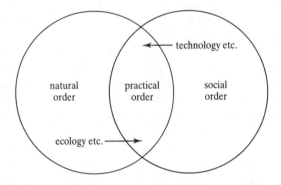

Figure 4.2

social constructionism), makes causal agency impossible. We have in effect here in this polarity the 'unity of opposites' in two forms of *de-agentification* — one issuing in *reification* and the other leading, via disembodiment, to effective *voluntarism*. This is already prefigured in the close association of the former with (Laplacean) determinism and the latter with advocacy of (unconstrained) 'free-will' — as in the Kantian injunction: 'ought implies [NB: not presupposes] can'.

Emergence makes possible the important phenomena of *dual* and *multiple control*. Physical laws set limits to and my physiological state enables me to write this precise sentence. But outside the special context of a closure the situation is rather, as Anscombe has expressed it, 'like the rules of chess; the play is seldom determined, though nobody breaks the rules'.[6] Chemical reactions are only partially constrained by Dulong and Petit's law and black bodies conduct themselves in all kinds of manner that are not specified by the Stefan–Boltzmann law. The use of machines is subject to control by the laws of economics as well as those of mechanics. But it is the former that determine when and where the latter apply, i.e. set the 'boundary conditions' for the use of machines. Closely connected with this topic is the Marxian aporiai of the *superstructures*. A superstructure–base relationship may be looked at in two ways. First, the polity, for instance, may be regarded as setting the boundary conditions for the relations of production which in turn set the boundary conditions for the forces of production (including science), the development of which initiates or enables transformation in the relations of production and so on. Second, the economic base may be regarded as setting the framework conditions of possibility within which cultural traditions and tendencies, for instance, mature or decay — in which event, we may regard culture as an *'intrastructure'*. These two models may be employed in complementary fashion in, say, a materialist explanation of the globalization of superveillance techniques.

We are now in the 3L domain of *totality*. Totalities are systems of internally related elements or aspects. A may be said to be internally related to B if it is a necessary condition for the existence (weak form) or essence (strong form) of B, whether or not the converse is the case (i.e. the relation is symmetric). A locale, for example, may be regarded as an internally related spatial network. I will sometimes talk of 'intra-relationality' or 'intra-action' instead of internal relationality. There are three forms of intra-action:

(α) *Existential constitution*, in which one element is essential or intrinsic to another, in the sense in which a person's charm may be said to be essential to her, even though it is not contained within her spatial envelope. This is an analogue of the existential constitution (not just dependence) of a thing by its geo-historical process of formation.

(β) *Existential permeation*, in which one element merely contains another.

(γ) *Causal connection*, in which one element is merely causally efficacious on another.

The internal relation between the parts of a melody, a sentence or a Titian or Van Gogh (contrast, montage or pastiche) comprise paradigm totalities. But there are many different kinds of totalities. There are expressive-centrist totalities, characteristic, as Althusser pointed out, of Hegelian ones, but present in real life as, arguably, my body may be said now to be in my writing hand.[†] There are sub-totalities punctuated by blocks and barriers or holes-within-wholes. And there are *partial totalities* constituted by external as well as internal and contingent in addition to necessary relations.

Is it possible to give a transcendental deduction for totality, as we did in Chapter 3.2 for negativity and in Chapter 2.3 for stratification? This is not difficult for the social world. Thus consider the experimental research report again, with sentences whose elements are semantically bound in a network of paradigmatic and syntagmatic relations (electrode, conductor, Farrady's law), existentially constituted by a research programme, permeated by the trajectory of the science and causally dependent on a government grant to produce instrumentally useful results. But is a deduction possible for nature? It could be argued that it is a condition of the possibility of science that things are classifiable into natural kinds, so that the Leibnizian level of knowledge of natural necessity is achievable. Second, it could be maintained that unless there were internal contradictions in things, change, and a fortiori emergence, and thus science itself would be impossible. For even if the apparent source of the change is exogeneous, the thing changed must be *liable* to it. It cannot be totally impervious and so must possess a counter-conative tendency in respect of the condition changed. Such 'inner complicity' would suggest thorough-going internal relationality in nature too. I will consider the validity of this line in the next section, but, for the present, the existence of at least partial totalities in social life can be

---

† Arguably, because of distraction, symptomatic of the internally disjoint pluriverses that human beings under conditions of contemporary capitalism and late/ post-modernity typically are.[7]

taken as established. This takes us immediately into contention with the doctrine of *ontological extensionalism*, classically (and extremely) formulated by Hume in his claim that events are entirely 'loose and separate, conjoined but never connected'. We shall explore the consequences of this dogma, paralleling ontological actualism at 1M and ontological monovalence at 2E, anon.

The characteristic mode of operation of a totality is *holistic causality*. This may be said to occur when a complex coheres such that:

(a) the totality, i.e. the form or structure of the combination, causally determines the elements; and

(b) the form or structure of the elements causally codetermine each other and so causally codetermine the whole.

Totalities bound in holistic causality may be asymmetrically weighted or charged and may contain relatively autonomous sub-totalities or generate detached autonomous structures. In general one will have to research a totality at two margins of inquiry: (α) the *intensive margin*, in which one will find more and more of the other elements and/or the whole packed or 'reflected' into a particular element; and (β) the *extensive margin*, in which one will find an element's efficacy reflected in more and more of the other elements or the whole. In the transitive dimension such research helps to account for the continual re-landscaping of totalities and rewriting of histories, while in the intransitive dimension the inescapable fact of change and the openness of the future account for the chameleon-like configurationality of social life. But even this distinction is too neat. For in the social sphere, although the existential intransitivity of phenomena remains (as a condition, we have already seen, of any intelligible act, including utterance, at all), all investigation has the practical character of a relational dialectic, in which the investigator is in principle part of the totality she describes. This implies the irreducibility of perspective (cf. epistemic world-lines) and the necessity for continual *perspectival switches*, as one permeates a totality from an exponentially increasing multiplicity of angles, together with the necessity for rational *self-reflexivity*. The pre-existing/ongoing character and multiplicity of rhythmics in social life entails that entities such as people and institutions will typically have the character of *processes-in-products-in-processes*. There is need here to construct much more complex ontologies than the simple shallowness of atomism and closure, generating actualist-monovalent-extensionalist and in practice reductionist (prefigured by Comte) and/or complexificationist (anticipated by Mill) regresses, would permit.

Figure 4.3 Totality of Structures Co-influencing a Bound
Conjuncture of Events

The *concrete universal* (see Chapter 3.3) has the minimum character
of a multiple quadruplicity with each element:

(α) universality = structure;
(β) processuality = rhythmic;
(γ) mediation = totality;
(δ) singularity = agency in the human sphere; generally, result or
outcome,

subject in principle to multiple (and, as we shall see, contradictory)
determination and totality. This is illustrated in Figure 4.3, where a
complex of the components of a conjuncture or multi-compounded
result cohere in a totality. It is important to differentiate within the
class of (a) concrete singularities, conceived as compounds,
conjunctures, condensates, outcomes or results, (b) the concrete
singularity of the individual human agent. The latter will have (i) a
universal aspect, constituted by our shared species-being (which
gives grounds for a core equality), (ii) particular mediations
characterizing her by age, gender, nationality, ethnicity, class, etc.,
(iii) in various processes of rhythmic formation, (iv) with idiographic
features uniquely individuating her. As a concrete singular she will be

defined by her dispositional identity with her rhythmically changing causal powers. This is represented in Figure 4.4.

There is a danger lurking here in the concept of the concrete, however. This is to give it an actualist interpretation. It is important to stress the concrete ≠ the actual ≠ the empirical. Indeed the concept of the concrete, insofar as it does not mean 'balanced' or 'well-rounded', makes full sense only in relation to its antipode, the abstract. Thus it was, I believe, the mature Marx's intention to construct a pan-concrete theoretical totality of the fundamental dynamics of the capitalist mode of production, which could be called capital-in-concretion, not to predict in actualist detail the future course of events. I have already referred to several other key 3L concepts such as mediation, constellationality and perspectival switches. But it is worth mentioning the figure of duality-with-a-difference or -with-a-hiatus preventing in the former case a reductionist collapse of theoretical to practical reason (or vice versa) and in the latter case of social structure to human agency (or vice versa). I will refer to these configurations again.

The phenomenon of reflexivity, which is the inwardized form of totality, has already been invoked in Chapter 1 in the concept of a meta-reflexively totalizing situation which allows us to think, for instance, the unity of world and language articulated in language within, from the standpoint of transcendental detachment (viz. detachment of the conclusions from the premises of one's argument), an over-reaching material objectivity. The stratification of the personality, which I will discuss in the next section, plays a key role in this — as it does in avoiding the need for Nietzschean forgetting or Heideggerian erasure (being) — a stratification which depends upon the rejection of actualism. Reflexivity is an ambivalent world-historical phenomenon manifest, on the one hand, as a sense of geo-historicity and, on the other, in the growth of surveillance techniques, restricting at once, to use Habermasian language,[8] the scope of the *Lebenswelt* or 'life-world' and access to the 'public

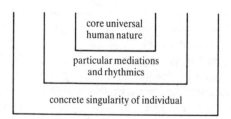

Figure 4.4 The Concrete Singularity of the Human Agent

sphere'. In direct opposition to superveillance conceived as an instrument of potential and actual manipulation is the existential of *trust*. This plays a philosophically significant role both (a) in what I have called primary polyadization, which is only the first — even if originally biographically the most important — instant of the systematic intra-subjectivity (existential constitution by others) that shapes our lives; and (b) in the dialectic of solidarity implicit in the expressively veracious judgement, and, by a perspectival switch, every practical deed (which is quasi-propositional in character). But trust is a complex existential and in addition to the personalized and concrete trust which correspond to (δ) and (γ) there are (α) the abstract trust we have in impersonal systems we know little about, and (β) the qualified mediated trust we might show in a system or person on which/whom we depend but which/who we have some, and perhaps good, reason to distrust, be it a mode of economic production or be he a politician, doctor or second-hand car salesman.

Since totalities are structures, there is an affinity between 3L and 1M approaches to the characteristically actualist and extensionalist problems of philosophy. Indeed we have already seen how one class of self-referential paradoxes can be resolved by reference to ontological stratification and we have witnessed the stratified self over distanciated space-time functioning as a resolution to the aporia of Nietzschean forgetting. Both the set-theoretic and related self-referential paradoxes are dissolved by the distinction between totalities, characterized by an emergent principle of structure, and aggregates (of which a heap is a prize example) which are not. Thus the heap paradox is not really a paradox at all. Whether we call something a heap or not depends on context and convention alone. More generally we can say that whereas the resolution of 1M problems of philosophy turns on a correct understanding of the relation of *cause to effect* (or inner to outer, primary to secondary quality, essence to accident, reality to appearance), chiefly via the concepts of ontological stratification or depth, the resolution of 3L problems turns on a correct understanding of the relation of *part to whole*, and hence the chief villain is ontological extensionalism or more generally detotalization and a misunderstanding of relationality (internal and external alike). If at 1M the prize mistake is the illicit *fusion* of the epistemic fallacy, actualism and identity theory, at 3L it is illicit *fission* implicit in detotalization or split, which may take the 4D form of an alienated split-off in the human realm and ontological extensionalism. At 2E the great problems are (a) those of opposites which can be explained in terms of a common dialectical ground and resolved by a suitable sublating mediation such as provided by the figure of constellationality, in the case of materialism v. dualism in the form of an emergent powers materialism; and (b) those of critical or limit situations, such as provided by the nodal point in a transition or the question of ultimata. I have already discussed the latter. But how do we understand the resolution of an anomaly or contradiction? At the point of transition, as the conceptual field is enlarged by the introduction of a new sublating notion, model or metaphor, positive contraries (actual and present) become negative sub-contraries (actual and absent), so completing the traditional table of opposition.[9]† This is clearly only intelligible if we adopt a non-punctualist view of 'space-time'. The new sublating concept offers a greater totalization in Gödelian fashion as indicated in Chapter 2, so totality as emergent structure plays a role in both paradigms.

In thematizing the problems of philosophy I have stressed that there can be extra-philosophical problems too. So how can dialectical critical realism play a part in illuminating the problems of, say, contemporary physics? For instance, it might be held that all we can speak about are the effects revealed by our experimental apparatus (conceived as part of our *Umwelt* or environment[10]). But if these effects are replicable, as they are, under experimentally closed contexts, then if we are to avoid invoking miracles, we *must* posit a cause for these effects and a realist interpretation of fundamental physics is saved, even if we can never empirically ascertain these

---

† It is, however, worth pointing out that for transcendental realism there is an easier way of completing the table of opposition. When two tendencies counteract each other but are nevertheless efficacious in codetermining a result, then at the level of the real they are positive contraries (both present) while at the level of the actual, as unmanifest, they are negative sub-contraries (both absent). It is of course the notion of negative sub-contraries, turning on the concept of reference to absence, and hence the critique of ontological monovalence, which allows the dialectical completion of the table of opposition. It is further worth mentioning that the two characteristic problems of philosophy at 2E, the problem of opposition and the problem of change, are thus united by the fact that the first (exemplified by Marxian dialectic) completes the traditional table of opposition in the mode of ontological stratification (the exercised tendencies explicable in terms of a common underlying causal ground are really efficacious but not actualized), while the second (exemplified by Hegelian dialectic) completes it in the mode of distanciated time (through the co-inclusion of the switched positive contraries to negative sub-contraries within the expanded discursive domain or conceptual field). Both turn, moreover, on the concept of negative reference — or, more precisely, referential detachment of the absent, whether unactualized or past (outside). At this point it is worth mentioning that when Plato analysed negation and change in terms of difference he reversed the traditional pre-Socratic analysis of difference as change from an assumed original unity, an analysis resumed by neo-Platonists such as Plotinus and given currency in Hegel's generation by Schiller. Both reductions must be rejected. If Plato's theory of Forms set the pattern for foundationalist epistemology to its present incarnations, it is his third period analysis of negation that structured the trajectory of subsequent ontology.

causes. We can allow, for instance, that the ultimata-for-us consists in the constellational identity of things (fields, forces) with their causal powers, including their powers to affect our sense-extending apparatus. As for the issue of indeterminacy, such a response may be supplemented by a concept of contextual or joint inter-action, in effect a form of holistic causality. If it is said that it is our interference which creates the indeterminacy, the case for transcendental realism is further strengthened in two ways. First, it allows us to re-emphasize that experimental activity is always the active demediation of nature — a demediation which, when successful, enables us to identify transfactually efficacious tendencies which apply to us too. Second, it makes it easier to reject that cognitive triumphalism, sometimes transposed as instrumentalist practical Prometheanism, which has gathered pace with the scientific and bourgeois revolutions from the seventeenth century on. There is no necessity that the world should be knowable to us, even if it is understandable why it should seem to be so. We are contingent temporary flotsam on a sea of being.

§ 3 Causality and Contradiction

To cause is to change is to negate is to absent (in any of the four senses, and four modes, of absenting). But causality is itself a multi-componential concept. Apart from the distinction between (i) antecedent condition stimulating, releasing or enabling the operation of a (ii) generative mechanism, we have used it polysemically to refer to:

(α)   the transfactual efficacy or generative mechanism of a structure;

(β)   the rhythmic (spatio-temporal) exercise of its causal powers;

(γ)   intra-active holistic causality within a totality;

(δ)   the intentionality of agency (corresponding respectively to 1M−4D); and

(ϵ)   the codetermination of a more or less unique result, a concrete singularity (corresponding to the moments of the concrete universal) — in the form of a conjuncture or compound (e.g. in the last case, a possibly uniquely laminated structuratum, such as only idiographically describable human agents).

We can illustrate the causal chain typical of open systems (in the case of (δ) in the social sphere) in Figure 4.5, remembering that each moment of the causal chain may be characterized by multiple

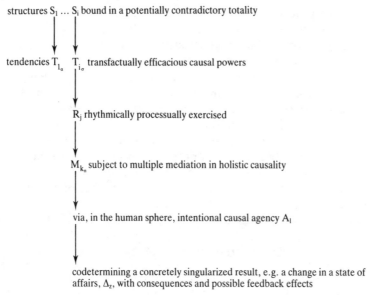

structures $S_1 \ldots S_i$ bound in a potentially contradictory totality

tendencies T_{1_a} T_{i_a} transfactually efficacious causal powers

R_j rhythmically processually exercised

M_{k_n} subject to multiple mediation in holistic causality

via, in the human sphere, intentional causal agency A_l

codetermining a concretely singularized result, e.g. a change in a state of affairs, Δ_z, with consequences and possible feedback effects

Figure 4.5 The Complexity of Causality

determination and totality. Corresponding to the distinct moments of the causal chain, we might want to differentiate distinct concepts of tendency:

(a) tendency$_a$ — a transfactually efficacious (or normically qualified) power;
(b) tendency$_b$ — the qualified directionality of a process;
(c) tendency$_c$ — the mediation of a (para-spatial) moment or a (para-temporal) determination;
(d) tendency$_d$ — a human disposition;
(e) tendency$_e$ — incorporating the effects of tendencies (a)–(d) plus conjunctural influences; all of which must be distinguished from
(f) tendency$_f$ — a tendency realized in all normal circumstances, and
(g) tendency$_g$ — a constant conjunction of events.

Within tendencies (a)–(f) further discriminations may be made. Thus the matrix set out in Figure 4.6 permits us in the case considered to identify the power a_2, a power *ready* to be exercised. If we allow that reasons can be causes, as I shall argue in the next chapter, and that absences (e.g. of food or shelter) can act as constraints, then, via the mediation of the concept of generation, we can work our way to a definition of the axiology of freedom as the *absenting of absences*. But thanks to our generalized concept of existence, which permits, inter alia, non-substantial process and reference to the existence of laws, and the critique of ontological monovalence, which enables reference to (absolute or relative) non-existents or absences, we have already achieved a unification of the concepts of existence, causality, space and time. And we are now in a position to see that real negation or absence is the hub not only, as argued in Chapter 3, of existence but also of causality.

Let us, by way of a stage summary, record some relevant theorems:

[1] $D_r > D_a > D_s$, whether D_s is empirical or conceptual.

[2] Ontology > ontics > onts.

[3] Real negation > transformative negation > radical negation > linear negation.

[4] To reason can be to cause = negate = absent which can be seen as to absent an absence acting as a constraint = to liberate.

Absences can be recursively embedded within absences, and wholes within wholes. In the 2E domain of negativity, which itself connotes ill-being in addition to absent-being (brought together in [4]), and the 3L domain of totality, further discriminations may be made. Thus radical negation stretches all the way from suicide to self-realization, auto-subversive tendency to self-overcoming process-in-product-in-process. Absences may be present in a negative (memory) or a

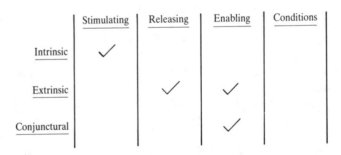

Figure 4.6

positive (not there) mode. All this indicates the need for a much more complex ontology than received philosophy provides.

Discussion of some slogans is to the point. Hegel famously inverted Spinoza to coin 'all negation is determination'. But this is not so — at least as Hegel meant it; for we have to distinguish real (natural) from logical negation, which Hegel's commitment to subject—object identity theory precludes, and definition from determination, a distinction Hegel elides. Moreover, we have to recognize that negations may be indeterminate in outcome and multiple, contrary to the linear autogenetics Hegel formally deploys. Then there is the celebrated/notorious 'negation of the negation', which Stalin saw fit to purge. In social life this can be simply interpreted as the geo-historical transformation of geo-historical products. This might be taken to re-establish a parity between the positive and the negative — until we remember that the initial and resultant product is radically constituted both by its process of formation, that is to say (to look at the matter synchronically), by its past and exterior, and by its inscription in a totality inhabited by entities and their relations other than itself.

I now want to say something about the vexed topic of contradiction. Apart from noting its use as a metaphor to designate any tension or strain, the first step to conceptual clarity here is to distinguish (a) *external contradictions*, which are binds or constraints, and, as such pervasive, from (b) *internal contradictions*, which are double-binds or self-constraints. This may be exemplified by the case where a system is blocked from pursuing a course of action T because it is pursuing an opposed course of action T'. As briefly indicated in the previous section, it is possible to construct an argument to show that for the very fact of change to be possible, internal contradictions are necessary. If the source is endogenous, then clearly the contradiction is internal. But if it is exogenous, a change in the thing, relative to the process concerned, will occur only if it is not completely impervious to the change. It must be at the very least liable to it. This is supported by my earlier argument in Chapter 3.2 against atomism. I will call this type of internal contradiction (c) *'inner complicity'*.

The most basic kind of (d) *existential contradiction* is established by finitude. (e) *Formal logical contradiction* must be rigorously distinguished from (f) *dialectical contradiction* as two distinct species of internal contradiction, although the classes intersect. The consequence of formal logical contradiction is axiological indeterminacy. To assert 'a' and 'not a' leaves the course of action indeterminate. If the subject must act, that is to say, what I have elsewhere called the 'axiological imperative' applies, then she is faced with a 'problematic axiological choice situation' — a 2E limit situation — in which, after a non-valent response, she must find some way of redescribing or changing the terms and/or expanding the relevant conceptualized terrain, so that the erstwhile positive contraries become negative sub-contraries, the contradiction is removed and she now has rational grounds for action. Note that even if this does not happen this does not mean either that nothing occurs or that the subject can do anything (you can't go anywhere from x or get to y from everywhere); it just means that the rationality of her praxis is subverted. I have argued that anomalies abound in science and I am going to argue that naturalistic ethics depends upon science, so it is important to see that logical contradiction does not leave us bereft of criteria, subject to spatio-temporal and resource constraints. One may have good grounds for opting for a non-valent/Socratic strategy on one tack angled in a particular direction if one rather than another research programme has proved its resilience or explanatory power, that is to say, is progressive in roughly Lakatos's sense,[11] or if it offers better hope of freedom, grounded in a 'concrete utopian' exercise. This last consists in the construction of modes of alternative ways of living on the basis of some assumed set of resources. In this way it counterbalances actualism and underpins hope.

Dialectical contradictions may best be introduced as a species of the more general 3L category of (g) *dialectical connections*. The latter are internally related elements of a totality or ensemble such that they are in principle distinct but inseparable. As such they may of course hold between absences as well as presences, and the causal connections and existential dependencies may be transfactual or actual. More-over, the connections may be absolute, epochal, local-periodized, conjunctural or spatio-temporary. Most dialectical contradictions possess all these features of dialectical connections but their elements are also *opposed*, in the sense that one of their aspects negates another or the whole or its ground, so that they are *tendentially mutually exclusive*, and perhaps harbingers and/or conveyors of change. They are typically radically, but not normally linearly, negational (possessing a tendency to proliferate throughout a system). Dialectical contradictions are not per se, nor do they depend upon, logical contradictions. On the other hand, however, logical contradictions can be dialectical contradictions, insofar as the terms that constitute the logical contradiction are *grounded in a common mistake*. However, this can only be shown coherently when the mistake is isolated and its contradictoriness removed. Figure 4.7 illustrates a contradiction tree. Dialectical contradictions, in the sense of radically transforma-tive auto-subversive tendencies to change, are not necessary for

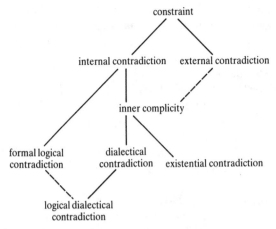

Figure 4.7 Species of Contradiction

change per se, in the way in which inner complicities or liabilities are. But they are pervasive in totalities, and hence must occur in the cosmos, insofar as its ultimate explananda are internally related (as it seems plausible to suppose they are).

Dialectical contradictions may be synchronic or diachronic; they may be more or less asymmetric; they may hold within or between structures; they may be more or less reversible; they may be more or less antagonistic, and more or less manifest in overt conflict. Conversely, not all conflicts may be grounded in dialectical contradictions. Conflicts may take a discursive, hermeneutical (where hermeneutics means the art — more generically, process — of interpretation) or more material shape. However, in the latter case they will be conceptualized, i.e. known or interpreted under some or other descriptions. If we return to our concept of power$_2$ or generalized master—slave-type relations, which may be hidden or obvious, we can thus develop the concept of *hermeneutic struggles over power$_2$ relations*, a theme I will resume when I take up the concept of ideology. In fact, insofar as the dialectical contradictions are hidden, they will be typically tied to a mystifying mode or modes of appearance, such as the commodity fetishism, on Marx's analysis, intrinsic to the capitalist mode of production. Here such hermeneutical struggles will play a crucial role in motivating their overthrow. Dialectical contradictions of the type Marx analysed must be distinguished from opposed forms of independent, externally related (although perhaps necessarily connected) origins, which Kant called 'Realrepugnanz'. There is thus a fallacy in the tendency of positivistically minded critics of Marx from Bernstein to Colletti to dismiss dialectical contradiction as unscientific, or, as in Colletti's case, to attempt to reduce it to *Realrepugnanz*. We can now write

[5] connections > necessary connections > dialectical connections > dialectical contradictions > antagonistic dialectical contradictions > antagonistic dialectical contradictions manifest in overt (conceptualized) conflict (where the category of *Realrepugnanz* falls under necessary but not dialectically necessary contradictions, insofar as the terms of a *Realrepugnanz* are, though distinct, not inseparable).

Protagoras (490–421 BC) said 'in every question, there [are] two sides to the argument, exactly opposite to each other'. As a theory of argument or rhetoric this does not seem very plausible, but taken ontologically, if it means that every momentary state is in temporary equilibrium, in transition, it might seem to have some dialectical plausibility. However, what it misses is the typical directional asymmetry of processes, the movement of the mole under the ground. It is in fact an eristic aphorism of stasis, which, as we shall see later on, is the opposite of the thrust of dialectic. We now turn to the social zone, where the concept of dialectical contradiction is most patently at home.

Making It Happen
(Social Agency)

Eleanor Rigby picks up the rice in the church where a wedding
    has been,
Lives in a dream,
Waits at the window, wearing a face that she keeps in a jar by the
    door.
Who is it for?
All the lonely people, where do they all come from?
LENNON AND McCARTNEY

§ 1 The Problem of Naturalism and the Nature of Society

Naturalism has usually connoted three related ideas:

1. the dependence of social, and more generally human, life upon
   nature (i.e. ontological materialism);
2. the susceptibilities of society and nature to explanation in
   essentially the same way (i.e. scientifically);
3. the cognate character of statements of fact and value, and in
   particular the absence of an unbridgeable gulf between them of
   the kind maintained by Hume, Max Weber and G.E. Moore.

This section is mainly concerned with the second issue, which has
been the dominant one in the philosophy and the practice of the
human sciences. Naturalism, in this sense, must be distinguished
from two extreme versions of it: scientism, which claims a complete
unity, and reductionism, which asserts an actual identity of subject
matter, between the natural and the social sciences.

Three broad positions can be delineated:

(α) a more or less unqualified naturalism, usually associated with
    positivism;
(β) an anti-naturalist hermeneutics;

(γ)   a qualified critical naturalism, underpinned by a realist theory
      of science and a transformational conception of society, which
      has come to the fore in the last quarter of the century, and
      which I will be advocating here.

Positivism finds expression in the sociological tradition associated
with Émile Durkheim and in behaviourism, functionalism and
structuralism. Early harbingers of hermeneutics (originally the art of
textual interpretation) are Vico (1688–1744), who maintained the
anti-Cartesian position that human beings can know society because
they have made it in a way in which only God can know nature, and
Schleirmacher (1768–1830). But its immediate philosophical ancestry
comes from Dilthey, Simmel, Rickert and Weber. They fused Kantian
and Hegelian distinctions so as to produce a contrast between the
phenomenal world of nature and the intelligible world of freedom,
grounding distinctions between causal explanation (*Erklären*) and
interpretive understanding (*Verstehen*), the nomothetic and the
idiographic, the repeatable and the unique, the realms of physics and
of history. It informs the Weberian sociological tradition and
phenomenological and ethnomethodological studies. A distinction
must be made within this second strand between those who seek to
combine positivist and hermeneutical principles, such as Weber and
Habermas, and those dualists who would deny positivism any
applicability in the human sphere, such as the Wittgensteinian Peter
Winch and the Heidegger-influenced H.-G. Gadamer.
    One feature uniting both groups must be immediately noted. They
both share the backdrop of an essentially positivist view of natural
science. Consider, for instance, Winch's influential *The Idea of a Social
Science*.[1] His arguments for a contrast between the social and the
natural sciences boil down, in essence, to just two. The first is an
argument to the effect that constant conjunctions are neither
sufficient nor (contrary to Weber) necessary for social scientific
explanation, which is achieved instead by the discovery of intelligible
connections in its subject matter (pp. 114–15). This may be granted;
but the required contrast is forthcoming only if one assumes that the
discovery of intelligible connections in *its* subject matter is not equally
the goal of natural scientific explanation (or that constant
conjunctions could be necessary and sufficient for this). Winch's
second point is that social things have no existence, other than a
purely physical existence, that is, as social things, apart from the
concept that agents possess of them (pp. 118–19). Apart from leaving
the ontological status of concepts unclear, the posited contrast only
gets off the ground if one assumes that in natural science *esse est*

percipi. Winch's anti-naturalism thus depends entirely on empiricist theories of existence and causality. Realists can deny that the conceptual and empirical jointly exhaust the real. And realism can allow that conceptuality is distinctive, without supposing that it is exhaustive, of social life. On the contrary, the very conceptuality of social life may sometimes mask or distort what is going on, which is why critical realists insist on a critical hermeneutics (to purloin the title of John Thompson's book[2]). While hermeneuticists have grounded their anti-naturalism in ontological considerations, particularly the meaningful or rule-governed character of social reality, positivists — in the complete absence of laws and explanations conforming to the positivist canon — resting on a priori epistemological grounds, have to make out a separate case, in the face of the dilemmas of actualism already investigated, as to why positivism should be uniquely (and most implausibily) applicable in the human realm.

I now want to broaden the scope of this section by bringing in two other long-standing oppositions or dichotomies in the social sciences, besides

(a) that between positivism and hermeneutics to be resolved in a dialectical critical naturalism, viz.:

(b) that between the voluntarism characteristic of the Weberian tradition, and the reification typical of the Durkheimian school, to be resolved in what I will style the transformational model of social activity (henceforth TMSA); and

(c) the individualism, implicit in the utilitarian and Weberian traditions, intrinsic to neo-classical economic theory and championed as methodological individualism by Popper, which we can write as [1] $S = f[i]$ and the collectivism, which we can write as [2] $I = f[s]$, inherent in Durkheimian practice and typified by the ideologies of many right-wing organicists and left-wing collectivists, to be sublated in a social relationism.

Whereas on the Weberian stereotype social objects are seen as the results of, or constituted by, intentional or meaningful behaviour, tending to voluntarism (see Figure 5.1), and on the Durkheimian stereotype social objects are viewed as possessing a life of their own, external to and coercing the individual, tending to reification (see Figure 5.2), on the critical naturalist's conception society is envisaged as both pre-existing as a (transcendentally and causally) necessary condition for it (Durkheim's insight) but equally as existing and

Figure 5.1 The Weberian
Stereotype: 'Voluntarism'

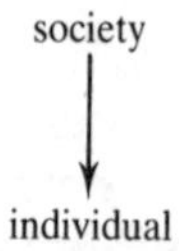

Figure 5.2 The Durkheimian
Stereotype: 'Reification'

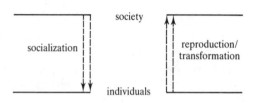

Figure 5.3

ongoing only in virtue of it. Society is thus both the condition and outcome of human agency (the duality of structure to use Anthony Giddens's terminology[3]) and human agency both the production and reproduction (or transformation) of society (the duality of agency) as depicted in Figure 5.3.

Thus (b) is argued by showing that intentional activity would be impossible without prior 'material causes' (to invoke the Aristotelian jargon), on which it means that out of which something is formed, but that some material causes exist only in virtue of the 'efficient causality' of the human agency which reproduces or transforms them, so that we have a conception of social science pre-existing/ ongoing the agency necessary for it, as depicted in Figure 5.4. At the heart of this conception is the idea of human agency or *praxis* as transformative negation of the given (think of cooking a meal, mending a bike); and at the same time as both enabled and constrained by and reproductive or transformative of the very

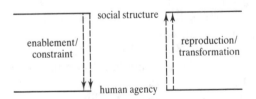

Figure 5.4 The TMSA

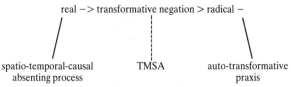

real −> transformative negation > radical −

spatio-temporal-causal   TMSA   auto-transformative
absenting process   praxis

Figure 5.5   The TMSA as Transformative Negation

conditions of this praxis, so that these conditions are *activity-dependent* or auto-poietic, *conceptualized* (concept-dependent but not concept-exhausted) and *geo-historically dependent* (and thus themselves possible objects of transformation). Figures 5.3−5.5 illustrate the relationships between society and individual, social structure and agency, and the character of praxis as transformative negation respectively.

(c) maintains that all social life is embodied in a network of *social relations*. This may be demonstrated by the mental experiment of subtracting from society the human agency required for it to be an ongoing affair. What we are left with are *dual points of articulation* of structure and agency, which are differentiated and processually changing *positioned-practices* human agents occupied, engaged, reproduced or transformed, defining the (changing) system of social relations in which human praxis is embedded. Here again, on this relational model, we have the figure of a duality-with-a-hiatus, preventing a reductionist collapse in either direction.

(b) contends that the social sciences can be seen as sciences in the *same sense* as the experimental sciences of nature, such as in organic chemistry, but in *ways* which are as *different* from the latter as they are specific to the nature of societies. Here one can divide the relevant differences into (α) *ontological*, (β) *epistemological*, (γ) *relational* and (δ) *critical* ones, as so many limits on naturalism:

(α) We have already situated the auto-poietic (activity-dependent), conceptualized, geo-historical and social relation — dependence of social structures as ontological *differentiae*.

(β) Epistemologically, the openness of social systems is entailed by the complete absence of universal empirical generalizations of any cognitive import. This leaves the social sciences without the possibility of crucial experiments to investigate the necessary transfactuality of its subject matter (if it is to be the object of science). On the other hand, its conceptuality establishes the necessity for a hermeneutic moment in (and starting-point for) inquiry, while its geo-historicity implies the local and transient character of social structures. This sets the basis for *dialectical explanations*, as we shall see in more detail anon, and encompasses, inter alia, concepts of contradiction, crisis and struggle, including hermeneutical struggles over generalized master—slave-type relations. A dialectical explanation typically explains some tendency or outcome in terms of a dialectically contradictory ground or condition of possibility or some complex, combination or totality of them. As a complex may be hierarchicized, this opens the way for concepts of hegemony and counter-hegemony, and a fortiori for counter-hegemonic hermeneutical struggles. It also lays the ground for dialectical arguments, where a *dialectical argument* is a species of transcendental argument characterized by the condition that it establishes the ontological necessity of false (or limited) categories of results, as is exemplified by Marx's analysis of the wage (false) and value (limited) forms.

(γ) Relationally, the co-incidence of the causal efficacy of ideas (implied by the mere fact of intentional embodied agency) and their material structural conditioning will lend to social science the character of a relational dialectic between subject and object of inquiry.

(δ) Finally, in virtue of their conceptuality (quasi-propositionality), social forms will be liable to both (1) immanent and (2) dialectical explanatory metacritique. The former will play a key role in counter-hegemonic hermeneutic struggles, in isolating, for instance, theory/practice inconsistencies. The fourth critical difference, necessitated by the fact that the subject matter of social science includes not just objects but beliefs about the objects, in principle corrigible, makes possible the latter, viz. an *explanatory critique* of consciousness and being, entailing judgements of value and action, without parallel in the domain of natural science, including a modified form of substantive ethical naturalism as will be explored in §2. However, it seems vital to see such critique, and such science, as constituted by human beings' dependency on the natural order (see Chapter 4.2 above), that is, materialism or naturalism in sense (1) above.

Subject to these differences, both the DREI(C) and RRREI(C) models of theoretical and applied explanations hold in the social zone.

The TMSA, which already exemplifies transformative negation, must be further negatively generalized or dialecticized to allow for the following:

1. The tensed geo-historical character of the social process, which is illustrated in Figure 5.6, showing how unacknowledged conditions,

unconscious motivation, tacit skills and unintended consequences may all serve to make it opaque to social agents (and so affords social science a putatively emancipatory role).

2. The fact that the pre-existence of the social structure (think of the religious rites established by the practices of the long dead) means that social structures may survive as a result of omission or inaction, or despite our actions (two difference cases, of course). Does this vitiate the one premiss from which I have derived the principal characteristics of social science, viz. the activity-dependence of social structure? Not a bit. The negative or dialectical generalization of the TMSA does not commit the error of reification. For the TMSA requires that the present actions which serve to reproduce social structure only be intentional under *some* description, not under the description of reproducing the structure concerned (which would make all social reproduction or persistence the product of conscious acts). Pre-existent structures, established perhaps by the long-since dead, continue to be reproduced by our agency, but the class of activities is expanded to include inactions as well as actions, and of acts to include omissions (we refrain from altering grammar or the architecture of the city square) as well as commissions. Just as non-being exists, in omissions one acts. We may, as one instance of the presence of the past (cf. Chapter 4.1), inherit structures reproduced, transformed (or created as the transform of a pre-existent reproduct or transform) as a pre-existent that may survive, or be ongoing, without any positive actions on our part. Hence we can talk of *persistence through inaction in virtue of our agency*. Any other position leads back to voluntarism. Society is a pre-existing prior to/ongoing in virtue of our agency affair. We can recall, here, Adorno's adage that even the absence of theory can become a material force when it seizes the masses. We can now further elaborate Figure 5.4 as in Figures 5.6 and 5.7. Structure is always pre-existing for any act, individual, cohort or generation but one can think the levels of structural

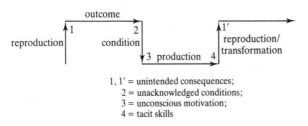

1, 1' = unintended consequences;
2 = unacknowledged conditions;
3 = unconscious motivation;
4 = tacit skills

Figure 5.6 The Social Process

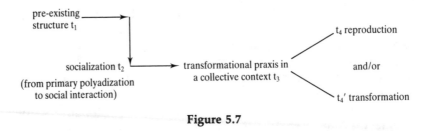

Figure 5.7

conditioning, socio-cultural interaction and structural elaboration as in Figure 5.8.[4]

Four inter-dependent planes constitute social life, which together I will refer to as four-planar social being or sometimes as human nature simpliciter. These four planes are:

[a]   the plane of material transactions with nature;
[b]   the plane of inter-/intra-subjective (personal) actions;
[c]   the plane of social relations;
[d]   the plane of the subjectivity of the agent.

These are depicted in Figure 5.9. Planes [b] and [c] constitute the social cube. The importance of not conflating the social structure and human agency should be clear. I have provided an argument for the dislocated duality of structure and agency. But the inexorable spatio-temporality (and multiplicity of rhythmics) of the social process is equally important. Thus the social cube should be thought of as a cubic spatial spread and temporal stretch or flow. Both [a] and [b] are the site of power$_2$ relations, though those at [c] may not be visible (as is arguably the case in capitalism as a result of reification and fetishism, and alienation generally), in which case their exposure and

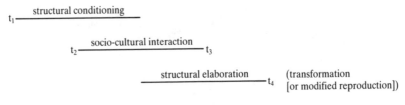

Figure 5.8

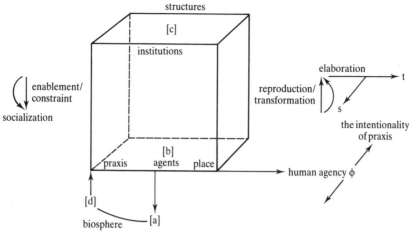

Figure 5.9 Four-Planar Social Being Encompassing the Social Cube

overthrow requires of necessity a depth explanatory social science. The social cube may be layered in many ways. Thus if one views ideology as characteristically discursively legitimating $power_2$ relations, one can see it as an intersect of three sub-dimensions of the social cube as depicted in Figure 5.10. It is of the greatest moment for the argument of this book that the moral evolution of the species, like the future generally, be regarded as open. Further substantialization of this model depends upon empirically controlled research into the geo-historical dynamic of four-planar social being; and, for any given topic of inquiry, space-time span and level of abstraction, on the differential weights of the moment of the social totality — and in particular on any hierarchicization revealed. This will also depend in

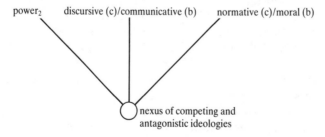

Figure 5.10 Ideology as an Intersect of Three
Sub-dimensions of the Social Cube

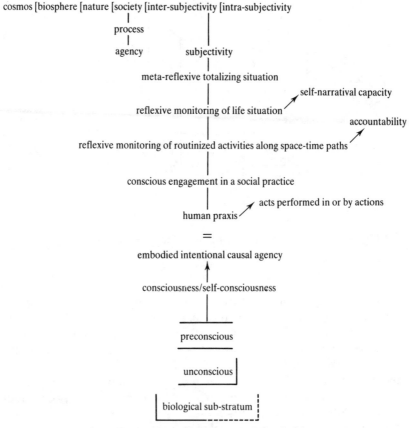

Figure 5.11 The Stratification of the Subject

part on which of the two models of superstructure I delineated in Chapter 4.2 one deploys. Thus does one conceive the global capitalist economy as setting boundary conditions on the nation-state, or capitalist relations of production as constituting the conditions of possibility of the intra/international order? It is worth emphasizing the multiplicity of rhythmics at work in a single episode, such as the design of a book jacket, from the spatio-temporality of that process to the narrative of the designer's life, the lagged causal efficacy of her unconscious, her life-cycle as an organism and specifically as a woman, her daily space-time paths, the *longue durée* of differentially structurally sedimented social institutions and that of the social relations upon which they depend, the development of specifically civilized geo-history in the context of human history embedded in the

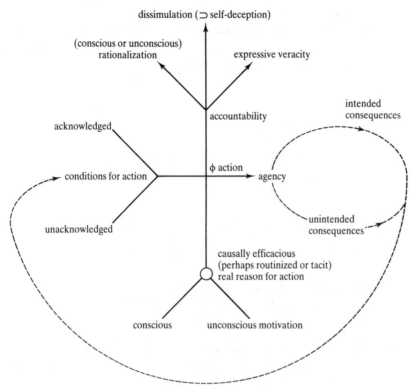

Figure 5.12 The Stratification of Action

rhythmics of species, genera and kinds, located in the physical development of a solar system, unravelling itself in the entropy of an expanding universe.

I now want to home in on plane [b]. Figure 5.11 depicts the stratification of the personality, or more properly subjectivity. On this model the self is nothing other than the dispositional identity of the subject with her changing causal powers. But this model does not do justice to the open systemic, multiply and conflictually determined character of the agent's life in our internal dialectical pluriverses; or the degree of alienation, destratification or fragmentation of the subject. Properly conceived, actions should be seen as cognitive-affective-conative-expressive-performative vectors, with a form, content, mood, style and efficacy of their own.[5] The transformative capacity of the agent depends upon competences and facilities (access to resources), while the acts performed in or by her actions will depend upon the extent and manner in which she is able to mobilize

these resources (including 'inner' ones — curiosity, hope, imagination, drive, bodily gesture, self-esteem) and the circumstances of her
action. Figure 5.12 is a very rudimentary model of the stratification of
action which I have elaborated elsewhere.

§ 2 Problems of Agency

I am going to consider eight main, interconnected problems, or
problem-areas, which I shall summarily list at the outset:

(α)   the mind—body problem;
(β)   the problem of whether reasons can be causes;
(γ)   the problem of free-will and determinism, already touched on
      in Chapter 1;
(δ)   the problem of personal identity;
(ϵ)   the problems of interpretation, which we have already
      breached in the guise of Meno's paradox;
(ζ)   the problem of solipsism;
(η)   the problem-field of subjectivity, and of erasure;
(θ)   the problem of the seeming primacy of structure over agency,
      the past over the present, of power$_2$ relations, of fragmentation
      v. totality, and of emancipation, which for many on the left has
      become known as the 'world-historical problem of agency'.

We are in the domain of the abode of 4D, unified by the category of
transformative praxis or agency (upon which 5C is supervenient). Just
as 3L has a special affinity with 1M, 4D has a special resonance with
2E, since agency, which is intentional causality, consists in absenting;
that is, more specifically, the transformative negation of the given.
Agency may be defined in the simplest way as embodied intentional
causality or process, which issues in a state of affairs that, unless it
was overdetermined (as in a firing squad), would not have occurred
otherwise, even if the real reasons which cause it (cf. Figure 5.12) are
routinized, unconscious, multiple, contradictory and/or anterior
(including lagged, delayed, long prior) ones. Philosophically, this is
sustained by an emergent powers materialist orientation — itself a
figure of constellationality; and substantively by the concept of four-
planar social being in nature discussed in the previous section.
Metacritically, we have pinpointed two complementary kinds of

ontological de-agentification (this is the dialectical duplicity of antagonistic counterparts, notionally at loggerheads): dualistic disembodiment, typical of (e.g. discourse in) the intrinsic aspect, or the first person intentional stance; and reductionist reification, characteristic of the extrinsic aspect.

This takes us immediately into problem group (α): materialism v. idealism. First let me differentiate four different kinds of materialism which I take to be heuristically acceptable:

(a) Epistemological materialism, which asserts the existential intransitivity and transfactual efficacy (relative or absolute) of the objects of scientific thought. This makes it equivalent to transcendental realism as articulated in Chapter 2.

(b) Ontological materialism, which asserts the unilateral dependence of social upon biological (and thence physical) being and the emergence of the former from the latter. This makes it consistent with the emergent powers materialism defended here and in particular upon the taxonomic and causal irreducibility of the human to the natural sciences.

(c) Practical materialism, which asserts the constitutive role of human transformative agency in the production, reproduction and transformation of social forms. This is congruent with the TMSA — insofar as we understand both in the negatively generalized way I outlined in §1. This is the meta-sociological basis of Marx's materialism, which takes the substantive form of

(d) geo-historical materialism, a research programme nucleated by the core idea of the causal primacy of men's and women's mode of production and reproduction of their natural (physical) being, or of the labour process more generally, in the development of human (four-planar) species-being.

Opposing classical dualistic Cartesianism, behaviourists argued that mind consists in outer acts (or even, in the extreme form endorsed by B.F. Skinner, movements). This traded, to say the least, on a confusion between meaning and empirical grounds. The perhaps dominant form of philosophical materialism, the central state materialism (CSM) mooted by Armstrong, Place and Smart, involved three steps:

1. the analysis of prima facie mental states, such as 'I am thinking now', as 'topic-neutral', that is, as saying nothing about the nature of the process concerned;

2. the definition of the mental state, in opposition to both the classical view of it as an inner arena and behavourism as an outward act, as a (real) state of the person apt for the production of certain sorts of physical behaviour (so that the mind is conceived as an inner arena identified by its causal relations to the outward act); and

3. the speculative identification of these inner processes with the physico-chemical workings of the brain, or, more fully, the central nervous system.

CSM may be regarded as a research programme, backed by neurophysiological evidence. But the notion of the reduction involved in step (3) is suspect, especially if it entails predictability (and if it does not, a gap appears in the physiological chain). Moreover, it seems to face insuperable difficulties in dealing with inter-subjective communication, for here the causal link between two or more persons is mediated by hermeneutic understanding and there is no necessary physiological interaction involved in the exchange between a bank clerk and a client. Indeed it would seem to have to fall back on a miraculous Leibnizian harmony of monads. Eliminative materialism (ELM), persuasively contended by Churchland, following up on the earlier work of Feyerabend, Quine and Rorty, rejects the topic-neutral analysis (step 1), not offering a revisionary analysis of prima facie mentalistic terms, but denying that the statements in which they occur can be true. But it is not clear that ELM can be consistently stated — the statement would seem to be a self-eliminating performative contradiction or theory/practice inconsistency. Human beings need intentionalistic truth-talk to get about the world. Underlying both forms of reductionist materialism is a Laplacean-Humean determinism, which confounds ontological determination and epistemological predetermination, and denies the phenomena of emergence, novelty and dual, multiple and complex control, for which I hope I have made a watertight case in the previous chapter. On the synchronic emergent powers materialism (SEPM) I defend, mind is conceived not as a substance, whether material (reductionism) or immaterial (dualistic idealism), but as a complex of powers. This has analogies with Putnam's 'functionalism'.

Double-aspect theories, which hark back to Spinoza, have been revived in the second half of the twentieth century by Strawson. On them, mind and matter are two modes of a single substance. But such theories suffer from an ambivalent ontological commitment. If the mental attributes are real, i.e. irreducibly causally efficacious, then this amounts to SEPM; if not to CSM. On the other hand, if the question is evaded, then there is no non-subjective criterion for the attribution of any mental states at all. Epiphenomenalism, still supported in some quarters, has difficulty in doing justice to our *agency*. In fact what other theories lack and SEPM has is a robust theory of *intentional causality*. If we link this to the closely interwoven issue of (β) and face the question of how human beings make things happen, i.e. change the world, both individually and collectively, accepting that emergence is a widespread phenomenon and a realist analysis of causality, there is no need to resort either to a Cartesian pineal gland or to talk, as I once did, of transcategorial causality.

The logical connection argument is generally regarded as the strongest in the anti-causalist position. This asserts that (a) causes must be logically distinct from effects, but (b) reasons are not logically distinct from the actions they explain, so that (c) reasons cannot be causes. Both premisses are faulty. It is quite improper to talk of events, as distinct from their descriptions, being logically connected or not. Such talk betrays the hand of the epistemic fallacy. Moreover, natural events can likewise be redescribed in terms of their causes, e.g. toast as burnt. But actions can normally be redescribed independently of their reasons. 'Flicking the switch' is logically independent of my 'turning on the light', but my *reason* for flicking the switch (e.g. my desire to illuminate the room) is always and in principle independent of the act with which it is performed. Furthermore, unless reasons were causally efficacious in producing one rather than another sequence of wordly movements, sounds or marks, it is difficult to see how there can be *grounds* for preferring one reason explanation to another, and indeed eventually the whole practice of giving reason-explanations, and with it the notions of accountability and responsibility, not to mention morality, must come to appear as without rationale. Similar objections apply to the 'language stratum' argument, viz. that reasons and causes differentiate not different types of events, but distinctive sorts of explanations. This has a decidedly Kantian air and is compatible with Davidson's 'anomalous monism' and Rorty's so-called 'hermeneutics'. The main point offered here is that reasons are normally cited in justificatory contexts where natural causes would be inappropriate. But it would seem to be a necessary condition for an adequate justification R of an action ϕ_t that R was the reason why the agent performed that action at t. For, in contradiction from other causes, we *appraise* reasons qua beliefs, and more generally as wants or dispositions to act, for consistency, truth, coherence, etc. And we appraise them for their suitability for acting on, their *actionability*. Such appraisals are necessitated by the irreducibility of intentionality, viz. that what I am to do will happen, in part, because of any decision I take or grounds for this process. The appropriate picture is not one of two series: one (S_1), in the extrinsic aspect, in which it is determined what is going to happen; and the other (S_2), in the intrinsic aspect, in which the agent has projects and beliefs, desires and generally cogitates her life. Of course if this picture were appropriate there would be a problem of how, if S_1 existed (irrespective of the degree of our access to it), there was any room for S_2. But there is only one series, ontologically speaking, and it is continuous with S_2. The intrinsic aspect is constellationally contained within, i.e. it is a part of, the intrinsic domain of causality. In short, reasons are causes, and agents possess, in any given context, greater or lesser degrees of freedom, a topic to which I will return later.

The problem of personal identity, graphically formulated by Locke as a problem of what warrant we have for our consciousness of being the same thinking self [NB] at different times and places, was taken to its reductio by Hume, who argued that the self is nothing but a 'bundle of perceptions'. Even this is not coherent — for it is not clear how at any moment we can get from one part of the bundle to another. Ultimately, Hume must be forced to a punctualist ego-present-centrism, denying memory, embodiment and human agency, solipsistically disengaged from the possibility of practice or exchange with other minds. Kant posited a continuing 'I think', inter alia, to overcome this problem, but its ontological status remained (to say the least) obscure. Contemporary materialists want no truck with a thinking self and are content to rely on purely bodily criteria. But thought experiments, not too distinct from actualization, cast doubt on this line. Brain transplants, genetic cloning and virtual duplicates all threaten it, as the work of Williams and Parfitt has made clear. On the other hand, the very idea of the unity, as distinct from the uniqueness, of a self is questionable from studies on schizophrenia, paranormal psychology, Goffmanesque sociology, on which selves become a bundle of roles, and modernist literature from at least Joyce on, a point well made by Dennett. When we take into account the fact that our geo-historical constitution by the processes of our formation is an ongoing affair (we are processes-in-product-in-process) at 2E, and that from primary polyadization on we are radically constituted by our internal relations with others at 3L (i.e. combine Bakhtin and Vygotsky or, if one likes, Klein[6]), we have to theorize a person's identity as her dispositional identity with her changing and intra-active causal powers, some of which will be in internal dislocation and others of which will be stereotyped (the social truth of cloning).

These powers will be exercised only in virtue of our embodied intentional causal agency. On the one hand, then, our received conception of personal identity collapses. Persons ain't what they used to be. In particular we are geo-historical products, globally interconnected and, as reflexively monitoring, rationally accountable for our actions in rhythmic processes of transformation or letting be (which is equally absenting a state of affairs that might otherwise have occurred). But, on the other, there is no conflict but necessary complementarity between physical and psychological criteria.

It will be remembered that our resolution of Meno's paradox turned on the fact that we are thrown into the world, and in the course of what I have called primary polyadization we are not normally (although we may be occasionally) faced with situations concerning which we have no prior understanding, the ultimate basis for which lies in our shared species-being and the common core rationality with which we are all endowed. But patently interpretive stumbling blocks may arise. Hermeneutics gets its force from the fact that saying 'hello', like the act of chopping wood, is a meaningful act which requires interpretive understanding prior to, and as a necessary condition for, any causal explanation (and, if the action syndrome is compulsive or otherwise unwanted, unnecessary and transformable, for any liberation). Hermeneutics is thus the necessary starting point for any explanatory, and a fortiori emancipatory, human science. This is sometimes, somewhat misleadingly, put by saying that social science requires a double hermeneutic — in fact, it requires a triple hermeneutic: into the potential scientist's own social world, into the neophyte's scientific trade and into her subject matter, and hermeneutics may be required while doing physics or chemistry, particularly in periods of turmoil or 'revolutionary science'. In fact there are four distinct hermeneutical circles: of inquiry, of communication (both of which are putatively universal), of inquiry into (the culture of) communicating subjects and finally into that of textual objects. These are 'circles' because they always already presuppose some pre-understanding; they are putatively or actually dialogical; they are indexicalized (place—time-specific); and always subject to a meta-hermeneutic (and so on recursively) if the base hermeneutic breaks down.

Solipsism is a problem that results inexorably from the 'analogical grammars' that presaged or followed Descartes's subjective turn. These included the Renaissance, the Reformation, the secularization of science, the rise of an artisan class, the market economy, a bourgeois-individualist-atomist conception of man, Newtonian celestial closure, a corpuscularian world-view and the classical paradigm of action by contiguous contact.[†] Problems about the existence of an external world, other minds, personal identity, the past should have logically extended to doubt about doubt itself, which to be intelligible would have to be considered as referentially detachable and so existentially intransitive. But rationalist fundamentalist criteria of knowledge, incorrigibility about the universal and necessary, were easy targets for an empiricist line of sceptical attack that must be continued from Locke, Berkeley and Hume to Kant. This by no means prevented dogmatic complacency in practice — in fact, faith in Newtonian science and the Laplacean outlook reached its apogee in this period. The reaction of and to the nineteenth century, dominated by an alliance of positivism and historicism, after the eclipse of reason in the Hegelian *Götterdämmerung*, laid the ground for the *judgemental* relativism and irrationalism that was the inevitable outcome of the collapse of science's most successful system. Wittgenstein's private language argument and Heideggerian existential phenomenology both laid stress on being-with-others in a common (inter-subjective) world as a condition for any being at all. Hegel had in effect said that to exist we must be recognized. This was the argument of Strawson and Hampshire and Harré and Secord in the Oxford of the 1960s, strengthened by the successes of post-Vygotskian psychology and its emphasis on the necessity for dyadization (primary polyadization) for individuation, that is, for being an individual at all, and hence for the very intelligibility of solipsism and the ego-ethno-anthropo-centric 'predicament' in the first place.

We have already seen how the *stratification* of the subject, as represented in Figure 5.11, at the level of a meta-reflexively totalizing situation, allows a rational resolution of the problem of subjectivity and objectivity, viz. as only articulated within language but via a strategy of transcendental detachment as coherently and necessarily conceivable as pertaining within an over-reaching objectivity. It is the same stratification that allows the post-Nietzschean subject to remember the dependency of ontogenetic (language-tied) truth upon metaphor and that obviates, from the critical realist standpoint I have been articulating here, the need for the erasure of being. Ontology, I have insisted, is inexorable, and on the post-positivist transmutation

---

[†] At this point it is worth remarking that though I have argued that Parmenidean monism — the source of the doctrine of ontological monovalence — has as its only plausible avatar punctualist solipsism and must reduce to it via Cratylan silence, there is no evidence that any ancient Greek — either in the serious and dialectical scepticisms of Pyrrhonism or the academy or the cynicism of Diogenes — argued for solipsism (the self-refuting position); their object was to teach imperturbability or other virtues.

route I describe in Chapter 2.3 the failure to rethematize ontology leads merely to the secretion and repetition of the Humean actualist, monovalent, extensionalist and reificatory and/or voluntaristic one.

All of this accentuates the impact of the effects of the depthlessness, naturalization, homogenization, atemporalization and emotivism/ decisionism/personalism characteristic of the late/post-modern world of fin-de-siècle contemporaneity. It is in this context that we have to think the so-called 'world historical problem of agency'. This usually refers to the greater majority of the agents, in E.P. Thompson's redolent phrase, of an 'unmastered history' as being agents of a geo-history that they merely suffer and do not affect. It also refers to the detotalization, division and fragmentation, of those who are the subjects of some or other oppression, at the subaltern poles of power$_2$ relations. It refers to the dislocated primary of structural conditioning over agents' lives, to the massive presence of the past and the outside, to the bewitchment of our intelligence by the ideological intersect, to the fact that we cannot access the resources for emancipation, and to the existence of an actualist blanket suffocating hope. For the Marxist left, the more specific meaning of the world historical problem of agency was the apparent absence of agents of revolution against capitalism that was probably prematurely thought to be late, and in particular the domestication of the bourgeoisie in the leading industrial powers (their failure to play their allotted roles), which the Hobson—Lenin explanation of the phenomena did little to allay. Later in this book I will consider whether there are counter-tendencies at work to this problem of agency, and how they are connected to the preceding ones. But it is now time to turn our attention to the critical functions of social science and to consider their role in exposing some typical ideological tropes and manoeuvres.

§ 3 Alienation and the Problem of Value

I have touched briefly on reification and fetishism — in philosophy and substantive social life. But before we can thematize the 'problem of value' — in essence the problem of an is/ought divide — we need another figure on the scene, the 3L detotalized one of alienation. Alienation is the condition of being estranged or separated from what is constitutive of or essential to one's nature, causal powers or wellbeing. Its source lies in the Hegelian figure of the Beautiful Soul, alienated from her community. This is eventually developed in Hegel's mature system to become the self-alienation of the absolute idea, to be restored to itself and recognized for the first time as absolute spirit in Hegel's system. But in Hegel's early writings of the 1790s the Beautiful Soul is Jesus, who is placed in the dilemmatic situation of either retaining the purity of his Kantian teaching or of accepting the cult of authority among the people he would instruct. In Hegel's essay 'The Positivity of the Christian Religion' (1795–96), in order to avoid the fate of the Beautiful Soul, Jesus chooses to don the mantle of the Messiah, an after-life (*Jenseits*) is posited, and his teachings are accepted, not on the basis of reason, but on that of authority, so heavily 'positivized' are the Jewish people, and later the Roman slaves, amongst whom his disciples spread his gospel. This is the origin of the Unhappy Consciousness, equally split (detotalized) but now *within* itself.

Years later, in 1844, reading *The Phenomenology of Mind* (1806), Marx is fired by the final section on 'absolute knowledge', in which the diremption of absolute spirit is overcome after its odyssey from its humble beginnings in sense-experience. Marx substitutes labour for spirit; distinguishes (contra Hegel) objectification from alienation, that is, the production of social forms as such from the alienation of producing subjects, recognizing that alienation is only one possible (geo-)historically determined mode of objectification; and, noting that in the 'labour of the negative' that drives the dialectics of the *Phenomenology* on Hegel sees only 'abstract mental labour', Marx begins his own odyssey to *Capital Volume 1* (1867). In Marx's mature writing a *generative separation* or split estranges the immediate producers from their own labour, and as a result of this primordial separation a fivefold (second-order) alienation results, separating the immediate producers both from their products and the four planes comprising social being — in the shape of the means and materials of production (cf. [a]), each other (cf. [b]), the nexus of social relations (cf. [c]) and ultimately themselves (cf. [d]).

The full relevance of these figures for our story will become clear in Chapter 7. But here I want to look at the alienation characteristic of the ethical realm. It will be easiest to do this if I first adumbrate the general character of my critical realist position. This is defined by a combination of moral realism and ethical naturalism. Moral realism entails that the objects of morality, like knowledge in epistemological realism or what I called in the previous section epistemological materialism (which is essentially transcendental realism), are real and in this sense intransitive. There is thus a potential distinction between moral reality (and at the ontological, including alethic level, moral truth), dm_r, and actually existing morality, dm_a. At the same time, morality signifies an action-guiding relationship to four-planar social being. (This means that, unlike knowledge, it is necessarily anthropic or social relation-dependent.) As such, again like knowledge, as distinct from the objects of knowledge, morality itself lies on the transitive-relational side of the transitive/intransitive divide. But as morality is practical, it is more natural to talk of its objective than its object — provided we do not make the mistake of thinking objectives subjectively or that they cannot be real or ontologically, including potentially alethically, true.[†] Thus we can distinguish descriptive, redescriptive and explanatory critical morality on an agent's ethical world-line from that of some actually existing society or group, which is an object of critical naturalist investigation. (This can of course reflexively incorporate the agent's own morality too.) This distinction sustains [1] the contingent irreducibility of what really ought to be with what actually is, i.e. dm_r to dm_a, i.e. the possibility of criticism and a fortiori critique (in contrast to moral reductionism or actualism). Note that [1] is not the same as [2] the independence of 'factual' from 'evaluative' statements, a position with which I sharply disagree. Moral realists hold that there is an objective morality. But how can it be known? This is where ethical naturalism comes in. Ethical naturalism holds that it is possible to derive the moral truth from facts (including of course well-confirmed theories), and in particular our knowledge of natural necessities, alethic truths, etc.; that is to say, that there is no inseparable barrier between 'is' and 'ought' statements of the kind posited by Hume, Weber and Moore, i.e. to affirm [3] the derivability of what really and actually ought to be from what really is; which has the corollary of [4] the dependence of 'evaluative' upon 'factual' statements. Note that [3] is consistent with [1]. Alongside the transition of facts to values is a transition from theory to practice. Just because I contend we can get, through the practice of *explanatory critique*, from fact to value, the first-person action-guiding character of morality poses no problem for moral realism. At the same time, the anti-naturalistic fallacy argument often functions merely to screen the generation of an implicit emotivist or conventionalist morality reflecting the status quo ante of actually existing morality. It thus demoralizes, *de-values* reality, *alienating* us from the moral good, the ethical alethia, ultimately grounded in conceptions of human nature, in the context of developing four-planar social being, with the moral consciousness of the species in principle open. Moral irrealism secretes an implicit realism, normally the status quo ante, or one bit of it, an analogue of the ontic fallacy (more usually in emotivist, decisionist or personalist and/or

---

[†] In *Dialectic*, Chapter 3, I did not make the necessary distinction between morality and its object/ive and so the status of my moral realism was there left unclear.

traditionalist guises), and, as one would expect, a Tina compromise form. It is worth remarking that if it is ethical naturalism that grounds and substantiates moral realism, it is the axiological imperative and in particular the situation that we cannot help but act in an always already moralized world that imperiously demands a grounding or critique of our values. Notice that the combination of the moral realist [1] with the ethically naturalist [3] opens up the possibility of demonstrating the necessity of the falsity of (or just the false) actually existing morality/moralities of a society in the manner of an explanatory critical dialectical argument. Thus in particular we should notice that the contingent irreducibility of 'ought' to 'is', taken together with the derivability of 'ought' from 'is', holds open the possibility of demonstrating the actually existing morality of the society to be *false* and at the same time *necessary*.

I want in fact to argue from a base conception of social science as neutral, to a conception of it as explanatory critique, and then to a conception of it, through the dialectics of assertorically sensitized solidarity, as emancipatory axiology. It is first necessary to refute [2]. Social scientific discourse will not be evaluatively neutral, because of the always already moralized character of what it is about. Social scientific discourse is 'value-impregnated' because of the 'value-saturated' character of its subject matter. Thus consider a well-known example of Isaiah Berlin's. Contrast the following statements of what happened in Germany under Nazi rule.

(α) 'The country was depopulated.'
(β) 'Millions of people died.'
(γ) 'Millions of people were killed.'
(δ) 'Millions of people were murdered.'

All four statements are true but (δ) is not only the most evaluative, it is also the best (i.e. the most precise and accurate) description of what actually happened. And in virtue of this, all but (δ) convey the wrong perlocutionary force. For to say of someone that they died normally carries the presumption that they were *not* killed by human agency. And to say that millions were killed does not imply that their deaths were part of a single organized campaign of brutal killing. In general one can say that the most adequate description of a phenomenon will be that entailed by the theory which *maximizes explanatory power*, for which hermeneutic adequacy is a necessary, but not a sufficient, condition. Note that this argument turns not on the subject's interest in the subject matter, but on the nature of the subject matter itself and criteria for its adequate description and explanation.

Now my argument for [3] and, a fortiori, [4] turns in the first instance on the critical limit to naturalism delineated in §1 above. It depends upon the condition that the subject matter of social science contains not only social objects but also beliefs about their social objects. It is certainly part of the mandate of social science to assess beliefs about a subject matter (including of course its own) and to explain that subject matter. And if we can explain the necessity for some systematically false belief, then we can pass, ceteris paribus, to a negative evaluation on the object (e.g. structure, or system of social relations) generating that belief and, ceteris paribus again, to action rationally directed at removing it. Thus one moves from fact to value, and theory to practice. This is the model of explanatory critique. It may be obviously generalized to include the non-satisfaction of other interests besides truth, e.g. for food, health care or shelter; but then it does not violate Hume's law (i.e. 'no ought from an is'), or, at any rate, not so neatly, because one can always argue either that the satisfaction of these interests or needs is a necessary condition for truth and/or the failure to satisfy them amounts to untruths to human nature. A paradigm of an explanatory critique is provided by Marx's critique of political economy, which is a triple critique of capitalism and the ideological categories and forms it generates, such as the value form or the wage form, as well as the doctrines that legitimate it.

But it is in fact even simpler to move from fact to value. For to criticize an action is to criticize the belief that informs it, and any judgement — even a purely technical one — needs to be *grounded* in virtue of the fourfold character of the judgement form, so that a proto-explanatory critical moment is intrinsic to it. At the same time its theoretico-practical duality commits the judgement-maker, through its normative-fiduciary aspect, to an assertorically imperatively sensitized dialectic of solidarity with the addresse of her remark, and hence to a proto-emancipatory axiology. In practice this means that if there is a constraint on an agent X performing a class of actions ϕ, the judgement-maker assists X to rid the cause of that constraint, insofar as those actions are intrinsic to her concretely singularized human flourishing, i.e. insofar as she is at present alienated from something intrinsic to her wellbeing. Ceteris paribus, a constraint on human wellbeing is an ill, and to absent that constraint, and, if recalcitrant, its causes, is good. Moreover, by the logic of dialectical universalizability, both the judgement-maker's remark and the addressee's absenting practice commit them to getting rid of all dialectically similar constraints; and, then, by a further step, to getting rid of all unwanted, unnecessary and remedial constraints as such, precisely

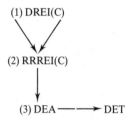

Figure 5.13

insofar as they are dialectically similar, viz. as constraints. Thus the goal of concretely singularized universal emancipation may be seen to be implicit in every fiduciary remark or absentive practice — that is, in every judgement or practical deed. In Chapter 7 I will work through this argument and its implications, which establish the supreme good and the conditions for the highest good, the ultimate moral alethia, in detail.

What are the implications of sticking to Hume's law? The endless regress of decisionism, the caprice of emotivism, the unconcretized, undialectical universalizability of personalism; an acceptance of actually existing morality of one kind or another. It is not difficult to see the de-evaluation of reality as alienation. What is the non-alienating praxis demanded? In any situation of constraint on human wellbeing or flourishing (which includes the satisfaction not just of needs but also of the conditions of possibility of development), *Diagnosis, Explanation* and *Action*, informed by explanatory critique, a concretely utopian alternative and a theory and practice of transition.† This is the DEA model of practical problem resolution. Insofar as it involves normative change, we have *Description, Explanation* and *Transformation* (DET) in the schema represented in Figure 5.13. How might this apply to those at the subaltern pole of discursively moralized power$_2$ relations? Through a dialectic of morality which may be schematized thus:

descriptive morality → immanent critique (theory/practice inconsistency) → redescriptive morality → hermeneutic and material counter-hegemonic struggle → metacritique$_1$ → explanatory critical morality (metacritique$_2$) → totalizing depth praxis (incorporating a

---

† The necessity for what I have called the concrete utopian exercise is precisely to pinpoint the real, but non-actualized, possibilities inherent in a situation, thus inspiring grounded hope to inform emancipatory praxis.

self-reflexive monitoring-learning process and satisfaction of a prefigurative condition stipulating [a] that the means be as far as possible consistent with the end-state or process, and [b] that they in some manner embody or express the values of that end) → emancipatory axiology.

One might envisage a rapprochement of the conflicting approaches of de-ontology, consequentionalism and virtue theory in the ethical circle depicted in Figure 5.14, understood as situated in the context of the transformational model of social activity.

Light may perhaps be cast on another long-running dispute in ethics, viz. that between universalists and particularists. Universalizability is both (a) a test of consistency (and a fortiori sincerity) and (b) a criterion of truth, but the universality involved must be dialectical, i.e. transfactual, concrete, agentive in the twofold sense explicated in Chapter 3.3 and directionally transformative. In particular the requirement of concretion entails that full account must be taken of space-time-specific processes and contextually specific mediations, where these are relevant and oriented to the concrete singularities (including their transformative capacities) of the agents involved. We may assume a core universal human nature, and thus grounds for a core equality, but it will always be manifest at a particular time and place, as mediated and as singularized. This is the basis of the dialectical critique of abstract universalist ethics, based on the corresponding dialectical critique of deductivism (see Figure 4.4 on p. 79). The communitarians are also right to insist both on the epistemic relativity of moral judgement and on the diversity of actually existing moralities. Epistemic relativity is, however, as we have seen, quite consistent with judgemental rationality (and a fortiori the dialectical universalizability of ethical judgements) here, in the practico-ethical realm, as in the descriptive-explanatory work of science (including the description and explanation of actually existing moralities).

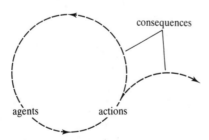

Figure 5.14 The Ethical Circle

As a résumé of this chapter, let me ask in what sense the position I have been expounding can be called 'dialectical critical naturalism'. It is *naturalist* (1) in that it is consistent and coupled with an emergent powers materialism, in which society is seen as materialized ultimately embodied intentional causal agency reacting back on the materials out of which is was formed; (2) in that, subject to the differentiations specifically noted earlier, it legitimates the possibility of an explanatory social science; and (3) in that it licenses us to pass from purely factual to evaluative conclusions. It is *critical* (1) insofar as it is both established by, and legitimates the possibility of, substantive[†] transcendental arguments in social science; (2) inasmuch as the explanatory social science it indicates is contingently critical; and (3) in that the model of explanatory critique I have outlined can be generalized to cover the failure to satisfy concretely singularized human needs and interests. It is *dialectical* (1) insofar as it situates the possibility of dialectical explanatory critical argument, in which the necessity of some false or partial form is situated; (2) insofar as it non-monovalently situates the dislocated dialectics of structure and agency, with structure a transform of past praxis and a reproduct or transform of present praxis in virtue of our agency, and allows more generally for discrepant and discordant processes and struggles; and (3) insofar as it paves the way for a dialectic to be explored in Chapter 7 of transformative praxis, paradigmatically informed by desire, transforming the given in the shape of the constraints on the realization of concretely singularized human wellbeing and flourishing in a society in which the free development of each is a condition for the free development of all; that is, of a dialectic from desire to freedom via truth mediated by wisdom.

[†] For example what are the conditions of the possibility of generalized commodity production?

Dialectic

> In its mystified form, the dialectic became the fashion in Germany because it seemed to transfigure and glorify what exists. In its rational form it is a scandal and abomination to the bourgeoisie and their doctrinaire spokesmen, because it includes in its understanding of what exists a simultaneous recognition of its negative, its inevitable destruction; because it regards every historically developed form as being in a fluid state; in motion, and therefore grasps its transient aspect as well, and because it does not let itself be impressed by anything, being in its very essence critical and revolutionary.
>
> MARX

§ 1 Hegelian Dialectic

In its most general sense, dialectic has come to signify any more or less intricate process of conceptual, social or even natural conflict, interconnection and change, in which the generation, interpenetration and/or clash of opposites, leading to their transcendence in a fuller mode of thought or being, plays a key role. Most contemporary discussion of this old, complex and contested concept revolves around the figures of Hegel and Marx, to which the first two sections are dedicated, before I turn to consider whether we can give a 'real definition' of dialectic and the nature of the dialectical critique of analytical reason.

There are two principal inflections of the dialectic in Hegel: (α) as a logical process of reason; and (β), more narrowly, as a dynamo of this process, the method, practice or experience of determinate negation. But to understand (α) one must go back to its roots in ancient Greek thought. For, in Hegel two ancient strands of dialectic, (a) the Eleatic idea of dialectic as reason, and (b) the Ionian idea of it as process, are united in the idea of dialectic as a logical process of reason.

(a) Aristotle credited Zeno of Elea with the invention of dialectic (derived from the Greek *dialectikē* — the art of conversation) in his famous paradoxes which were designed to vindicate the Eleatic cosmology by drawing intellectually unacceptable conclusions from its rejection. But the term was first generally applied in a recognizably philosophical context to Socrates' mode of argument, or elenchus, which was differentiated from the Sophistic purely rhetorical eristic, by the orientation of the Socratic dialogue towards the disinterested pursuit of truth. Plato himself regarded dialectic as the supreme philosophical method and the 'coping-stone' of the sciences; and used it to designate both the definition of ideas by genus and species (founding logic), and their interconnection in the light of a single principle, the Form of the Good (instituting metaphysics). Aristotle's opinion of dialectic was considerably less exalted, regarding it as a mere propaedeutic to the syllogistic reasoning expounded in his *Analytics*. The sense of dialectic as conversational interplay and exchange, involving the assertion, contradiction, distinction and qualification of theses, was retained in the practice of medieval disputation. Kant regarded dialectic as that part of transcendental logic which showed the mutually contradictory or antinomic state into which the intellect fell when not harnessed to the data of experience. This spread of connotations of dialectic includes, then, argument and conflict, dialogue and exchange, but also probative progress, enlightenment and the critique of illusion.

(b) The second Ionian strand typically assumed a dual form: in an *ascending* dialectic, the existence of a higher reality (e.g. the Forms or God) was demonstrated; and in a *descending* dialectic its manifestation in the phenomenal world was explained. Combination of the ascending and descending phases results in a pattern of original unity, loss or alienation and return or reunification, graphically portrayed in Schiller's *Letters on the Aesthetic Education of Mankind*, which heavily influenced Hegel's generation. Combination of the Eleatic and Ionian strands yields the Hegelian absolute — a logical process or *dialectic* which actualizes itself by alienating or becoming something other than itself, and which restores its self-unity by recognizing this alienation as nothing other than its true expression or manifestation — a self-generating, self-differentiating and self-particularizing process of reason that is recapitulated and completed in the Hegelian system (which demonstrates this) itself.

We now have to step back a bit and consider the evolution of Hegel as a thinker who, by 1800, i.e. after the period described at the beginning of the last section, wanted to attain three objectives:

1. to realize the traditional goals of philosophy — in particular to *realize idealism*, but from the standpoint of transcendental subjectivity, i.e. within an immanent metaphysics of experience, i.e. without sacrificing Kantian gains. But the outcome of

the first dialectical thread in Kant was a view of human beings as bifurcated, disengaged from nature and inherently limited in both cognitive and moral powers. Hegel's generation longed for the restoration of the 'expressive unity' of the idealized ancient Greek world, but, as Schiller and the Scottish Enlightenment had prefigured, one which would be

2. a unity-in-diversity, identity-in-difference, harmony-in-conflict, i.e. which would not forgo the complexities of modernity or the autonomy that the Enlightenment had striven for. At the same time Hegel wanted

3. to develop a technique of transfiguration which would overcome the contradictions, splits and illusions of the contemporary world, of which the Unhappy Consciousness of the Kantian philosophy was the index, while avoiding the fate of the Beautiful Soul (the self-diagnosed 'hypochondria' he had himself experienced in the 1790s).

For Hegel, the problem of elaborating a subjective and non-reductionist monism gradually became tantamount to the problem of developing a self-consistent idealism, which, in fusing the finite in the infinite, would retain no dualistic or non-rational residues, thereby finally realizing and vindicating the primordial postulate of the identity of being and thought in thought (and for the sake of thought), at the same time underpinned by a progressivist view of history. Neither Fichte nor Schelling had been able to accomplish this. In Fichte, the non-ego or otherness of being, although originally posited by mind, remained as a permanent barrier to it; so that the principle of idealism became a mere *Sollen* or regulative ideal. Fichte, Hegel opined, is 'stuck fast on an ought'. Schelling, on the other hand, genuinely transcended dualism in his 'point of indifference' uniting man and nature but less than fully rationally. For Schelling, the identity was achieved only in intuition rather than conceptual thought, and its highest manifestation was in art, not philosophy. By contrast, in the Hegelian spiritual odyssey of infinite, petrified and finite mind, the speculative understanding of reality as absolute spirit shows, in response to the problem posed by the descending phase of the Ionian strand, how the world exists (and, at least in the human sphere, develops) as a rational totality *precisely* so as (infinite) spirit can come to philosophical consciousness in the Hegelian system demonstrating this. The effect of the Hegelian perspective (*Ansicht*) is, on Hegel's own account, 'more than a comfort: it reconciles, it transfigures the actual which seems unjust into the rational'. 'To recognize reason as the rose in the cross of the present and thereby to enjoy the present, this is the rational insight which reconciles us to the actual, the reconciliation which philosophy affords.' 'The dissonances of the world' then appear in his friend the poet Hölderlin's words in *Hyperion*, 'like the quarrels of lovers. Reconciliation is in the midst of strife, and everything that is separated finds itself again' — in the movement of self-restoring sameness or self-reinstating identity, which is the life of absolute spirit.

(1) – (3) will become respectively the principles of realized idealism, spiritual constellational monism and immanent teleology. In the second figure the major idealist term (e.g. thought) over-reaches, envelops and contains the minor, more materialist term (e.g. being). Constellationality (which is my, not Hegel's) term, is in Hegel inevitably a figure of closure.

(β) The motor of this process is dialectic more narrowly conceived, the second, essentially negative, moment of 'actual thought', which Hegel characterizes as 'the grasping of opposites in their unity or of the positive in the negative'. This is the method which enables the dialectical commentator to observe the process by which categories, notions or forms arise out of each other to form ever more inclusive totalities, until the system as a whole is completed. For Hegel, truth is the whole and error lies in one-sidedness, incompleteness and abstraction; its symptom is the contradictions it generates and its cure their incorporation into fuller, richer, more concrete and highly mediated totalities. In the course of this process the famous principle of preservative dialectical sublation is observed; as the dialectic unfolds no partial insight is ever lost. In fact the Hegelian dialectic progresses in two basic modes: (1) by bringing out what is implicit, but not explicitly articulated in some notion; or (2) by repairing some want, lack or inadequacy in it, the first comprising immanent, the latter omissive critique. 'Dialectical', in contrast to 'reflective' (or analytical), thought grasps conceptual forms in their systematic interconnections, not just their determinate differences, and conceives each development as a product of a previous, less developed, phase, whose necessary truth or fulfilment it is, so that there is always some tension, latent irony or incipient surprise between any form and what it is in the process of becoming.

Let us go into the fine structure of (β) in more detail. Although the principle of the mutual exclusion of opposites, entailing rigid definitions and fixed polarities, is adequate for the finite objects grasped by common sense and the empirical sciences, the infinite totalities of reason (which, of course, constellationally embrace the former) require the dialectical principle of the identity of exclusive opposites. And Hegel's central logical claim is that the identity of

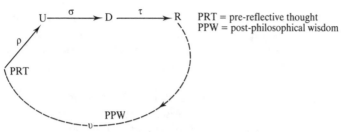

Figure 6.1 The Logic of Hegel's Dialectic

opposites is not incompatible with their exclusion, *but rather depends upon it*. For it is the experience of what in non-dialectical terms would be a logical contradiction which at once indicates a need for an expansion of the universe of discourse and at the same time yields the required concept. It is *this* experience in which the dialectical moment proper, which I shall write as γ, consists as the second moment of a triad composed of:

[1]   the understanding [henceforth U], dialectic or negative reason [henceforth D], and speculative or positive reason [henceforth R]. Now it is clear enough that if we stay at the level of U we will not find or recognize contradictions in our concepts of experience. In general it takes a quantum leap — in what we may call a σ transform — to find the contradictions, anomalies or inadequacies; and another quantum leap — in a τ transform — to resolve them. However, the understanding, which, at one point, Hegel characterizes as an 'almighty power', is a great advance on the pre-reflective reasonableness of everyday life, to which *after* the passage to dialectical and speculative philosophy Hegel believes we have to return, in what we could call the ρ and υ transforms.

The structure of any Hegelian dialectical movement will be as depicted in Figure 6.1.

Now, from the consideration that the Hegelian determinate negation is simultaneously both a *transformation* in the observer's consciousness and an *expansion* of the whole conceptual field, it follows that the latter can be held only in the mode of 'negative presence' — what Kosok has denominated 'negative referral'. Consider a triadic dialectic, where the base conceptual form is (e) and (−e) is the determinate negation of (e) and (o) is the sublation of (e) and (−e). In principle it seems we have a choice: either (1) we can say neither (e) nor (−e) apply in the transition state or boundary zone, thus rejecting the law of excluded middle and/or bivalence, assigning a third value (e.g. ontologically indeterminate, underdetermined or fuzzy; or epistemologically undecidable); or (2) we can say that both (e) and (−e) apply, thereby rejecting the law of non-contradiction.

On (1) we must sacrifice completeness, which Hegel cannot allow, but on (2), for which Hegel must plump, we seem to sacrifice consistency. It is the way in which Hegel takes (2) that is truly instructive. This is the node within the node (δ). The contradiction between the positive contraries (e) and (−e) becomes a signalling device for the expansion of the previous conceptual field. With this expansion in the conceptual field the erstwhile positive contraries are retained as negative sub-contraries in a cumulative memory store. There are a number of interesting consequences of this. First, it is a prototype of a genuine epistemological dialectic in science:

[2]   inconsistency → greater depth and/or totality → restoration of consistency.

Second, in the expanded field, the erstwhile contraries are reinstated in their full *distinctiveness*; yet they remain *inseparable* moments of the totality which transcends them. In other words, Hegel achieves an analytical reinstatement within a dialectical connection. In general Hegel wants to assert all of the following: 'a is a', 'a is (i.e. passes over into) not a', 'a is b (the determinate result of the transition)' and 'a is after all a'. This is the reconciliation to actuality the Hegelian dialectic, via logical contradiction, affords. Third, such dialectical opposites illustrate, as we have already noticed in Chapter 4.3, one way in which the traditional table of oppositions can be completed. For if contraries do not permit both (e) and (−e) and sub-contraries neither (e) nor (−e) and contradictions do not permit either, dialectical opposites permit both, though not at the same time, i.e. only within a distanciated stretch of (space-)time. But there is a simpler way of completing the table of oppositions. If the exercise of two (or more) tendencies is invoked to explain a multiply determined result, they are both really present (i.e. transfactually efficacious) and actually absent; at once, insofar as they are tendentially negating, positive contraries and, insofar as they are not actually manifest, negative sub-contraries. Moreover, insofar as they are grounded in a common condition of existence or totality, they are dialectical and contradictory at the same time. Critical realism can thus situate and sublate Hegel's logical innovation.

It is now time to turn from exposition of Hegelian dialectic to critique. I shall use two sets of coordinates. First Hegel's dialectic is supposed to satisfy crtieria of (a) seriousness (the lack of which is the gravamen of his own critique of Kant), (b) totality and (c) clarity. I am going to use (a) to generate an immanent critique, (b) to yield an omissive critique (metacritique₁) and (c) to establish an antinomial critique. My second set aligns the three motivations for his system, viz. (1)–(3), to generate critique of the principles to which they give rise, viz. realized idealism, spiritual constellational monism and preservative dialectical sublation (immanent teleology). It will be convenient to concentrate in this section on the first dimension of ordination and to postpone the second until the next section, when I will associate it with Marx's critique of Hegel's dialectic. Except to mention here that in virtue of (1), *intransitivity* is lost and we have a series of illicit fusions or conflations between natural and conceptual necessity, negation and dialectic; in virtue of (2), *transfactuality* disappears and we have a whole group of problems stemming from Hegel's actualism (also implied by [1]) and constellational monism; and in virtue of (3), *transformative praxis* vanishes, and there arise aporiai generated by his denegation of incompleteness (also implied by [1]) and change (implied by both [1] and [2]), again producing recalcitrant surds and splits. It should be noted here and now that Hegel is a deeply ambiguous figure, split between what I have elsewhere called Hegel Mark I, who can be interpreted as a radical atheist this-worldly humanist, as the Left Hegelians interpreted his method, which corresponds to Hegel roughly up to 1800, when his emphasis became *Geist*-centred and increasingly rationalist, absolutist, logico-spiritualist and apologetic (Hegel Mark II). Although there is a temporal transition, one can say that this tension is constitutive of his system, which manifests all the symptoms of the Unhappy Consciousness, while he personally adopted the posture of the Stoic, whose contradictions, mediated by the theory/practice inconsistencies and Tina compromises of the Sceptic, the Unhappy Consciousness brings out.

First, some simple points. It is obvious that Hegel's dialectics do not conform to the criteria of ex ante autogenetics and that many of his crucial transitions are faulty, arbitrary, unclear and/or presuppose what they have to prove. This has been documented in my *Dialectic* and by others. Next one could examine his cardinal argument from *Dasein* or finite being to infinite being which determines the static evanescence of Hegel's system, and is the archetype for the conceptual realist gloss with which Hegel coats his empirical realism. In immanentizing transcendent reality, Hegel collapses the intransitive, structured, transfactual and ontologically bi/polyvalent reality of scientific investigation to actuality; while in transcendentizing actuality, Hegel eternalizes it, transmuting it *sub specie aeternitatis*. The effect of this double substitution of the logical present for a tensed geo-history and of spirit for structure is to undermine the possibility of science and change alike. Then we could look at Hegel's epistemological method. If (a) it is transformationalist, i.e. it operates on pre-given data (which is the most reasonable interpretation of it), then Hegel does not succeed in generating content out of form alone and is subject to his own strictures against Kant. If (b) it is, to use Rosen's term, hyperintuitive, as Hegel claims it to be, then one can only accept the charge made by Marx and Trendlenberg that unreflected empirical data are tacitly absorbed and projected onto the play of the parthenogenic process, betraying a contradiction between Hegel's theory and practice. Finally, if (c) it is purely phenomenological, as Kojève has claimed, then aside from the fact that this is only plausible for the *Phenomenology of Mind* and perhaps his histories, one can only say that Hegel has not justified his claim to unilinearity or uniqueness. Next one could take Hegel's theories of totality and truth. Hegel's totality is closed; an open totality conjures up for him an infinite regress, which implies the homologous more of the same. But why rule out significant change? Even if it is admitted that there is some kind of inadequacy or lack in an open totality (viz. tautologically a lack of completeness), there is no inadequacy in the thought of an open totality — which is what is at stake in Hegel — which includes the thought of a closed totality as a special case. For Hegel, truth is the conformity of an object to its notion. But incoherence in Hegel is always resolved in thought. There is no 4D, but transfiguration, in Hegel. But if reality is out of joint with its notion, it is reality which should be adjusted, not its truth, on Hegel's own theory of truth.

Let us look at Hegel in the second book of the *Logics* on 'Essence', from the perspective of the experimental natural sciences. Thought applies to, but is not intrinsically constitutive of, being. Existence becomes intransitive, and so it must be conceded that there exist whole domains of being which are not essentially related to thought. The transfactuality of laws and the openness of systems implies that we must have the categories of non-apparent essence and non-actual essentialities, which Hegel cannot allow. Contingencies, like Krug's pen or the number of species of parrot — indeed anything that Hegel cannot explain or rationally transfigure — must be put down as irrational existents, demi-actualities, and the future as demi-present (my terms).† Now suppose it is pointed out that Hegel's idealism and monism are of a constellational kind, so that they are there for the sake of *Geist*. This now generates the recurrence of a Fichtean endless regress in the vain search for closure; or the obscurity of a Schellingian point of indifference. Then there is the shortfall in his resolution of the master−slave dialectic. Mutual recognition is consistent with the persistence of a host of generalized master−slave-type relations.‡ Closely akin to this it is patently obvious that there are many resolutions of contradictions besides preservative determinate sublations. In general the Hegelian schema is a special case of a more general one which we may write as

$$[3] \quad dr^0 \geq dr^* \geq dr' \geq dr'' \geq dr''' \geq dr'''',$$

where dr^0 is an outcome, dr^* is a rational outcome, dr' is a preservative determinate rational outcome, which satisfies criteria of essentiality, significance or value, dr'', affording us reconciliation to life, dr''', and encouraging mutual recognition in a liberal democratic state, dr''''.

I have entered the terrain of the omissive critique. The category of determinate absence is a void at the heart of the Hegelian system. Contradiction cancels itself. Hegel's freedom is fate, his reason rationalization or transfiguration of the actually existing order of things. Subject to primal squeeze, he lacks the concept of natural necessity and alethic truth. His realized idealism collapses the distinction between reference and sense; and his point of identity becomes a point of duplicity or ideological plasticity. His totalities are expressive-centrist and closed in the three dimensions of depth, systematicity and spatio-temporality. His concept of causality is intrinsically teleological. Another perspective on the omissive critique can be obtained by looking at the absences at the various stadia of his system, of intransitivity in Being, of essential transfactuality in

---

† Genevieve Lloyd[1] has shown how deeply in his thought the figure of the demi-(which is nothing but a reprise of Aristotelian non-being, matter, accident) permeates through Hegel. Thus in his social philosophy women, confined to the sphere of the family, only achieve full actuality as mediated by their relationship with men participating in the spheres of civil society and the state. If the comparison with Aristotle seems far-fetched, then one can ask what are Hegel's demi's but recrudescences of the Kantian unknowable thing in itself.

‡ This has been disputed by Joseph McCarney,[2] who argues that only a radical egalitarianism is consistent with it. Although I have argued in *Dialectic*, Chapter 4.5, that the logic of the master−slave dialectic is a concretely singularized egalitarianism, Hegel does not have the conceptual tools to develop it. In the first place, the emphasis in the *Phenomenology* is on mutual forgiveness, rather than recognition per se. Second, his concept of recognition embodies the valid insight that recognition must be between non-identicals, which is only consistent with radical egalitarianism if the egalitarianism is in principle and practice concretely singularized.

Essence, of essential transformability in Objective Spirit, where praxis, consisting in the transformative negation of the given, cannot do anything but transform the conditions of the possibility of the given, undermining Hegel's theory that (geo-)history has reached a plateau, a theme to be re-echoed again and again.

It is arguable that opacity is essential to art; certainly the multiple possibilities of interpretation are.

Let us now turn to the antinomial critique. Focusing on the principles of spiritual constellational monism, we have the problem of monism, the transition to nature, the deduction of Krug's pen, the demi-actual and a host of others. The problem here is Hegel's failure to achieve an *absolute absolute*, which divides reality into two, the half that he can account for and the half that he cannot. The normal Hegelian reply that the various species of parrot, or contingency, are there for the sake of categorial completion would do were it not for the claim that Hegel makes for his system and his strictures against the dualisms and/or shortfalls of other philosophies. For left with the irrational half of reality, Hegel is no better off, as we have seen, than a Kant, Fichte or Schelling. Further supposing the irrational existent is consigned to the domain of the empirical sciences, what guarantee does he have that work here will not seep back essentially on to his system and produce what I have called 'endosmotic refutation', as the harbingers or conveyors of conceptual change, in the way in which relativity theory has affected our concepts of space and time, and feminism men's of women. As already remarked, Hegel uses the figure of constellationality as a device of closure, but also as one of teleology and one in which it must be asked how the minor materialist term, say nature, can sustain any genuine autonomy, if it is conceived as petrified mind. The same figure is heavily implicated in Hegel's response to the problem of completeness and change. It is true that I have praised him for his epistemological dialectic, but in the final analysis this is eristic in that it always ends in completion. There is no genuine concept of ontological stratification independently of mind or of contradiction uncancelled. Once more in respect of change we have the possibility, actualized, of endosmotic refutation. Finally, it is worth re-emphasizing the countless alternatives to the preservative *Aufhebung*, from transformative negation through existential contradiction to the 'mutual ruin' of the contending parties.

§ 2 Marxian Dialectic

Four main issues have dominated intellectual discussion about dialectic in the Marxist tradition:

1. the difference between the Marxian (materialist) and Hegelian
   dialectics;
2. the role of the dialectic within Marx's work, and more broadly in
   any Marxian social science;
3. the compatibility of dialectics with formal logic, materialism,
   scientific practice and rationality generally; and
4. the status of Engel's attempt to extend Marx's dialectic from the
   social realm to encompass nature and the whole of being
   generally.

The three most frequent emphases of the concept of dialectic in the
Marxist tradition are as a method, most usually scientific method,
instancing *epistemological* dialectics; a set of laws or principles,
governing the whole or some sector of reality, *ontological* dialectics;
and the movement of geo-history, *relational* dialectics. All of these are
to be found in Marx. But their paradigms are Marx's methodological
comments in *Capital*, the philosophy of nature expounded by Engels
in *Anti-Dühring* and the 'out-Hegeling Hegelianism' of the early
Lukács of *History and Class Consciousness* (1923) — texts which may be
regarded as the founding documents of Marxian social science,
dialectical materialism and western Marxism respectively.

Whatever Marx's positive debt to Hegel, there is a remarkable
consistency in Marx's criticism of Hegel.

(a) *Formally*, there are three chief targets — Hegel's principle of
identity, his logical mysticism and his inversions (which I shall
connect to the other two and the components of his substantive
critique). Each will be related to the three principal motifs of Hegel's
philosophy: viz. (1) realized idealism, (2) spiritual (constellational)
monism and (3) preservative determinative sublation in an immanent
teleological way, which it will be recalled I connected to the three
principal motivations for Hegel's system at the beginning of the last
section and which are also connectable to the Eleatic and ascending
and descending phases of the Ionian strands. Each of Marx's
criticisms of (1)–(3) will be related to the three principal forms of
philosophical materialism, viz. epistemological, ontological and
practical materialism, adumbrated in Chapter 5.2, to which Marx is
(or ought to be) committed. Further, Hegel's failure to sustain these
will be linked to his centrism, triumphalism and endism. And I shall
argue that Marx's critique of Hegel can be organized in dialectical
critical realist terms as proleptically critiques of the epistemic fallacy,
the speculative illusion (the sublimation of social life and especially
irreducibly empirically controlled scientific theory into philosophy)
and ontological monovalence.

Hegelian principle	Formal critique	Form of materialism	Philosophical critique	DCR organization	Substantive critique
(1) Realized idealism	(1) Principle of identity	(1) Epistemological	(1) Centrism/ expressivism	(1) Critique of epistemic fallacy	(1) Lack of autonomy of nature
(2) Spiritual monism	(2) Logical mysticism	(2) Ontological	(2) Triumphalism	(2) Critique of speculative illusion	(2) Cognitivism
(3) Preservative sublation (immanent teleology)	(3) Subject– predicate inversions	(3) Practical	(3) Endism	(5) Critique of ontological monovalence	(3) Lack of geo-historicity

Figure 6.2

(b) *Substantively*, Marx once more pinpoints three principal failings, viz. his inability to sustain the autonomy of nature, his cognitivism and his failure to sustain the irreducible geo-historicity of social forms, which I will relate to Marx's formal critique as schematized in Figure 6.2.

Marx's critique of Hegel's principle of identity, the identity of being and thought in being, is duplex. In his *exoteric* critique, which follows the line of Feuerbach's transformative method, Marx shows how the empirical world appears as a *consequence* of Hegel's hypostatization of thought; but in his *esoteric* critique, Marx contends that the empirical world is really its secret *condition*. Thus Marx notes how Hegel presents his own activity or the process of thinking generally, transformed into an independent subject (the idea), as the demiurge of the empirical world. He then argues that the content of the speculative philosopher's thought actually consists in uncritically received empirical data, absorbed from the existing state of affairs, which is in this way reified and eternalized. Figure 6.3 illustrates the logic of Marx's objection.

Marx's analysis has a number of interesting corollaries. First, it implies that conservatism or apologetics is intrinsic to the Hegelian method, not, as the Left Hegelians thought, or not only, a result of some personal weakness or compromise. Second, it entails that Hegel's logical theory is inconsistent with his actual practice, in that his dialectical pirouettes turn out to be motivated by more or less crudely empirical considerations. Third, it opens up the possibility of a *materialist diffraction* of the dialectic: that is to say, that the dialectic in Marx (and Marxism) may specify not a *unitary* phenomenon, but a

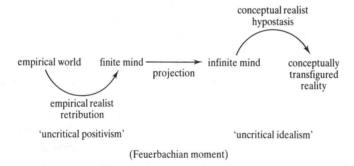

Figure 6.3 Marx's Critique of Hegel's Principle of Identity

number of *diverse* figures and topics. Thus it may refer to patterns or processes in philosophy, science or the world; being, thought or their relation; nature or society; structures, rhythmics, totalities or conjunctures, etc. It is also worth noting here that the term 'dialectic', as customarily employed, has systematic transitive/intransitive and intrinsic/extrinsic ambiguities to it. And within these categories further divisions may be of moment. Thus an epistemic dialectic may be metaconceptual, methodological (critical or systematic), heuristic or substantive (descriptive or explanatory); a relational dialectic may be conceived primarily as an ontological process (as in Lukács) or as an epistemological critique (as in Marcuse). Such dialectical modes may be related by (a) a common ancestry and (b) their systematic connections within Marxism *without* being related by their possession of a common essence, kernel or germ, still less (c) one that can be read back unchanged into Hegel. Marx may still have been positively indebted to Hegelian dialectic, even if in his work it were to have been utterly transformed, so that neither of the famous kernel or inversion images would apply, and/or developed in a variety of ways.

Marx's critique is epistemologically materialist insofar as it presupposes his commitment to scientific realism, viz. the assertion of the existential intransitivity and transfactual efficacy of the objects of scientific thought. I shall later argue that this is in fact his mature position. For the moment we may note, on our own account, that transcendental realism entails a critique of the epistemic fallacy, of subject–object identity theory, whether in anthropocentric or *Geist*-centric (i.e. by Feuerbachian criticism anthropomorphic) form, and that, as Althusser has correctly argued, Marx's totality is not expressive, and, as Della Volpe has stressed, it is subject to rigorous empirical controls. It is perhaps worth noting here the complementarity (and tacit duplicity) of dialectical antagonists in objective idealism which epistemologically presupposes the reified facts of classical (subjective) empiricism, and classical (subjective) empiricism which ontologically presupposes that these reified facts are in effect hypostatized ideas.

Marx's epistemological materialism meshes with the first aspect of Marx's substantive critique, essayed in the *1844 Paris Manuscripts*, the introduction to the *Grundrisse* and innumerable other places, namely his incapacity to sustain the *objectivity* of nature and being generally, conceived as radically alterior to thought and neither causally dependent upon nor teleologically necessitated by any kind of mind.

1. Marx's critique of Hegel's 'logical mysticism', and the parthogenesis of concepts and ideological conjuring tricks it allows, turns on the critique of the notion of the autonomy or final self-sufficiency of philosophy (and ideas generally). But it is unclear whether Marx is advocating a literal inversion, viz. the absorption of philosophy (or its positivistic supercession) by science, as is suggested by the polemics of the German ideology (1844) period; or rather

2. a transformed practice of philosophy as heteronomous, i.e. as dependent upon science and other social practices but with relatively autonomous functions of its own, as is indicated by his (and Engel's) own practice. In any event, this line of attack amounts to a critique of the speculative illusion, and of Hegel's theoretical triumphalism, i.e. his claims for absolute idealism. Substantively, Marx's critique is oriented against Hegel's cognitivism, for whom 'the only labour . . . is *abstract mental labour*', and is rooted in his ontological materialism, asserting the unilateral dependence of social upon biological being and the emergence of the former from the latter.

3. Hegel is guilty, according to Marx, of a triple inversion of 'subject' and 'predicate'. In each respect Marx describes Hegel's position as an inversion (of the real situation) and his own position as an inversion of Hegel's — the inversion of the inversion. Thus Marx counterposes to Hegel's absolute idealist ontology, speculative rationalist epistemology and substantive idealist sociology, a conception of universals as properties of particular things, knowledge as irreducibly empirical and civil society (later, modes of production) as the foundation of the state. But here again it is unclear whether Marx is merely affirming the contrary of Hegel's position or rather transforming its problematic. In fact he is normally doing the latter. Marx conceives infinite mind as an illusory projection of (alienated) finite beings and nature as transcendentally real; and the Hegelian

immanent spiritual teleology of infinite, petrified and finite mind is replaced by a methodological commitment to the empirically controlled investigation of the causal relations within and between geo-historically emergent, developing humanity and intransitively real, but modifiable nature. But Marx, following Hegel here, does not clearly differentiate ontology, epistemology and sociology, and so, a fortiori, the different inversions at stake, as I have done. Their distinctiveness is, however, implied by Marx's first and second lines of attack, which I have interpreted as hinging on critiques of the epistemic fallacy (the reduction of being to knowledge) and of the speculative illusion (that of science to philosophy) respectively.

It is his criticism of the third inversion which I want to associate with (i) the most characteristically Marxian species of philosophical materialism, (ii) the main animus of his substantive critique, (iii) my critique of ontological monovalence, and finally (iv) his criticism of Hegel's endist immanent teleology. (i) Historical materialism presupposes epistemological, is grounded in ontological but consists in a substantive elaboration of practical materialism.[3] (ii) It was Lukács who first pointed out that the crux of Marx's critique of Hegel's phenomenology was the absence of the distinction between objectification and alienation. For in identifying the two, Hegel had rationalized the present geo-historically specific forms of human objectification as the self-alienation of an absolute subject, thereby pre-empting the possibility of a more truly human, non-alienated mode of objectification. More generally, Marx insists that labour not only presupposes 'a material substratum . . . furnished without the help of man', but also entails at once (a) irreducible loss and finitude yet also (b) the possibility of genuine novelty and change, that is, of transformative non-preservative negation. (iii) This connects directly with Hegel's elimination of post-Mark II sublation, his absenting of the notion of absence, checking genuine change, betraying the positivity of absolute idealism and rendering Hegel vulnerable to my critique of ontological monovalence. The very most a Hegelian could say is that Hegel is only constellationally monovalent. But as Hegel is not concerned with the demi-actual, the demi-present (i.e. the future), this is a very weak response. (iv) In Marx's major theoretical and applied conjunctural analysis, his emphasis is on causal and not conceptual necessity and teleology is limited to its proper place, viz. in the intentional causality of embodied human agency, and its appearance elsewhere is, as he writes as an avowed admirer of Darwin, to be 'rationally explained'. Moreover, this whole strand of critique entails that any Marxian dialectic will have to be both objectively conditioned and non-endist, that is to say, absolutely finitist and prospectively open, i.e. unfinished.

Despite the consistency of Marx's criticism of Hegel from 1843 to 1873, a definite positive re-evaluation of Hegelian dialectic occurs from the time of the *Grundrisse* (1857–58) on. Unfortunately Marx never realized his wish 'to make accessible to the ordinary human intelligence, in two or three printers' sheets, what is *rational* in the method which Hegel discovered and at the same time mystified'.[4] There is little doubt that in Marx's self-understanding the primary emphasis of the concept is epistemological. Indeed he often uses 'dialectical' as a synonym for 'scientific' method. In the Preface to the Second Edition of *Capital* (1873) he quotes the St Petersburg reviewer's distinctively positivistic descrption of his method, commenting 'when the writer describes so aptly . . . the method I have actually used, what else is he describing but the dialectical method?' However, it is important to my argument that Marx's method, though materialist and empirical, is not positivist, but *realist*. For I want to argue that scientific realism, more precisely an unelaborated dialectical critical realism, is the *absent* methodological fulcrum of his work. It is not difficult to establish that Marx is committed to 1M realism. This maintains, inter alia, that explanatory structures, or (in Marx's favoured terminology) essential relations, are (a) distinct from (b) often, and even normally out of phase with (i.e. disjoint from) and (c) perhaps in opposition to the phenomena (or phenomenal forms) they generate. Thus Marx remarks that 'all science would be superfluous if the outward appearance and essence of things directly coincided' and comments that 'in their appearance things often represent themselves in inverted form is well known in every science except political economy'. But Marx never satisfactorily theorized his scientific, as distinct from simple material object, realism. It is this which, combined with four other asymmetries in his intellectual formation, helped to account for his mature return to Hegel, both (a) for his epistemological dialectics, with its progress by superstructuration and its concepts of immanent and omissive critique and the quasi-realist polarities and categories in the doctrine of Essence (where, for instance, necessity is sustained although it is logico-divine not natural); and (b) for his concept of dialectical explanation in terms of contradictory forces stemming from an (itself dialectically) common causal ground. The other asymmetries in Marx's intellectual formation were underdevelopment of his critque of empiricism as distinct from idealism, of the theme of objectivity as distinct from that of labour (i.e. of the intransitive in contrast to the transitive dimension); of normativity in comparison to (geo-)historicity (i.e. of the intrinsic within the extrinsic aspect); and of the research programme of (geo-)historical materialism in comparison with the critique of political economy.

So far I have only gone some way to

(a) justifying my claim that Marx was a proto-dialectical critical realist;
(b) explaining his Hegelian residues.

Marx had two moments of great intellectual affinity with Hegel. The first was in 1844, when, as I have already said, fired by the *Phenomenology*, he, with the appropriate corrections, substitutes the alienation of labour for that of spirit. A sympathetic interpretation of Marx would have seen the emphasis of labour in the context of determinate negation as providing core elements of 2E and 4D realism. The second was in 1857, when he re-read the *Logic* and was inspired by the analogy between it and capitalism conceived as an intra-active totality, constituting a process in motion, again most vividly exemplified by its final sections. Here, coupled with the proleptic critiques of monovalence and closure which I have attributed to Marx, one can glean core elements of 2E and 3L realism. But we still have to account for the quasi-linear theoretical presentational dialectical form of *Capital*. Marx himself makes the relevant distinction here between his empirically controlled method of inquiry and his quasi-deductive mode of exposition, when he says 'it may appear to us as if we have here before us an a priori construction'[5] (cf. the Leibnizian moment in science).

I have elsewhere examined the deleterious effects of Marx's Hegelian residues.[6] Let me conclude this discussion on a positive note. Marx understood his dialectic as *scientific*, because it set out to explain the contradictions and crises in socio-economic life and thought in terms of the particular contradictory essential relations generating them; as *(geo-)historical*, because it was both rooted in, and (conditionally) an agent of, the changes in the very relations and circumstances it described; as *critical*, because it demonstrated the historical conditions of validity and limits of adequacy of the categories, doctrines and practices it explained; and as *systematic*, because it sought to trace the various historical tendencies of capitalism back to certain structurally constitutive contradictions of its mode of production. The most important of these are the contradictions between the use-value and value of the commodity, and between the concrete useful and abstract social aspects of the labour it embodies. These contradictions, together with the other structural geo-historical contradictions they ground, are both (α) *real inclusive oppositions*, in that the terms or poles of the contradictions existentially presuppose one another, and (β) *internally related* to a mystified form of *appearance*. Such *dialectical contradictions* do not violate the principle of non-contradiction, for they may be consistently described; nor are they scientifically absurd, for the notion of a real inverted, or otherwise mystificatory, misrepresentation of a real object, generated by the object concerned, is readily accommodated within a dialectical critical realist, *stratified* and *totalizing* ontology in which thought is included within reality, not hypostatized.

§ 3 On the Real Definition of Dialectic

Hegelian dialectic has as its terms identity, negativity and totality. The critical realist dialectic, which I have elaborated and which will be resumed in Chapter 8, has as its moments: non-identity (1M), negativity (2E), totality (3L) and praxis or transformative agency (4D). But the content of the terms notionally shared in common are very different. In Hegelian dialectic negativity is cancelled and positivity restored; and a critical realist totality is open, not closed. In this section I am going to essay a real definition of dialectic designed to capture its essence, or essential structures, as distinct from the purely nominal one issued in the opening paragraph (of which even weaker variants are possible, such as any relation between differentiable elements). Dialectic could be treated historically, intra-systematically or topically. Thus one could start from Heraclitian dialectical contradiction, move through Socratic-Platonic-Aristotelian dialectical argument with its characteristic figure of the dialectical distinction (dd'), or thematize specifically Platonic dialectical reason (dr') or Aristotelian dialectical propaedeutics, move through Platonism to Schillerian dialectical process (dp') or Kantian dialectical limit (dl'), which has a modern equivalent in the Derridean inversion, chiasmus and erasure of the traditional hierarchies of philosophy, viz. the (anti-)dialectical remark (drk), to Hegelian dialectical totality (dt') and sublation (ds'), which progresses by the continual reiterated application of U-D-R schemata, in which an immanent meta-critical dialectical comment (dc') on the preceding phase isolates a theory/practice inconsistency in it, through to Marxian dialectical explanatory argument, in which the ontological necessity of false or partial categories of forms are demonstrated (da') in terms of their dialectically contradictory causal grounds (dg') to the 4D notion of dialectical praxis (dφ), as the coherence of theory and practice in practice (absolute reason [dr$_a$']), or the dialectic of freedom, the roots of which can be traced back to Plato but begins its recognizably modern form in Hegel, which I will discuss in Chapter 7.

Within a critical realist framework, one can note its extensions — longitudinal 2E−4D (5C), scalar (de-simplifying) and lateral (through alethic, moral and spatio-temporal realism), which permit dialectical figures as striking as existentially constitutive geo-historical process and/or intra-activity, constitutive falsity, morality and perspectivity. Whether we are concerned with argument, change or freedom, all dialecticians agree that it is negativity (most simply — real negation or absence) that holds the key. Critical realism brings to bear its revindication of ontology to dialectic in its critique of ontological monovalence and it is here we will find the key to the definition of dialectic, the unified resolution of the problems of philosophy; the metacritique of philosophy and the axiology of freedom. Each moment of critical reason has its characteristic dialectics — those of 1M of alterity, superstructuration, ground and/or their inversions; those of 2E dialectics of oppositionality and transition or limit, or more generally absence and/or presence; those of 3L dialectics of totality or detotalization, alienation and split, of centre and periphery, form and content, figure and ground; those of 4D of transformed transformative praxis or of reification or disembodiment and/or voluntarism, of emancipatory critique or repressive ideologies. (One should think of not the bipolarity but the polypolarity of dialectics.) There is a special affinity between 3L and 1M, since totality is a structure, and between 4D and 2E, since intentional causal agency is transformative negation. Some dialecticians can themselves be located specifically within these categories, e.g. Hegel within 3L.

I am going to give a real definition of dialectic as the *absenting of absences*, via a retroductive-explanatory argument from the genealogy of the concept. But it is just worth considering some other candidates, which I would argue my real definition can illuminate, if not exhaust. For although, through its 1M−4D (5C) relations, dialectical critical realism attempts to explicate the essence of the concept, it has no wish to be proprietorial about it. Some other candidates to my preferred real definition are (seeing) the negative in the positive (which inverts Hegel), the concrete in the abstract, the complex in the simple, the totality in its aspects (and vice versa), the real in the apparent (and vice versa), the co-incidence of distinctions and connections (cf. when we have to think the co-incidence of identity and change or of identity and difference), the co-existence of positive contraries and negative sub-contraries, the presence of the past and/

or exterior in the moment of becoming. What about Engels's famous three laws? The transformation of quantity into quality (and vice versa), based on Hegel's nodal line of measure relations, is a case of dialectical thresholds (cf. σ and τ transform of Hegel's epistemological dialectic). The unity of opposites is most fruitfully thought under the aspect of the internal relationality of dialectical counterparts in a structure of domination with differential interests — the one ultimately in the overthrow of that structure. As for the negation of the negation, this is most concretely caught by the formula already given as the geo-historical transformation of geo-historical products (so long as we realize that process has indeterminate moments, multiple determinations, unintended consequences and is almost always partial). In articulating dialectic as the positive identification and elimination of absence, this is perhaps the place to stress that dialectic is the *process*, or, given the multiple diffraction of the concept that Marx's critique of Hegel's principle of identity allows, the set of processes, or more generally phenomena (in the intransitive dimension), which critical realist, like Hegelian, dialectic sets out to *describe* (in the transitive dimension) and dialectically and reflexively connect in the philosophical *system* or network of dialectical critical realism.

The affinities between Aristotelian dialectical distinction (dd'), Kantian dialectical limits (dl') and Hegelian dialectical comment (dc') as species of dialectical remark and civilized dialogue or communication are apparent. But in the relatively unknown Ionian tradition which I earlier differentiated from the Eleatic mainstream, dialectic — literally meaning splitting into two — connotes contradiction, conflict and change. From communication as distinct from conflict, the practice of the argumentative tourney, arguably as a species of rhetoric, embodied conflict *as* communication, as a putative alternative or complement to force, in the sense of dialectic as argument, a sense which could be naturally invoked as late as John Stuart Mill, despite his anti-Hegelianism. It is this sense that I have conceptualized around the idea of hermeneutic struggles. Dialectic understood as essentially involving contradiction, and as a dynamic of conceptual and social change, was heavily reinforced by Hegel, Marx and the Marxist tradition and a century dominated by class conflict, war and increasing global intradependence, partial colonial and female emancipation and arguments about rights. These may be seen as occurring in the context of generalized master–slave-type or power$_2$ relations of exploitation, oppression, domination and control, whether maintained directly or indirectly by force, superveillance and/or ideological legitimation. So we have here dialectic as the 'logic of change'. But also, from Hegel, dialectic as immanent critique and hence upon the detection of theory/practice inconsistencies (and a consequential lack of dialetical universalizability). Thus also the motif of the unity of theory and practice in absolute reason.

But change involves transformative negation, and hence the absenting of constraints (such as those flowing from power$_2$ relations) on desires, wants, needs and interests. However, since constraint can be seen as absence (tautologically of freedom), and since all ills can be seen as constraints and so functioning as absences; hence the definition of dialectic as absenting absentive agency, or as the axiology of freedom. Or reverting to dialectic as argument, whether it takes the form of ideology-critique or not, it is easy to see that this too depends upon the positive identification and elimination of mistakes. Definitionally these depend upon absences, whether they take the form of and/or are based on inconsistencies, incompletenesses and/or irrelevances. And this too, as schematized in

[4] argument → immanent critique → explanatory metacritique$_2$ → emancipatory axiology → change → freedom,

is part of the process of liberation. A real definition of dialectic as the absenting of absences and, socio-substantively, as the process of the development of freedom suggests itself inexorably, as Figure 6.4 illustrates. This definition can then be applied recursively as the absenting of constraints (and hence absences) on absenting lower-order constraints (or absences), e.g. as absenting their grounds. And so we have the meta-definition of dialectic as the absenting of absences on absenting absences.

Now the theorem of the duality of theory and critique entails that dialectic can only achieve its full purchase in relation to its analytical antipode. Thus in dialectical practice what is absented is absence itself. And absenting is the intentionally causally efficacious transformative negation or spatio-temporal (rhythmically processual) distanciation of more or less holistically mediated blocks on possible change. From this standpoint, analytics expresses the ontology of stasis, and an implicit ideology of repression: that is to say, it assumes the shape of an unselfconscious legitimator normalizing past (and local) changes and freedoms, and denegating present and future (and general) ones.

But this, although true, is too fast We first need to look at the traditional ('transcendent') dialectical critique of analytical reason, and next engage an immanent critique of it. I will then be in a position

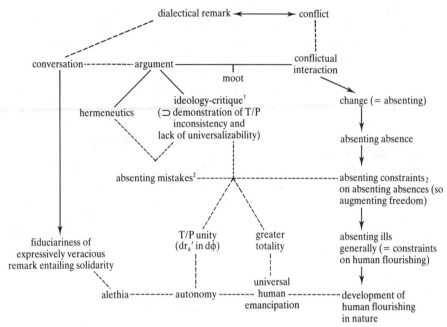

† involving immanent critique (demonstrating T/P inconsistencies and lack
of dialectical universalizability)
‡ e.g. those grounded in incompleteness

Figure 6.4 A Genealogy of Dialectic

to display the anatomy and diagnose the pathology of the analytic
problematic (at the level of a proto-metacritique$_2$, which will situate it
in the context of the history of irrealism). The essence of the
traditional critique is that the principles of identity and non-
contradiction falsely abstract from organic categories such as process,
interconnection, context, ground, totality, vital to the understanding
of social life. Although I agree with their thrust they are rarely stated
with rigour,[7] they are non-immanent and hermeneutically suspect in
their exegesis of dialecticians such as Hegel and Marx. Thus, for
instance, on my exegesis, Hegel entirely accepts the archetypal
critique of dialectical reason, just as he epistemologizes being in his
principle of (subject—object) identity. His novelty is that he uses it as
the motor of his (constellationally ubiquitous) dialectics, which
progresses from the identification of an inconsistency, or more
usually a convenient incompleteness, at the nodal moment in the
U-D-R schema, to its repair in speculative reason.

The immanent critique is altogether more satisfactory. From the most elementary to the most recondite forms of it, analytical reasoning is entirely *dialectically dependent* upon processes of absentive agency (transformative negation) necessary to ascertain, in an open-ended meta-hermeneutics, 'what x means' or when two instances of A are to count as the same, and a meta-semiology explicating the changing intra-relationality of a nexus of signs. Identity presupposes non-identity, and non-contradiction incompleteness and change. Thus identity is always an abstraction from a (set of) process(es) of formation; and reidentification of a token (say a grapheme or phoneme) not only depends upon differentiation from others of the token's type but also turns on the possibility of a situation in which the individual is becoming something other than it was (the co-incidence of identity and change) and/or constituted by something other than itself (the co-incidence of identity and difference). Remember, too, that when the Lockian or Leibnizian moment arises in the epistemological dialectic of dialectical and analytical reasoning in science, this at once depends upon and ushers in a new round of inconsistency and conceptual change in the search for greater depth and/or totality. Dialectic over-reaches and contains analytical reason as a precious gem vital for grounding truth claims and attributions of natural necessity and deducing consequences for experimental tests. But logic is only one (vital) moment in the process of scientific thought.

What is the categorial error crucial to the *analytical problematic*? It is the irrealist

1. epistemologization of being, implicit in subject — object identity theory, undergirded by the epistemic fallacy — in its anthropocentric form, an anthroporealism (such as empirical or conceptual realism) — and to be objectified and generalized as actualism.

This goes together with

2. the ontological contra-position (or transposition) of the logical principles of identity and non-contradiction, which we have just situated as contextually valid principles of thought (i.e. in the transitive, not the intransitive, dimension).

There then follows

3. the ontification of knowledge, overseen by the ontic fallacy (the reciprocating dual of the epistemic fallacy, jointly producing

subject—object equivalents) characteristically spawning what, following Adorno, can be called 'identity-thinking', which can then be read back into the world as

4. Butler's principle of self-identity.

This ensemble has presuppositions, consequences and effects. Thus it immediately generates in its wake

5. Tina compromise formations, defence mechanisms (e.g. metaphysical λ clauses) and connective supports (such as the tacit duplicities of dialectical counterparts, e.g. the mutual interdependency of objective idealism and subjective empiricism observed in the previous section), to cover the aporiai, antinomies and theory/practice inconsistencies generated by the analytic problematic.

Let us examine the fine structure of the consequences of identity-thinking as depicted in Figure 6.5. This can be classified into (a) token—token identity, presupposing the constancy of particulars; (b) token—type identity, presupposing that the particular tokens instantiate one and only one universal or generalization, i.e. closed systems and the fetishism of conjunctions that the latter entails; and

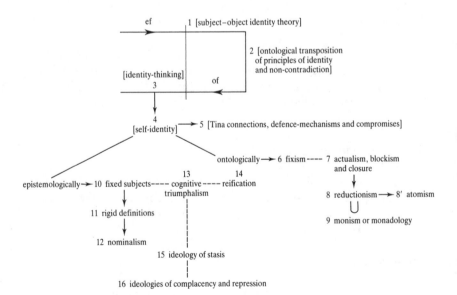

Figure 6.5 The Analytic Problematic

(c) type–type identity, presupposing that the universal or generalization is unchanging. Ontologically (a) entails fixism and (b) and (c) actualism, blockism and fetishism. If there is a single particular, (a) implies monism or solipsism, and if there is a plurality, it implies a monadology. If there is a single type, (b) implies reductionism and tendentially atomism. So we have the theorem: actualism > reductionism > monism. Epistemologically (a) pre-supposes fixed subjects in contrast to the Hegelian 'speculative proposition', Fischer's concept of contradictio in subjecto and my category of subject-developmental negation, all of which are designed to capture the subject, in a network of relations, in a process of formation. It presupposes, moreover, that they are rigidly, and therefore arbitrarily, defined, leading to a tendential nominalism. At (b), that these are subsumable under known generalizations, i.e. cognitive triumphalism. At (c), that these generalizations are reified, naturalized and eternalized. The net effect of this problematic is the impossibility of accommodating either ontic or epistemic change; that is to say, stasis and complacency, leading on to an ideology of repression. And the upshot of my argument could be summed up by saying that *the very concept of analytical reason embodies mystification and con-fusion*.

So prevalent is the analytic problematic that one might be tempted to define philosophy as the unconscious and aporetic normalization of past changes (and freedoms) and the denegation of present and future ones. This helps to explain why in the ethical field, *within* a given polity, only changes from the status quo ante, not differences within it, are characteristically required to be justified. This is as true of Rawlsian practice[†] as it is of Paretian theory. And I will argue that it is a combination of alienation, reification and the fear of change, as manifest in the doctrine of ontological monovalence, that is the real basis of the problems of philosophy. For it is ontological monovalence that explains the epistemic fallacy which underpins both the analytic problematic (see Figure 6.5) and the history of irrealism. None of this is inconsistent with saying that by normalizing the recent and local, philosophy can play a potentially emancipatory role, or to deny its

---

[†] For in this the removal of the veil of ignorance acts as a mechanism which substitutes for the formal principle of difference the substantial question of change, sequestered by the analytical problematic, the roots of which lie in the Platonic analysis of negation and change in terms of difference (to untie the naughty Parmenidean [k]not) by making negations safe in theory but not in practice, de-ontologizing it, thus at once reifying the status quo and hypostatizing thought. The result of the epistemological naturalization of the actually existing order of things, the status quo, is that only changes, not differences, have in practice to be justified.

Janus-faced character. For the recent and local will contain new beginnings as well as dead-ends.

However, so great has been the dominance of analytics and so irrealist has been most philosophical dialectic (in contrast to the dialectical critical realism I will outline in Chapter 8 and my sympathetic realist interpretation of Marx in §2) that it makes sense to talk of the constellational unity of analytics and dialectics within irrealism under the dominance of analytics. For irrealist dialectics cannot think diremption as a contemporaneously existing fact. It is irredeemably endist. Hegel Mark II is continually repeated in the thematics of the end of history and the end of ideology.

=======7=======

Living Well

Man was born free, and everywhere he is in chains.
ROUSSEAU

Oh, lift me as a wave, a leaf, a cloud!
I fall upon the thorns of life! I bleed!
SHELLEY

Imagine there's no heaven,
It's easy if you try.
No hell below us,
Above us only sky.
Imagine all the people,
Living for today.[†]
LENNON

§ 1 The Practical Presuppositions of Agency and Discourse

We are at once desiring acting creatures and judging speaking beings. Although agency has discursive presuppositions and judgement practical ones, we can derive the formal criteriology for the good society from either alone.[‡] Paradigmatically it is informed desire, experienced as an absence or lack, that drives praxis on. Now it is analytic to the concept of desire that we seek to absent constraints on it, i.e. to be autonomous or self-determining in some relevant respect or class of respects. In seeking to satisfy my desire, I am logically committed to the satisfaction of all dialectically similar desires. (This does not depend upon the judgement form, but is implicit in action as such.) Now theory/practice consistency in a praxis in a process entails that the act performed in or by it be practical, directionally

---

[†] This is a sentiment I concur with in the sense of the denial of an after-life or the affirmation of the finitude of human existence, not if taken literally, where it would result in ecological and economic catastrophe.

[‡] In my recent *Dialectic*, Chapter 3, I gave the impression that it was upon the dialectical universalizability of the judgement form that the argument had to turn. But as I shall shortly show, this is not so.

141

progressive and universalizably *accountable* such that it is trans-factually, concretely, actionably and transformatively grounded. These are the discursive presuppositions of praxis. I shall shortly come on to the practical presuppositions of discourse. In absenting a constraint I am thus committed to the removal of all dialectically similar constraints; and thence to the removal of all (remediable) constraints as constraints, i.e. of constraints insofar as they are dialectically similar in being constraints; and thence to the realization of assertorically sensitized concretely singularized equality of autonomy. This is the basic form of the *dialectic of agency*.

Now to the dialectic of speech action. In Chapter 3.3 we saw that universalizability was implicit in the fiduciary nature of the expressively veracious remark and we moved progressively through the logic of simple universalizability (equality simpliciter) to that of assertorically sensitized concretely singularized equality and thence to that of assertorically sensitized concretely singularized equality of autonomy, insofar as the speaking creature asserts a judgement as to what another (paradigmatically the addressee of her remark) should do or what should be the case. This implies a commitment to solidarity, and insofar as 'ought' presupposes not just that the agent can but that the addressee will, a commitment to the totalizing depth praxis that I have elsewhere schematized in terms of the ethical tetrapolity, viz.:

[axiological commitment in the expressively veracious remark] →
(1) fiduciariness (trustworthiness) → (2) explanatory critical theory complex* [= explanatory critical theory + concrete utopianism + theory of transition] ↔ (3) totalizing depth praxis → (4) emancipatory axiology oriented to freedom qua universal human emancipation.

These are the practical presuppositions of discourse and the argument just outlined gives the basic form of the *dialectic of speech action*. It is mediated by the judgement form; and a brief coda on the relationship between the most rudimentary form of Habermasian discourse ethics and the judgement form tetrapolity may be in order. For Habermas, in performing a speech act the speaker commits herself:

(a) to the meaningfulness of her utterance (which is for me a hermeneutic presupposition, not a component of the judgement form, but a condition for the logic of dialectical universalizability to apply);

(b) to the claim that it is true (this corresponds to descriptive adequacy, but although Habermas is committed to the redeemability of truth as of other claims, this would seem to be only under the special conditions of the ideal speech situation, or discourse or a life-world uncontaminated by system, and many critics[1] have focused on the lack of an 'evidential dimension' in Habermas's work);

(c) to the presupposition that it is sincere (this corresponds to my empirical veracity, but fiduciariness and the dialectical universalizability it presages is only implicit, or 'conversationally candid', to use Grice's expression);

(d) to the affirmation that she has the right to speak as she does (this raises a host of questions, and I will argue that only participatory democracy — or at least the surrogate for it which is participation-in-democracy — can guarantee the equal right of all agents in dialectically similar circumstances to employ relevant speech acts).

There are many side constraints on these two basic dialectics. First, the principle of self-emancipation. Solidarity is not substitutionism. This is entailed both by the objective of self-determination or autonomy and by the principle of prefiguration, which itself implies both means—ends consistency and anticipatory pre-embodiment (so that we can see the nature of the fiduciary remark as presaging a normative order based on care and trust). Just as the principle of prefigurationality anticipates the presence of the future, the principle of constitutionality pays homage to the presence of the past. The two-sided nature of the principle of actionability has already been discussed. The principle of unity-in-diversity is closely connected to the theme of concrete singularity, the dialectic of recognition necessary for solidarity (I must see an individual or situation as dialectically similar under the appropriate description, which presupposes recognition of underlying identities behind manifest but real differences) and both the dialectic of learning processes and the realm of unquestioned choice (personal freedom) in the three-sector polity I will subsequently outline. Then there is the principle of totality itself, applied to individuals, collectivities and the global inter-generational and trans-specific village which we inhabit, the consequences of which I shall briefly explore. Suffice it here to say that the dialectic of learning processes, mediated by reflexive self-monitoring of acts and their outcomes, implies, contrary to the ideology of the free-market right, that the only form of association consistent with concretely singularized autonomy is a radically democratic and egalitarian one. Finally, we may consider the dialectical indivisibility of freedom. For an increase in x's freedom is, ceteris paribus, an increase in y's right to freedom and hence, insofar as rights are freedoms, an increase in y's freedom simpliciter.

In this chapter I shall be showing how one gets from elemental desire to the eudaimonistic society, in which, to use Marx's words, 'the free development of each is a condition for the free development of all', mediated via the transition from fact to value, form to content, figure to ground, desire to freedom and centre to periphery. I shall be arguing for a position, as intimated in Chapter 5.3, which combines moral realism, on which morality is seen as an objective property of four-planar social being (contingently irreducible to actually existing morality, so that $dm_r \neq dm_a$), and ethical naturalism, on which moral propositions can come to be known, thus confuting Hume's law. *Formally*, the nature of moral truth (the alethia of which is universally concretely singularized human autonomy in nature) can be known by articulating the implications of the dialectical universalizability of agency and judgement (as briefly indicated above), but *substantively*, the formal criterion of what I will call the supreme good has to be fleshed out by an empirically grounded theory of the possibilities of developing four-planar social being in nature. On the position I am mooting, then, moral truth or alethia is universal concretely singularized freedom. But this is on the basis of a radically *positively* generalized concept of freedom to include such items as needs and possibilities for flourishing and such values in substance as rights, democracies and other autonomies; and of a correspondingly radically *negatively* generalized concept of constraint to include such formal items as (unwanted, unnecessary and remediable) absences and ills generally and in content inequities (conceived as constraints on universally concretely singularized autonomy), alienations and the totality of master – slave-type relations of exploitation, subjugation, domination and control.

The root notion of freedom I am operating with is *autonomy* or self-determination. An agent N may be said to be rational to the extent that she possesses the power, knowledge and disposition to act in her real interests (e.g. wanted needs, development, flourishing), including, for example, her wants for the needs of others. One can then say that if one uses one's freedom rationally and wisely (in accordance with the meta-ethical virtue of phronesis), then one will tend to be able to realize one's ideas and ideals (including desire for greater autonomy) in practice; so that autonomy functions as a theoretico-practical bridge concept linking truth to freedom.

I am now in a position to delineate various degrees, or ratchets, of freedom:

1. Agentive freedom, viz. the capacity to do otherwise analytic to the concept of action.
2. Formal legal freedom, which neither implies nor is implied by (1).
3. Negative freedom from constraints, which, since the absence of a capacity to do x can always be viewed as a constraint on x, is equivalent to
4. positive freedom (to do x, become y, etc.).
5. Emancipation from specific constraints, where emancipation is defined as the transformation from unwanted, unneeded and/or oppressive structures or states of affairs to wanted, needed and/or liberating ones, a special case of which is
5*. universal human emancipation.

If we now introduce the core concept of

6. autonomy qua self-determination, we can then form the derivative concepts of
6'. rational autonomy (just discussed) and
6". universal human autonomy in nature, which to be universalizable must be concretely singularized, i.e.
6*. universal concretely singularized human autonomy in nature, specifically subject to the rights of other species and future generations.

This can now be further elaborated in the concept of freedom as

7. wellbeing (oriented to the satisfaction of needs and the absence of remediable ills) and correspondingly
7'. universal concretely singularized wellbeing; and thence to freedom as
8. flourishing, with the emphasis turning to the presence of achievable goods and the realization of possibilities, including possibilities for development and
9. universal concretely singularized human flourishing in nature or the eudaimonistic society, to which the logic of dialectical universalizability inexorably points, or so I shall argue.

Let us focus on the dialectic of speech action. The first cardinal point to appreciate is to remember that every assertorically sensitized speech act implies, if it is expressively veracious and fiduciary (trustworthy), an axiological commitment, entraining a dialectic of solidarity, whether its content be explicitly moral or not. Second, an agent addressor A cannot say to an agent addressee B 'do ϕ' if A is not prepared to do ϕ in exactly the same circumstances, i.e. without committing reflexive or performative contradiction, theory/practice inconsistency. It is exactly the same point that accounts for the fact that an increase in your concretely singularized freedom means, ceteris paribus, an increase in my freedom, universalized out as an increase in my right to freedom and ultimately in every agent's freedom. It is this too — the indivisibility of freedom — that provides the transcendental deduction of the conditionality requirement in the formula for the good society; that is, which makes the realization of the concretely singularized freedom[†] of each a *condition* of the realization of the concretely singularized freedom of all. Conversely, not to concede to others the rights and benefits one appropriates to oneself or otherwise enjoys is to be guilty of theory/practice inconsistency, and to be untrue to oneself, heterological, heteronomous and alienated. The third point to stress is that universalizability is not just a test of consistency but a criterion of truth, with analogues in the natural world in the in principle replicability of a crucial experiment. And, as the dialectic of agency indicates, actions, and not just judgements (which are in any event just abstractions from [normally speech] actions), are universalizable. Fourth, the logic of dialectical universalizability, which can be derived equally from the accountability of absentive absenting agency and the assertorically sensitized judgement form, is implicit in every practical deed and every fiduciary remark (as prefigured in Chapter 3.3). Both alike are oriented to concretely singularized autonomy of action, and to the dialectics of solidarity and the causal research this presupposes.

We have already seen in Chapter 5.3 the way in which the nature of an explanatory critique is at the heart of the missing transcendental deduction of values from facts, and thence to practice, such that if theory T is better than theory P and explains its illusory character, we can pass without further ado to a negative evaluation of the system or

---

[†] It is here worthwhile stressing that if the logic of equality is to treat all alike except insofar as they are relatively different, the logic of concrete singularity is to treat all persons in their concrete singularity. Of course a concretely singular respect can always be glossed as a relevant difference, so one could put the same point by saying that if for Kant all individuals are ethically the same, for dialectical critical realism it would be more appropriate to say that all individuals are, qua individuals (uniquely laminated structurata), ethically different. This is different from saying with Nietzsche that only the overman is worthy of respect or with Rorty that only the few (e.g. Proust or Nehamas's Nietzsche) are unique.

structure S which explains its illusoriness and to a positive evaluation on any process rationally directed at transforming it. This is schematizable as

[1] $T > P. \ T \exp I(P) \rightarrow -V \ [S \rightarrow I(P)] \rightarrow V_{\phi(-S)}.$

But it is equally important to see that the conceptuality of action and/ or the theoretico-practical duality of the judgement form allows us to pass immediately to transformative negation of remediable structures or states of affairs — that, for instance, to affirm of the world 'p' is to imply a grounded commitment to act on the basis of p for all dialectically similar agents and/or in all dialectically similar situations.

[2] axiological commitment in praxis $\phi \rightarrow (F-V) \rightarrow x(px) \rightarrow y(\phi y).$

If the explanatory critique forms the basis of the *substantive* criterion for the good = freely flourishing society (in conjunction with a concretely utopian exercise and a theory, forged in tandom with the practice, of transition), it is the logical implications of either or both of the dialectical universalizable (transfactual, concrete, actionable, transformatively directional) praxis or judgement that furnishes us with the *formal* criterion. There are not, in the dialectics I am going to outline in the next section, two separate arguments from form to content, but two kinds of criteria and considerations pertinent to each.

It may help if we set these dialectics, the two basic forms of which I have already sketched, in the context of different levels of rationality. (1) At the lowest level is instrumental (including technical) rationality. (2) One may then move in one of two directions — along the lines of either (α) a depth explanatory and/or (β) a totalizing vector. Ultimately both are mandatory. (α) without (β) is non-universalizable and heterological; (β) without (α) is axiologically ungrounded and impotent. But the bare bones of dialectical universalizability are clearest from (β) alone. One moves from, say, a desire to absent an ill which is functioning as a constraint, to the commitment to absent all dialectically similar ills, and thence to a commitment to absent all ills as such, precisely in virtue of their being remedial ills or constraints. This already entails absenting their causes (i.e. vector α) and implies a commitment to absenting the absence of the society which will remedy them. (3) combines (α) and (β) at the level of totalizing depth explanatory critical reason. The logic of dialectical universalizability gets its purchase in the dialectic of agency in the transition from the absenting praxis, and in the dialectic of discourse from that of the grounds of the fiduciary remark, to that of the remoralization of the always already moralized world that is the objective of ethical action and judgement. To (3) we may append (4), the level of dialectical rationality or absolute reason, and (5), the contingent but not unimportant question of geo-historical or rhythmic directionality.

So the goal of universal human flourishing is implicit in every practical deed and every fiduciary remark. Let us examine the kinds of dialectics that can substantiate these claims and trace their implications.

§ 2 The Axiology of Freedom

I am going to divide dialectics of freedom into four types:

1. systematic dialectics;
2. intrinsic dialectics;
3. intrinsic extrinsic dialectics;
4. extrinsic intrinsic dialectics.

1. Systematic dialectics include the dialectic of agency, set off by absence, and the dialectic of judgement, entailing the dialectic of solidarity and the ethical tetrapolity, which we have already observed in the preceding section and whose systematic implications will be described in the next chapter. So I will say no more about this here save to make two points: (a) I want to stress the first and second person character of the principle of actionability — morality is practical; like natural laws it is both efficacious qua binding and universalizable; at the same time it is agent-specific (an implication of concrete singularity — ought presupposes, not implies, can); (b) democracy (and in principle participatory democracy) is the only form of association consistent with the goal of autonomy implied by the dialectics of agency and more indirectly of speech action.

2. Intrinsic dialectics are logically compelling but provide no causal grounds for their implementation. They may be exemplified by the dialectic of equity, or concretely singularized equality of autonomy. This may be motivated by considering once again the nature of the concrete singularity of individual human agents (see Figure 4.4 on p. 79). Now the principle of sufficient practical reason states there must be grounds for differences. But the epistemological naturalization of the status quo turns this almost inevitably into the requirement that it is *changes, not differences, that must be justified*. This is most overt on Pareto-optimal criteriology. But even on Rawls's

theory of justice the veil of ignorance acts as a screen whereby, once removed, the principle of difference is in effect transformed into a principle of change. We thus face in philosophy the remarkable phenomenon of the displacement or projection of negation, the 'not' generally, from epistemology to the ethical sphere, which becomes the realm of prohibition, of opposition (duty v. desire), dichotomies (fact and value), with action characteristically noumenalized (so that it doesn't conflict with the doctrine of ontological monovalence). I will call this phenomenon the 'negativity' of ethics. Its negativity must itself be negativized to incorporate the critique of differences as well as (un)changes and to justify and enact in our intentional causal absenting praxis justifiable and necessary change. It is the scouting of the difference between difference and change, originated by the Platonic analysis of change and negation in terms of difference, bolstered by the reification of the present (i.e. of recent and local past changes), that is, the epistemological naturalization of the status quo ante, underpinned by the fear of change, that is the real basis of the problems of philosophy and accounts for the negative generality of ethics alike. If it is the middle Plato's theory of Forms that creates the first philosophical foundationalism, it is the late Plato's analysis that I would argue has proved historically more decisive.

Consistently carried through, the principle of sufficient practical reason, following the logic of dialectical universalizability, will almost inevitably issue in the project of a society, or so I have argued elsewhere,[2] characterized by massive and global redistribution of resources, tending to a core equality in virtue of our common humanity (i.e. our shared species-being), with differences justified by particular mediations, specific rhythmics and individual singularities, involving a dialectic of de-alientation, the abolition of structurally sedimented master–slave-type relationships, a vast expansion of reciprocally, thence, in universally recognized and enjoyed rights, of participation-in-democracies (justified on the basis of autonomy and equality in the sense of equal rights to employ not just speech acts but leadership and organizational acts) and of the recognition of the conditionality requirement that it is only if I recognize the concrete singularity of each and every other individual that I am not guilty of theory/practice inconsistency and heterology in asserting my own.

Equality does not entail sameness. To the contrary. Elsewhere I have argued for a tripartite structure of (at the very least the transition to) eudaimonistic society:

(α) the realm of civic duty;
(β) the realm of social virtue; and

(γ) the realm of personal freedom.

(γ) The domain of personal freedom, of unquestioned choice subject
only to the recognition of those rights by others in a normative order
based on care, solidarity and trust, is entailed both by the hiatus in
the duality of structure and agency and by the difference between the
supreme and the highest good on to which I will come in the next
section, as well as the critique of over-socialized conceptions of man
(sic). The necessity for (β) the third mediating sector can be broached
in a number of ways. Diversity is a necessary condition for totality
and plurality for progress. Practically, the open nature of moral, social
and technological evolution implies a society which would be in a
state of *reflexively* self-monitoring *learning* (maturation, developmental) *processes* in which a premium would be placed on initiative
and enterprise, economies and ecologies, on the one hand, and
necessary but tedious or unpopular work, on the other (each of which
would benefit all). Democratically, for a multiplicity of independent
public spheres, in which competing conceptions of economy and
justice can be debated and particular interests find representation.
Politically, for transitional rhythmics in which newly emergent forms
of democracy must compete with authoritarian states and globalized
capitalism. Psycho-sociologically, for the realization of the agonistic
and expressive aspects of (still developing) human nature, an insight
Veblen captured, banefully manifest in amour propre. Finally, for
due recognition of that very concrete singularity that gives different
individuals different wants, needs and capacities, including capacities
for self-realization.

3. Intrinsic extrinsic dialectics are self-reflexive learning dialectics,
which are, like (2), logically compelling but come packaged with
causal grounds for their implementation. Here we can trace a dialectic
of morality, passing through descriptive, redescriptive and explanatory critical morality, moving via the practice of immanent critique,
coupled with the logic of dialectical universalizability, through
hermeneutic and material (although still conceptualized) counter-
hegemonic struggle of the increasingly totalizing depth praxis, to
explanatory metacritiques$_2$ and explanatorily critical/emancipatory
axiologically oriented social science; of empowerment and of
disposition (corresponding to the three components of rational
agency), in which, to take the last case, individual and particular
interests are seen to be shared and increasingly totalized, as the
reality principle imposes its education on desire, until there comes
that increasing distanciation of the moral imagination and ethical
conduct that makes the good society seem to totalizing depth

strugglers a feasible project, subject to the side constraints that it be pre-figurationally achieved and realized as a unity-in-diversity.

The dialectics of morality raises another major issue, the precise characterization of moral realism. No particular harm is done if one places morality, like knowledge, in the transitive dimension, as I did in *Dialectic*, provided:

(a) one realizes that this is constellationally embraced within the intransitive dimension;
(b) that every feature in the transitive dimension can be made existentially intransitive in respect of some act (e.g. of cognition);
(c) morality itself, like truth, has a properly ontological and alethic employment; and
(d) morality, like knowledge, has an intransitive object/ive (cf. Chapter 5.3).

The parallel here is exact with respect to tense.[†] Transitive/ intransitive are constellationally contrastive terms and should not be hypostatized, so that the social-relation-dependent nature of morality gives no more ground for placing it than society simpliciter on the transitive side of the divide. One consequence of the irrealism of most moral philosophy (our realism, it will be noted, is ultimately grounded naturalistically) is that irrealist moral philosophies will generate Tina compromise forms, transcendent duals and metaphysical λ's of their own — a consequence I will explore in *Philosophical Ideologies*. The world, we could say, is always already moralized; the point is to remoralize it.

Before turning to (4), it is just worth noting some limits on the logic of dialectical universalizability:

(a) that provided by the limits of our knowledge of the possibilities and tendencies of developing four-planar social being and the unfinished moral evolution of the species;
(b) that provided by the criterion of actionability, feasibility;
(c) that provided by the criterion of assertoric sensitivity in the dialectic of self and solidarity;
(d) the principle that emergent totalities are subject to control by meta-principles and in this case by a fold-back, which would have to be justified by (a)–(c), the requirements of pluralism (totality) and/or that of prefigurationality.

[†] Contrary to what I implied in *Dialectic*, Chapter 3.

4. Extrinsic intrinsic dialectics are also learning dialectics with a reflexively rational component, but here the leading edge is, in virtue of the dislocated duality of structure and agency, structural. But both (3) and (4) depend upon the reality principle imposing its truth on the dialectics of agency and judgement, particularly in the form of a dialectic of interests, which can be schematized as in Figure 7.1. Both also depend on the articulation of the logic of dialectical universalizability, in conjunction with the practice of immanent critique. And the dialectic of material interests will presage the transitions

egoistic desire → instrumental reason → totalizing depth explanatory critical reason → totalizing depth praxis → dialectical rationality.

Four factors in particular motivate a structural dialectic of freedom at the present:

(i)   a reduction in necessary and actual labour-time;
(ii) post-Fordist information technologies, coupled with flexible specialization and a reduction in the size of optimum scale;
(iii) the globalization of commodity production and, to an extent, culture;
(iv) radical externalization and globalization of internal dis-economies (e.g. the ecological effects of pollution).

(iii) and (iv), entailing increasing intra-activity, make transformation tendentially increasingly radically negational in character.

Let us consider (ii) in exemplification of the possibilities here. This is best taken in conjunction with the argument from (3) that

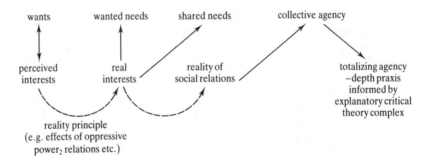

Figure 7.1 The Dialectic of Material Interests

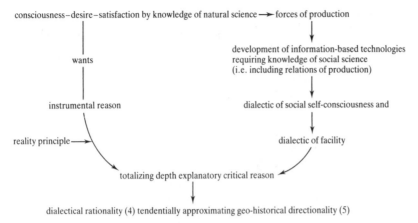

Figure 7.2

instrumental reason will see to it that the transition to totalizing depth explanatory critical reason and dialectical rationality is made, without which it will be inefficacious. Now an example of (4) might be given by the argument that the development of flexible information technologies in the age of post-Fordism/consumer capitalism requires operators with a knowledge of social science, and a fortiori of the relations, as well as the forces of production, leading to an increase in self-consciousness or sentient social self-awareness on the part of an increasingly globalized proletariat, faced with a reduction of necessary labour-time and with increasingly externalized internal diseconomies (providing releasing and stimulating conditions for knowledge of tendencies which are increasingly radical, i.e. auto-negational in character). One could schematize such a dialectic as in Figure 7.2.

§ 3 Aesthetics, Politics, Ethics — and Economics

The upshot of the argument of the last two sections may be put in the form of a dilemma: speak (or just act) or be committed to Cratylan silence. But the second horn of the dilemma cannot past muster. For even Cratylan silence (and, as we have seen, by repute he even engaged in figure-wagging) is a way of 'saying something', and so Cratylus must be guilty of theory/practice inconsistency, performative contradiction. But ethics is only part of living well. There are the fields of the other branches of the theory of value to consider, and

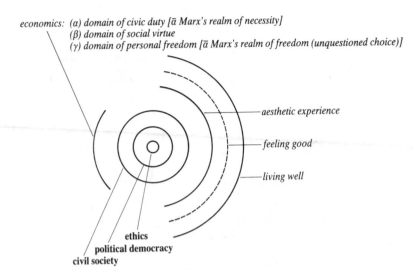

economics: (α) domain of civic duty [ā Marx's realm of necessity]
          (β) domain of social virtue
          (γ) domain of personal freedom [ā Marx's realm of freedom (unquestioned choice)]

aesthetic experience

feeling good

living well

ethics
political democracy
civil society

Figure 7.3

more besides. If *ethics*, in the form of the principle of universal human
emancipation, gives both the deep content of the judgement form and
the latent immanent teleology of praxis itself, *political* participatory
democracy is the only form of association consistent with autonomy
or self-determination. At the same time, *economies* of a sort I will come
on to provide the means, or at least sine qua non, of the ethical
supreme good, which, when it is *aesthetically* enjoyed in creative
flourishing, becomes, dialectically universalized, the *highest good*, as
part of the practical skill or wisdom (phronesis) of living well. By
associating democracy with politics I do not mean to imply that it
should not be radically extended to conventionally non-political, e.g.
economic, spheres of life. Figure 7.3 forms a rough prima facie
delineation of the scope of this section.

Actually to accord with our distanciated concept of time and the
Aristotelian principle that only a total life can be said to be a happy
one, we should reconstrue Figure 7.3 as what might be called the
eudaimonistic cylinder, as in Figure 7.4.[†] Figure 7.4 in turn should
be seen as extended laterally to include systematic intra-dependence;
longitudinally to include the implications of dialectical universalizability (and in particular the indivisibility of freedom) — in which

---

[†] Rom Harré argues in *Physical Being*[3] that while a person's personal being is
normally less than her physical being because of the time taken in individuation and
senility, her social being is greater in virtue of her works and others' memories.

Figure 7.4

event one might want just one cylinder for the entire human race, or if it is restricted to individual human agents, see it is as cylindrical flow within the stretch and spread of four-planar social being; and extended in a third dimension to include the rights of unborn generations and other species.

I want first to consider aesthetics. Here I must acknowledge my debt to Terry Eagleton's *Ideology of the Aesthetic*,[4] but I want to distinguish (α) ideologies of the aesthetic from (β) aesthetic experience, and both from (γ) the theory of art, and (δ) art-criticism. (β) may be more or less ideologically saturated, but its authenticity is not to be gainsaid on that ground alone. A world without aesthetic experience is inconceivable, be this the joys of a walk in the countryside or of a swim in the sea or the delight of a poetic turn of phrase or the recurrence of a motif in a Beethoven symphony. There is in aesthetic experience a genuine aspiration to concrete utopianism, neo-Blochian hope and prefigurationality. But the ideology of the aesthetic, understood as a discourse/normative/power$_2$ social intersect and/or that embodying categorial error plays a special role in the discursive argument of this book. For it is here, in the realm of the aesthetic, that masters grant slaves dummy resolutions of the insoluble aporiai that philosophical ideologies generate on the four planes of social being. Aesthetics is called upon — at least from Kant on — to act as mediator between mind and body, society and nature (cf. the first and second critiques reconciled in the weak teleologies of the third), intra-subjective, inter-subjective and social relations at the plane of society as well as individual and/or collective agencies sundered by class and other power$_2$ relational divides. There is no need to question the motives or sincerity with which these 'resolutions' are offered. Although after Schopenhauer and Nietzsche and the other two 'masters of suspicion', Freud and Marx, a more sceptical tone is apparent, it remains the case that their ideological effect is to attempt to solve the problems in practice that philosophy in theory cannot do; and to do so in a way that disguises the oppositional, fissional aporiai of 2E−4D/5C, generated by a power$_2$-stricken society. The effective response to this is not to deny the authenticity of aesthetic experience — although this is increasingly commercialized and bourgeoisified in consumer capitalist/post-modernist society — but to engage in counter-hegemonic struggle and the totalizing depth praxis that dialectical rationality demands.

I turn now to politics. Democracy is the only mode of government consistent with autonomy or self-determination, and within the range of democracy, participatory democracy as the limit form of participation-in-democracy is indicated. But here other things are not always equal: there are questions of scale, ergonic efficiency and global intra-dependence, which may indicate indirect and circuitous decision-making routes, to be borne in mind, so that accountability may have to act as a surrogate for autonomy. Moreover, there are at least four types of politics — life politics, movement politics, representative politics and emancipatory/transformist politics — which can be mapped on to the concrete universal as shown in Figure 7.5. Typically these politics will have different roles in respect to, say, rights — singularizing, extending, safeguarding and universalizing them respectively. The praxis of emancipatory/transformist politics will be transformed (alloplastic), transformative (autoplastic), trustworthy (fiduciary), totalizing, transformist (oriented to deep structural and global change) and transitional, based on the primary existential of trust and oriented to a normative order of care in a dialectic of solidarity.

Politics is characteristically conceived as essentially to do with power and its exercise. But there are many forms of power — civic, military, authoritative, symbolic, physical; and above all, perhaps,

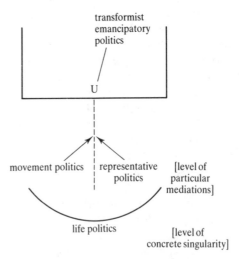

Figure 7.5 Four Types of Politics and the Concrete Universal

economic. I have already argued that the eudaimonistic society, presaged on concretely singularized universal human autonomy, must respect (γ) a domain of unquestioned choice, on the part of the individual citizen, subject only to the recognition that its exercise does not interfere with the universally reciprocally recognized rights of others to enjoy a similar domain. This corresponds roughly to what Marx called 'the realm of freedom'. But if citizens are to have both the rights and the opportunity to enjoy a geo-historically developing satisfying mode of life, there will, given the persistence of scarcity, the facts of finitude and/or necessary ecological limits plus the rights of other life-forms and future generations, remain a 'realm of necessity' — (α) a domain of civic duty, in which every concretely singularized individual must participate, say, in providing care and sustenance in exchange for a basic standard of living and, as the recipient of universal rights, access to public resources, health-care, education and so on. But the desiderata of pluralism, intrinsic to democracy and the concrete universal alike, and self-defined efficiency at a public level and, at a private level, the dictates of the expressive, agonistic and hedonistic dispositional springs of action, suggest the need for a socialized third sector, in which economic initiative and technological enterprise, scientific and cultural skills and political wisdom will be deployed and suitably rewarded, if not by the internal teleologies or intrinsic pleasures of their exercise themselves, then by access to a higher standard of living. This is the mediating (β) realm of social virtue, in which there will be space for a socialized market, without the compulsion to sell one's labour-power, the enjoyment of (relativized) luxuries, the encouragement of a society of individual talents and remuneration for (relatively) burdensome or unpopular tasks. As each will enjoy equal rights to participate in the third sector and as none will be forced to participate in it, the norm of universal concrete singularity is not breached, and as each participant will enjoy equal rights within it, the threat of a new order of power$_2$ relationships, which can never be constitutionally abolished but only practically watched out for, will be minimized. Ideally affairs will be organized so that there are overlaps between (α), (β) and (γ) such that individuals have as much choice as possible as to the way in which they perform their civic duties. (β) is especially associated with the learning processes vital in transitional rhythmics. It is noteworthy that both ecological and economic considerations point to the small-scale (I am here arguing associationalist) enterprise as the optimal production unit with the tacit knowledge of the immediate producers actively exploited in the organization of production. Management functions may then be coordinated on a rotating or selective, if not feasibily collective, basis. The enabling conditions for this include the abolition of the totality of structurally sedimented master—slave-type relations, including, vitally, those induced by the generative separation of the immediate producers from their labour and the means and materials of their production; the ending of the commodification and reification of labour-power (for which penetration through to the level of the explanatory critique of fetishism on the plane of social relations in the social cube is a necessary but not a sufficient condition); the socialization of tacit and discursive knowledge alike; the empowering of the powerless and the self-emancipation in the solidarity of the totalizing depth praxis of all who are oppressed. This will involve not just the dialectics from fact to value, theory to practice and form to content, but also the perspectival switches from centre to periphery and figure to (dialectical) ground.

I now turn to ethics. I have argued against the following:

(a) Ethical anti-naturalism, that the fact/value divide leaves ethics ungrounded — a matter of personal choice (emotivism, decisionism, existentialism, prescriptivism, nihilism, cynicism), diktat or received wisdom.

(b) Moral irrealism, that this merely results in the secretion of an implicit realism, most usually that of antecedently actually existing morality, so functioning to the same effect as sociological reductionism or descriptivism, and generating in its wake a range of ethical Tina compromise forms and unhappy consciousnesses.

(c) The negativization of ethics, most powerfully manifest in the consideration, bearing the heavy weight of the normalization of the status quo, that it is only changes, not differences, that have to be justified (a substitution effected in Rawls by the device of the veil of ignorance which in effect makes his principle of difference a principle for justifying changes, that which epistemology denies).

(d) The unactionability of ethics — closely connected to (c). (i) Personalistically it is argued that 'ought' implies 'can' so the specificity of agency is lost, and (ii) ethics is noumenalized, a matter for debate rather than action (the other side of the loss of actionability) — the ethical is not accorded its proper place among the real motives for action. The result is a doubly dogmatic — once epistemological, then ethical — normalization of the status quo and that ethics is not taken 'seriously' — in Hegelian parlance. Indeed one might be tempted, using our earlier formula, to write the schema depicted in Figure 7.6.

either (α'):   (2) + (3)   .   (4)   . .   (5) ⟶ (6)

      epistemology   ethics   aesthetics   socio-economic-political-ideological compromise forms
                           (the   (defensive
                 transcendent) shield)

or (β'):   (2) – (4)   .   (5) ⟶ (6)

     epistemology   ethics   ideology of the aesthetic sustaining and interwoven with
                   (defensive socio-economic-political-ideological compromise forms
                   shield)

Figure 7.6

I now want to conclude this chapter by effecting a critical retotalization of existing theories of ethics. First, consequentialism, which prioritizes the goodness of outcomes, deontology, stressing the rightness of acts, and virtue theory, of the sort recently championed by Alasdair MacIntyre, emphasizing the virtues of agents, are often seen as at loggerheads. But placed in the context of the TMSA, outlined in Chapter 5, these are not in opposition. Virtuous agents perform right acts with beneficial consequences, including the reinforcement of the virtues of the agent. Conversely, performing right acts encourages the disposition to do so — or, at least, this can be plausibly maintained. This is the beneficent ethical circle which I depicted in Chapter 5.3. A reconciliation with Habermas's communicative action theory can be effected by recognizing that axiological commitment and the dialectic of solidarity (i.e. a communicative and material politics of liberation) is implicit in every expressively veracious judgement or speech act. In the same way the feminist ethics mooted by Gilligan and other writers in a number of places, which prioritizes a normative order based on care rather than abstract universal rights and duties, can be brought under the auspices of the dialectic of freedom sketched in the previous section. This is by noting that the condition of prefigurationality reciprocally requires that the end be consistent with the means which it in some sense embodies; and the condition of fiduciariness, underpinning what I have elsewhere alliteratively called a dialectic of 7 E's — self-esteem ↔ mutual esteem ↔ existential security → ergonic efficiency → empowerment → emancipation → eudaimonia — is the pivotal core of the four components of the judgement form in the ethical tetrapolity. Communication and care are at the heart of the dialectic of freedom. At the same time, participatory democracy brings out the inner, but very hidden, truth of contractarian theories; while ecological theories (environmental ethics) are covered by the importance which should be granted to the rights of life-forms other than our own and of future generations (both ours and theirs). I have argued that a rapprochement between the ethics advocated here and Habermasian discourse ethics is possible. But it still remains the case that Habermasian ethics has only counterfactual, not transfactual, force. Rapprochement with Rawls is even more difficult. In one sense his principle of difference, viz. that economic inequalities are only justifiable if they work to the benefit of the disadvantaged, is very radical, for if consistently carried through it means that they will be tendentially self-eradicating, i.e. radically negating in my terms. But we have already seen how the veil of ignorance tacitly substitutes change for difference and there is no sign that economic equality either inter- or intra-nationally is diminishing. On the contrary. Moreover, what one counts as an advantage and a disadvantage will depend upon one's substantive theory of developing four-planar social being. As will what appears actionable and what appears not so. Moreover, the principles of equality and difference produce a split, reminiscent of the Unhappy Consciousness, which can only be accommodated by a radically generalized concept of equality, viz. that of concretely singularized equality of autonomy. It is noteworthy that both Habermas and Rawls have been forced to concede that their neo-Kantian procedures will only yield determinate results if institutionally specified traits are built into the 'ideal speech situation' or the 'original position' respectively.

At this juncture it might be felt that there is, however, no possible rapprochement with particularist communitarians, that I have indelibly thrown in my lot with the universalists. But this is not so. The communitarians are quite right to insist on two points:

(a) the diversity of moral belief;
(b) the relativity of moral truth — this last in virtue of the developing possibilities of four-planar social being.

Moreover, it should be stressed once more that the universalizability to which I am committed is not of the abstract personalist kind, but concretely singularized to allow the differentiations imposed by rhythmic processes, particular mediations and individual singularities. And that no more than Habermas or Rawls have I developed a substantive criterion for free flourishing in nature. This is a task of social science that I intend to undertake in *Dialectical Social Theory*.

8

Dialectical Critical Realism

1. Humanity is not the centre of the cosmos.
2. There are non-actual realities.
3. Non-beings exist.
4. Entities permeate one another.
5. Intentional causality occurs.
6. Values can be derived from facts.
7. The good society is implicit in elemental desire.

§ 1 The Nature and Derivability of Dialectical Critical Realism

Generally to be a realist in philosophy is to be committed to the existence of some disputed kind of being (e.g. material objects, causal laws, universals, moral facts, etc.). Thus one can be a realist about transfactually efficacious causal laws and an irrealist about propositions or God. Dialectical critical realism is committed to realism along four dimensionalities which may be classified as:

(α) longitudinal, in which along 1M–4D lines it is committed to the critique of ontological anthropism, actualism (1M), monovalence (2E), extensionalism (3L), de-agentification or disembodiment (4D) and at 5C to the critique of reification and voluntarism, individualism and collectivism, hypernaturalism and denaturalized hermeneutics;

(β) lateral, in which, in more orthodox terms, it is committed to an entity, causal, predicative, agentive and social realism (corresponding approximately to 1M–5C), extended to take in an alethic (truth), (more generally ontological truth), spatio-temporal (including rhythmic) and moral realism;

(γ) scalar, in which it is committed to the critique of simplistic (mostly implicit) ontologies, or, to put it in a nutshell, to doing justice to the complexity and differentiation of being; and

(δ) metacritical, in that it seeks out the explanatory critical grounds of causally efficacious disemancipatory irrealist philosophies.

Two questions of paramount importance stand out from this rudimentary list. The first is the character of, including the explicitness and grounds for, the realism in question. The second is the derivability of the realism at issue. Thus dialectical ·critical naturalism (at 5C) can be derived, as I sought to show in Chapter 5, from the sole premiss of the activity-dependence of social structure by transcendental argument, which is why I have in general subsumed it under 4D categories rather than given them formally co-equal status.

Let us dwell for a moment on the issue of derivability. It is often claimed that transcendental, and by extension critical, realism, whether in its non-dialectical (roughly pre-1993) or dialectical (post-1993) forms, is a scientistic philosophy. It is certainly true that transcendental realism can be derived by transcendental argument from scientific activities, in which event (to clinch the argument for transcendental realism) one has to go on to give an independent argument for science, e.g. in terms of its superior causal efficacy. But transcendental realism can equally be derived without recourse to science — from the intelligibility of lay activities like making a pot of coffee, using a shoe horn or playing football, all of which assume the relatively independent existence and stability of the causal powers of the substances and agents concerned and their susceptibility to transfactually efficacious laws not of the agent's making. Thus for the golf ball to land on the green it must be hit with the right degree of momentum, generated by swing, in the right position and subject to the non-intervention of extraneous forces such as a sudden gust of wind. Then there are intermediate positions from what I have elsewhere characterized as the pathology of everyday life. To take a Heideggerian example, N is hammering a nail into a door. She is in the domain of the Heideggerian ontological. The door breaks. By a short route she is transported into the domain of the Heideggerian ontic, which may indeed then be treated as an existential itself, employing categories. Or consider mending a bike, or changing a punctured car tyre. Or reference to a dietitian for a case of obesity. Any decision about domains seems entirely arbitrary. Two things can be established: whatever we do, we are always engaged in primordial pre-understood being-in-the-world-with-others; this world exists relatively independently of us (it will continue when we die, as it is present when we are absent) and is subject to transfactually efficacious laws (partly known or potentially knowable to science).

Transcendental realism comes as a triple synthesis to the demise of the positivist account of science hegemonic until *c.* 1970:

(a) The critique of the monistic theory of scientific development, initiated by Popper in the Anglo-Saxon and Bachelard in the Francophone world and carried through by Kuhn, Lakatos and Feyerabend. This provided the raw material for the development of a rational account of the logic of scientific discovery which would reconcile, in the context of ontological realism in the intransitive dimension, judgemental rationalism in the intrinsic or normative aspect of science with epistemic relativity in the extrinsic aspect of the transitive or social-epistemological dimension of science.

(b) The vertical or depth realism, existential structural realism, being elaborated by Putnam (prior to 1976) and Boyd in the USA and Hesse and Harré in England. The last in particular, reinforcing the tradition of Whewell and Campbell, mounted a scathing attack on the *sufficiency* of the deductivist theory of scientific structure, most notably in *The Principles of Scientific Thinking* (1970) and, with E.H. Madden, in *Causal Powers* (1975).

(c) Pursuing the critical hints of writers such as P.T. Geach, E. Anscombe, G.H. von Wright and the growing literature on the inapplicability of the deductive-nomological model to the social sciences, then the life sciences generally, I elaborated a horizontal or transfactual, causal generative mechanism realism questioning the *necessity* of Humean-Hempelian-Popperian criteriology, thus rounding off critiques of the other two strands, explicitly invoking transcendental arguments of a Strawsonian kind in my revindication of ontology.

But what exactly is at bottom the argument for ontology? Discourse must be *about* something other than itself or else it even cannot be about itself. (Cf. the arguments in Chapter 2.1 concerning the need to avoid homology if one is to evade self-referential paradox.) This establishes the case for referential detachment, existential intransitivity and ontology at one blow. In turn, the referentially detached entity, when propositions concerning it are optimally grounded (e.g. by the deducibility of its necessity from higher-order structure or more comprehensive totality), may come to possess its alethic truth, understood as the real reason or dialectical grounds for the phenomena of the world. Similarly, desire must possess an intentional object, in Brentano's sense; it must be *for* something other than itself. And it is this simple principle, subject to the logic of dialectical universalizability, which takes us, as we saw in Chapter 7.1, from the most primitive concept, absence, experienced as want, lack or need, but consisting, not in nothing, but, in real determinate non-being, to the eudaimonistic society. By the same token, praxis must be *on* (material causality), *with* (efficient causality) and *oriented* to (final causality) something *other* than itself (formal causality qua absenting of the given). This establishes at once (a) the basic structure of the transformational model of social activity, an isomorph of which (despite subsequent divergences) Anthony Giddens was independently developing, most notably in *Central Problems of Sociological Theory* (1979); and (b) a critique of every foundationalism. There can be no unhypothetical starting-point because we never start from scratch. What does this mean for science and for Plato? In science, experimental praxis, informed by theory and presupposing non-autonomized socialized minds, enables fallible access to the generative mechanisms of nature. This is the true world of forms, which account in all their complex, manifold and mediated determinations for all the phenomena of what identity theorists are pleased to call the sensate (which, to stress, is a category mistake) and non-sensate world. Such a position would have combined Platonic transcendence and Aristotelian immanence — sacrificing actualism, whether eidetic or kinetic, and incorporating change as irreducible as alterity (difference).

I now want to elaborate somewhat on the development of dialectical critical realism. Perceptual, causal and hermeneutical modes of access to reality must all be accepted, as must the differences between tacit, practical and discursive consciousness. We are concerned in dialectical critical realism with three kinds of ultimata. Constellational identity is the containment or co-inclusion of one thing within or by another thing or aspect, e.g. of a thing with its emergent causal powers. Dispositional identity is the identity of a thing with its changing (and intra-active) causal powers (whether emergent or not). Rhythmic identity is the identity of the thing with the exercise of its changing causal powers (whether these be emergent or intra-active or not). In dialectical critical realism we have existential constitution by absence (in its fourfold polysemy), by geo-historical process, including the presence of the past (and the presence of the future as mediated by the presence of the past) and outside in four basic modes (viz. by structural dislocation, lagged efficacy, co-inclusion as well as existential constitution proper), by intra-activity in holistic causality, by perspective, morality and falsity (as well as truth). We have the systematic breakdown of Butler's principle of self-identity in the co-incidence of identity and change in real 2E occurrences of the problem of induction and of identity and difference, e.g. at the intra-active frontier in real 3L occurrences of the problem of individuation. We have sustained a notion of ontological truth sui generis and argued for the concept of the alethic ellipse.

The unifying category of dialectical critical realism is that of absence. It is already implicit in discourse qua referential detachment, desire and praxis. It is presupposed by any world containing change, or that emerged (came into being) or that is finite; or that is not alone (unique), or not replete (voidless), i.e. that is not an all-pervasive Parmenidean token monism. It is implicit in alterity (1M), separateness or split (3L), agency (4D) and societal pre-existence (5C). It is the absence conceived as constraint, more generally ill, that entails the dialectically inexorable but geo-historically contingent conatus to the eudaimonistic society. Dialectically, entity realism presupposes absence in the guise of alterity and ubiquity determinism. Causal realism, presupposed by ubiquity determinism, presupposes rhythmic or the spatio-temporal material efficacy of a process on a thing, etc. and on through the causal chain outlined in Chapter 4. And A-serial spatializing tensed process is the mode of becoming of things, or, to put this another way, intra-cosmic constellational identity with the mode of manifestation of time. But it also presupposes a non-arbitrary principle of classification grounded realistically in terms of the presupposition of a common structure or totality, i.e. taxonomic realism in the 3L domain of internal relationality at the Leibnizian level in the dialectic of dialectical and analytical reasoning in science. Science presupposes 4D agentive realism, which presupposes 5C sociality. Sociality entails a critique of any solipsism/individualism/monism in terms of the primary polyadization necessary for any individuation and the social relations sui generis which are a condition of the possibility of the intra-subjectivity on which it continually depends. The social realm to which dialectical critical realism is committed is transformational, relational, conceptualized (but not conceptual-exhausted) and dependent upon the 4D agentive realism of embodied intentional causality. For moral realism we need the concept not just of the moral judgement form and the ethical tetrapolity, but also of its intransitively knowable, though social-relation-dependent, object/ive, which sustains the contingent irreducibility of moral truth to the mélange of actually existing moralities. Finally, it is worth re-emphasizing that in respect of the thematization of the problems of philosophy there is a special affinity between 3L and 1M since totality is a structure; and between 4D and 2E since agency is intentional causal absenting. The set-theoretic paradoxes fall notably into place with the self-referential ones; while the oppositional aporiai of 2E are at the heart of hegemonic/counter-hegemonic struggle over generalized master—slave-type power$_2$ relations of exploitation, subjugation, domination and control.

§ 2 Dialectics of Dialectical Critical Realism

1M dialectics are typically of superstucturation (including intrastructuration), stratification and ground, but also of inversion and virtualization (co-opted by dint of the fact that they are super-/intra-structures). 2E dialectics are either (a) dialectics of process, transition, frontier and node or (b) dialectics of opposition, including reversal (i.e. [b] + [a]). They are united by the fact that they both involve the characteristic combination of absence and presence, of positive contraries and negative sub-contraries, but that while (b) does so in the mode of ontological stratification (cf. the thematic of the 'unity of opposites' and the figure of the tacit duplicity of dialectical counterparts), (a) does so in the mode of distanciated space-time (cf. the thematic of the 'negation of the negation'). The dialectics of co-inclusion — of the non-actual real, of the past in the present, of inner complicity, of the totality in its aspects, of intentional causality, of the praxis of the dead, of duplicitous counterparts, of solidarizing intrasubjectivity — is perhaps the dialectically mediating figure par excellence, on a par with constellationality, the duality-with-a-hiatus, which, by a switch in perspective, it may indeed be seen to embrace. We shall see that it is dialectical contradictions, rooted in a common ground (viz. [b]), in the context of struggle over power$_2$ relations, that pave the way for the dialectics of transition (viz. [a]) that lead to the overthrow of oppressive systemic complexes, which may be as simple as a generative separation in which the dialectical contradictions and, via the theorem of the dislocated duality of structure and agency, the power$_2$ struggles to which they may give rise, are grounded. 3L dialectics combine aspects of 1M and 2E dialectics. We have, on the one hand, dialectics of centre and periphery, form and content, figure and ground, which can with some manoeuvring be situated within the 1M stereotype but also combine radical oppositionality in sense (b), e.g. as generative separation, alienation, marginalization, domination by repression or exclusion; and hold out the possibility of a reversal in sense (a) + (b), viz. of de-alienating retotalization in a unity-in-diversity. 4D dialectics combine all these aspects. They are at the sites of material and ideological struggles around oppressive power$_2$ relations. They include both emancipatory and metacritical dialectics. An archetype of the former is given by the sequence elemental desire—referential detachment—constraint—

Formal principle	Substantive content
1M Dialectics of non-identity	Superstructuration
2E Dialectics of negativity	Opposition (including reversal) and transition
3L Dialectics of totality	Holistic causality, reflexivity, universalizability
4D Dialectics of praxis	Emancipation; metacritics

Figure 8.1

understanding of the causes of the constraint—dialectic of solidarity (immanent critique and dialectical universalizability)—totalizing depth praxis—emancipatory axiology. An archetype of a metacritical dialectic is given by the following, which may be interpreted diachronically or systematically: repression of axiological necessity—symptom formation (Diderot's syndrome)—syntonic Tina compromise formation with reality principle—grafting/invocation of a metaphysical λ clause/Derridean supplementarity—split-off (dysntonic detotalization). Of course in most real dialectics these, or elements of these modes, will be combined. Thus a Hegelianesque epistemological dialectic involves superstructuration (at 1M) via the 2E σ and τ transforms (see Chapter 6.1), and within an epistemological dialectic there will be a Gödelian dialectic of incompleteness and inconsistency; a realist dialectic of explanatory and taxonomic knowledge; a social transformationalist dialectic of metaphor and metonymy; a linguistic dialectic of signifier and trace. Figure 8.1 provides a rough 1M—4D dimensional schematization of dialectics.

It would not be entirely misleading if we associated 1M dialectics with existence, with the arch problems resolved by the concepts of alethia and ontological stratification, turning on the repair of the absence of relevance, or homology, or vicious regress or incoherence (as in reductio ad absurdum) and the indexical key provided by epistemological dialectics; 2E dialectics with spatio-temporal-causality, with the arch problems of oppositionality (contradiction, dilemma, antinomy, etc.) and change resolved in theory by 3L mediating figures such as constellationality or the hiatus-in-the-duality or the dialectics of co-inclusion (of absence and presence) and in practice by ontological dialectics of rhythmic process; 3L dialectics with morality, with the key problems here the absence of parity, equality concretely singularized as equality of autonomy and the absence of completeness, and the absence of emergent principles of structure resolved by the figure of dialectical universalizability and the restricting conditions to which this is subject; 4D dialectics as dialectics of practice, especially in the domain of what I called in Chapter 7.2 intrinsic extrinsic and extrinsic intrinsic learning processes and, at a metacritically identifiable level, the dialectics induced by the inconsistent ensembles forged at 4D and 5C, especially in respect of the mind−body, reason−cause, structure−agency, individualist−collectivist, positivist−hermeneutical oppositions, the contexts of which ultimately 'explain' (though they require immanent philosophical principles to resolve) 'the problems of philosophy', whose most general characteristic is lack of progressive import.

The components of the judgement form may be loosely aligned along 1M−4D lines thus:

(a)   expressively veracious performative component = 4D;
(b)   trustworthiness (fiduciariness) performative component = 3L;
(c)   descriptive performative component = 2E (insofar as our object is change);
(d)   evidential performative component = 1M (insofar as our judgement is optimally grounded).

The logic of the ethical tetrapolity may be sketched as in Figure 8.2, while the logic of transition in the social sphere can be sketched as in Figure 8.3.

I have argued elsewhere that all the basic categories of dialectical critical realism are derivable from absence and in *Dialectic* I sketch three ways of packaging the categorial system of dialectical critical realism,[1] arguing that there is one particular way, which incorporates dialectical critical realism's dialectic of desire to freedom, which is the most natural one. I shall briefly recapitulate it here while repeating my warnings against hypostatizing a unilinear presentation.[2] The dialectic of freedom goes as follows. We start from absence in the context of primary polyadization manifesting itself as desire. This

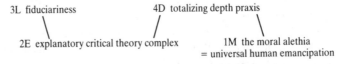

3L fiduciariness   4D totalizing depth praxis

2E explanatory critical theory complex   1M the moral alethia
                                                = universal human emancipation

Figure 8.2

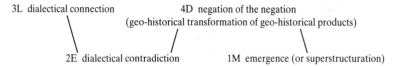

3L dialectical connection   4D negation of the negation
                                              (geo-historical transformation of geo-historical products)

          2E dialectical contradiction   1M emergence (or superstructuration)

Figure 8.3

entails referential detachment and we are soon into classification and causality and thence onto the plane of ontological stratification and alethic truth. Absence has already been presupposed (and in the dialectical circle agency entails it), and in the context of the contradictions[†] within and between differentiated and stratified entities, emergence and thence totalities result. The inner form of totality is reflexivity, which implies a stratified self in a social world capable of making assertoric judgements and acting on the world. The intentionality of praxis (in the dialectic of agency) and/or the fiduciariness of the expressively veracious judgement (in the dialectic of discourse) unleash the logic of dialectical universalizability which takes us by a multiplicity of routes, and subject to a variety of constraints, to the eudaimonistic society. The goal of this is concretely singularized universal human flourishing enjoyed as the highest good of a society in which the formal criterion of the supreme good is an association in which the free development of each is a condition — because unity presupposes diversity, and totality differentiation — of the free development of all. I have also given elsewhere[3] some indication of the variety of dialectics the materialist diffraction of dialectic makes possible. There is the dialectic of truth in which we go from (a) subjective certainty to (b) intersubjective facthood to (c) objective truth, at the point of referential detachment of the base structure S_i to (d) alethia, viz. the optimally grounded truth of S_j for S_i, occurring when referential detachment of the real reason or ground for S_i becomes possible. In the dialectic of morality we may go from (a) descriptive to (b) redescriptive to (c) explanatory critical morality and thence (d) to the totalizing depth praxis it entails. Dialectic is the logic of absence. But in satisfying my desire in absenting agency I am thereby committed to the project of universal human emancipation. This is the ultimate absence that *Plato Etcetera* aims to repair.

[†] Insofar as contradictions presuppose internal relations between structures, 3L categories are already implicit in this step too.

§ 3 The Implications of Irrealism

I want first to round out in this section my critique of irrealism, understood as ontologically anthropic, actualist, monovalent, extensionalist and de-agentifying and as involving alethic, spatio-temporal and moral irrealism, scalar irrealism (simplification and schematism) and metacritical irrealism (involving the hypostatization of ideas), by engaging respectively immanent, omissive, antinomial and meta-critical$_2$ critiques of irrealism, leading into some suggestions for its synchronic and diachronic explanation. Because if, as I have been arguing from Chapter 2.1 on, realism of the relevant genre is inexorable, then philosophical irrealism constitutes a prima facie paradox.[†]

(α) Wherever we start in the irrealist thicket we will end up with a reductio ad Cratylus. Suppose we deny the reality of tense. We will be forced to deny the reality of the difference between an event that has happened and an event that has not, and hence of the antecedence implicit in causality. We will now be pushed back into a punctualist ego-present-centrism, on which the reliability of even the testimony of my senses (for this to be used it depends upon memory which is subject to doubt) let alone the existence of my body or other minds, must be called into question. Or consider moral irrealism. If there is no moral truth, or, to put it less stridently, no better or worse or objective grounds for action, how can I ever act rationally at all? The only way to avoid the endless regress of decisionism and/or the ultimate arbitrariness of caprice is to accept conventionally generated a-morality/moralities or to fall back on the will-to-power — or, like Cratylus, to abstain from action insofar as it is possible. Kojève has aptly remarked that the real basis of scepticism is private property. For only those who can evade the pressure of the 'axiological imperative' is it a feasible option. Consider modern Cratylans such as Rorty, Putnam, Davidson and Quine who concede that there is something 'out there' causally impacting on us, but refuse to speculate as to its nature. They are at once mired in the failure to achieve referential detachment (once again a punctualist ego-present-centrism looms) and guilty of a variety of modes of theory/practice inconsistency, the sharpest of which is the commitment to a fully blown physicalistic materialism in the extrinsic aspect combined with

---

[†] Although I have separated out immanent and antinomial critiques, they are in fact integrally related. Both stem from theory/practice inconsistency. All forms of irrealism involve a quasi-ontic function, a transcendent realism, a defensive shield and a Tina compromise form (i.e. a (0)−(6) formulation), as I will show in my forthcoming *Philosophical Ideologies*.

(at least in the intrinsic aspect in the first person case) the hermeneutization of their discourse at 4D.

(β) Let us turn to the omissive critique of irrealism. There are two gaping omissions here — (a) of the absence of a concept of ontology and (b) of the absence of the concept of absence. I have already commented on the former in Chapter 2. So let me restrict my remarks to (b). This makes the whole categorial structure necessary for everyday life, not to mention science or human emancipation, impossible. At 1M we cannot sustain the concept of referential detachment (and so alterity) which depends upon the referrer absenting herself from that to which she refers. At 2E we need only note that all the categories of negativity from constraint to ill presuppose absence. At 3L we have the absence of a connection in detotalization (e.g. in alienation) or of a distinction in a relevant separation (e.g. in a partial totality). At 4D we have the absence of our intentional causal agentive activity which absents or negates the given and reproduces or transforms the conditions of possibility of the practice concerned (at 5C).

These absences deposit metacritical$_1$ voids. The 1M absence of structure normalizes or mystifies science and encourages a shallow depthless account of sociality, while the absence of differentiation uniformalizes or stereotypes social identities. The 2E absence of absence rationalizes, as I have already argued, recent past and local changes and liberties at the expense of the possibility of present and future ones; but it also deprocessualizes ontology generally and screens social conflict and contradiction and, to an extent, the existence of social inequities and ills. But palpably its most important effect is to sequester existential questions generally. The 3L absence of totality and reflexivity hides splits, inconsistencies, divisions, such as those of class, gender, ethnicity, etc., and alienation, the estrangement of part or the whole of one's essence or nature from oneself, generally. The 4D absence of intentional causality reifies and/or disembodies, fractures and enervates the self and human agency, individual, collective and totalizing alike.

But the metacritical$_1$ absences do not just generate voids with which surreptitiously to fill their positive content. They inevitably produce splits — of the actual and the not quite actual, of the fully self-present positive and the slightly less than positive, of the loose and unconnected and the not quite unconnected, of the language of body (yours) and the language of mind (mine). The splits of course render irrealism vulnerable once more to the theory/practice inconsistencies isolated in immanent critique, but they also presage the antinomial critique.

(γ) An antinomy occurs when one wants or finds grounds for asserting both of two opposed positions. Insofar as irrealist philosophy lacks, the absent, if it is axiologically necessary, must be repressed (leading to pathologies of praxis) or, as we have seen, be supplemented by ad hoc grafting (e.g. in the figure of the tacit duplicity of contraries which we have already witnessed at work in internally inconsistent irrealist ensembles) and further protected by a defensive shield (a metaphysical λ clause) to generate a Tina compromise formation with the reality principle, in the shape of the axiological necessity the absent violates. This can be accompanied by Stoic indifference, Sceptical denegation (denial in theory, affirmation in practice) or any manner of Unhappy Consciousness (the very sign of detotalization and split) — including the externalized form of repression, of compartmentalizing split-off. In any event the result is greater plasticity for potential ideological use.

(δ) In examining the metacritical$_2$ effect at the social intersect which is ideology, we have to distinguish:

(a) the irrealist social and moral consequences of irrealism, such as the virtualization of reason which follows from the de-valuation of reality, which may then be used to legitimate a commandist (Stalinist), elitist (social democratic), authoritarian (neo-liberal) or organicist (right conservative) state, for example;

(b) the immediate philosophical consequences of irrealism, such as its effects on the social sciences (where it encourages their already existing dichotomous character), the life sciences (where it lends itself to neglect of mixed determinations and mediations [cf. Chapter 4]) and the natural sciences (where it gives credence to irrealist interpretations of contemporary physics);

(c) covert as well as overt, resonance as well as injunctive, mediated and feedback (including mutually reinforcing) as well as direct social, including scientific, effects;

(d) reinforcement of existing substantive analogical and ideological grammars.

Let us now proceed first to sketch a diachronic analysis then a synchronic one. I have already ordinated the unholy trinity of ontological monovalence, epistemic fallacy and the primal squeeze as follows in Figure 8.4. Moreover, I have stressed that within this problematic irrealist dialectics will always be subordinated to analytics because it cannot think diremption as a contemporaneously

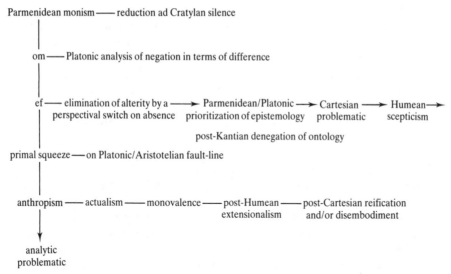

Parmenidean monism —— reduction ad Cratylan silence

om —— Platonic analysis of negation in terms of difference

ef —— elimination of alterity by a ——→ Parmenidean/Platonic ——→ Cartesian ——→ Humean—→
      perspectival switch on absence   prioritization of epistemology   problematic   scepticism

                            post-Kantian denegation of ontology

primal squeeze —— on Platonic/Aristotelian fault-line

anthropism —— actualism —— monovalence —— post-Humean —— post-Cartesian reification
                               extensionalism   and/or disembodiment

analytic
problematic

Figure 8.4

existing social fact and/or because it scouts alterity by accepting the
orthodox pre-Platonic analysis of differentiation in terms of change.
Synchronically we have to bear in mind the whole character of
philosophy as a theory problem-field solution set as depicted in
Figure 8.5.

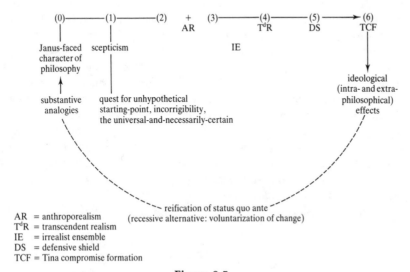

AR = anthroporealism
T^{d}R = transcendent realism
IE   = irrealist ensemble
DS = defensive shield
TCF = Tina compromise formation

Figure 8.5

The philosopher is typically disengaged from practice, a product of the class/gendered/ethnic, etc. division of labour, characteristically, but not always, a member of a dependent elite. He (sic) is imbued with the problematic, whose primeval moment is the quest for incorrigibility. With the collapse of this demand, given the fact of epistemic relativity without an explicitly revised ontology, philosophy follows the transmutation route from conventionalism to superidealism. Without an objective manifold (in the intransitive dimension) in which judgements could be classified as better or worse, the welcome collapse of epistemological foundationalism (in the transitive dimension) was accompanied by a judgemental irrationalism in which criteria of truth, objectivity and human need collapsed. The inevitable outcome of the primeval quest for incorrigibility was and is scepticism. This is further reinforced by the fact that, at least from the time of the Cartesian-Lockian-Humean-Kantian problematic, he starts from the immediate data of consciousness, which inevitably leads, with or without its blockist dual, to an ego-present-centrism. If he is a materialist, he is, in Marxian terms, a contemplative not a practical one.

What are the prospects for change? The 3L globalization of commodification and culture (not always homogenized) together with the world historical phenomena of reflexivity and new decentred (information-based) flexible technologies has generated a sense of both geo-historicity and accountability (in a post-traditional context), giving grounds for philosophy to resume its traditional goal of providing a *logos* or rational account or reason for what one does (the flip-side of which is the recrudescence of fundamentalisms, i.e. the acceptance of traditional modes on purely positive grounds, that is, on the authority of tradition). But this very process is giving rise to agents who are appraised of sentient socialized self-awareness of their relation to the relations and conditions of production and some of the power$_2$ relations at work; who have an interest in understanding social intransitivity and depth (cf. 1M), in recovering history and a sense of futuricity of their praxis, their species and its *Umwelt* (cf. 2E); who intuit the grounds for making connections rather than compartmentalizing and fragmenting (at 3L); who see themselves neither as (purely) machines nor as (purely) conversationalists (at 4D); who will demand to extend and democratize democracy, to emancipate freedom and to release the springs of solidarity (cf. 5C).

9

Socrates and So On?

When philosophy paints its grey on grey, then has a shape of life grown old. By philosophy's grey on grey it cannot be rejuvenated, only understood. The owl of Minerva spreads its wings only with the falling of the dusk.

HEGEL

§ 1 The Ancient World

(a) The pre-Socratics

It is conventional to divide the pre-Socratics into the characteristically more materialist eastern Greek or Ionian thinkers, such as Thales and Heraclitus, and the typically more idealist western Greek thinkers, of whom the most important are Pythagoras (himself an émigré from Samos to one of the Greek colonies in southern Italy) and the Eleatics. It has to be said at the outset that our knowledge of them is fragmentary and heavily dependent on Aristotle and his collaborator, Theophrastus. Despite this, something of a genealogy of their thought is possible.

The basic question for most of the early Greek thinkers is ontological: what is the nature of reality — in the sense of what is the world made of and/or from what did it originate and/or by what is it sustained. The earliest Milesian philosopher, Thales (c. 624−546 BC), in answering 'water', was probably giving a rational expression to an Egyptian and Babylonian belief, itself at least in the first case a reflection of the annual reappearance of the earth as the Nile recedes. What entitles Thales to be called a philosopher is his commitment to the presupposition that despite the diversity of its appearances, the world is coherent, intelligible and susceptible to rational explanation. In terms of the thematics of this book it is of some interest to note that the Ionians not only were explicitly ontological, but also, initially influenced by the Hesiodic seventh-century BC theogeny (in which the pantheon of gods issued from an originative gulf or gap or split called Chaos which generated Gaia or Mother Earth) they succumbed to the dialectical temptation of analysing difference in terms of the essential connection of opposites. (Both these tendencies were to be reversed by Plato, under the influence of the Eleatic Parmenides.) Thus Thales' immediate successor, Anaximander, argued that the originative material, which he referred to as the 'indefinite', had separated into mist and fire, whence the whole series of opposites (wet and dry, hot and cold) out of which the perceived world is made can ultimately be derived. But the Indefinite or Boundless is eternal and infinite. And we arrive at another important presupposition (this time accentuated by Plato) of Greek thought, that the ultimate or true objects of knowledge are of what is unchangeable. Anaximander's Milesian successor, Anaximenes, reverted to a monistic explanation of change and diversity, positing as his ur-stuff mist, which he anthropomorphically identified with 'breath' or human soul, susceptible to differentiated condensation or rarefaction. This is perhaps the place to point out that if the guiding analogy of post-Renaissance cosmological thought was mechanical, that of ancient Greek thought was organic or biological. The world was an animal animated by a soul.

The scene now shifts to southern Italy, where Phythagoras established c. 535 BC a semi-religious community, committed to abstinence from meat (believing in the inter-specific transmigration of souls) and the cultivation of music and mathematics — the link between which was established by the numerical nature of the musical scale — as a means to the purification of the soul. Aristotle typically represents Plato as a Pythagorean, committed to finding the principle of intelligibility of things in their form rather than matter. Xenophanes, like Phythagoras, an emigrant from Ionia, attacked the anthropomorphism of the traditional Homeric account of the gods, arguing that logically each species should envisage gods in their own shape. But the most important inroads on traditional assumptions were made by Heraclitus of Ephesus at the turn of the century. Heraclitus argued that the unity of things was to be found in their underlying, not superficially apparent, essential structure or *Logos* rather than in material. In this sense Heraclitus was a Pythagorean or vice versa. But although the structure underlying and accounting for change was for Heraclitus of paramount significance, he believed that the structure not only accounted for but depended on the ubiquity of change, analysed in terms of the essential connection (i.e. the dialectical contradiction) of and reaction between opposites, which he poetically termed strife or war. Knowledge of *Logos* was wisdom, which he distinguished from the perception of change. It is worth pondering what the subsequent trajectory of western philosophy might have been like if Plato had not come across Heraclitus' ideas in their absurdly one-sided Cratylan form.

Soon after — in the 490s — Parmenides wrote a poem articulating ontological monovalence, thus presaging the epistemic fallacy, and entailing monism (rejecting Pythagorean mind–body dualism), declaring that the predicate 'is not' is nonsense; that we can only say of something that 'it is'. This made absence, change, becoming, finitude, error, voids and motion, as his follower Zeno sought to show, impossible; but also alterity, diversity and multiplicity. It had a profound impact on Plato, who sought to defuse its more absurd conclusions while still working within a Parmenidean framework, rejecting ontological in order to save epistemological negation. The transition to epistemology which begins with Plato's distinction between *epistēmē* (knowledge) and *doxa* (belief) is also prefigured here in Parmenides' distinction between two ways of thinking, the way of truth and the way of belief. Parmenides hints at a pluralism in an appendix to his poem, a suggestion taken up by Empedocles, who proclaimed four kinds of matter — fire, water, earth and air — and two kinetic agencies — attraction, termed love, and repulsion, strife. Anaxagoras developed an even more complicated cosmology, like Empedocles, designed to avoid ineffable negation, at the pinnacle of which he placed mind.

This presages the Sophists, professional rhetoricians and teachers of wisdom, from whose midst arose Socrates, whom we know almost entirely through the writings of Plato (and his student and critic Aristotle). The Sophists, such as Protagoras and Gorgias, typically thought that 'man is a measure of all things' and that ontological speculation was fruitless. Yet about this time there appeared a far more cogent explanation of the physical world in the brilliant atomism of Leucippus and Democritus, which challenged the Eleatic implication that voids cannot exist, postulated constant atomic motion and interaction, and explained the differences in appearances (theoretically) in terms of posited differential constitutions. This a priori atomism, cursorily rejected by Aristotle, was revived by Gassendi in the seventeenth century. Socrates, however, shared the Sophist distaste for physics and concentrated his energies on questions of ethics and the nature of the soul.

(b) Plato

The two dozen or so dialogues which can be attributed with confidence to Plato fall naturally into three groups, which may be taken as corresponding to early, middle and late periods of his development. In each period 'dialectic' plays a key role, but whereas in the first 'Socratic' period it is distinguishable only from Sophistic 'eristic' by its orientation to the disinterested pursuit of truth rather than rhetorical success, in the second it is the means of access to the Forms, while in the third it is a method of collection and division, a taxonomic procedure rather than a putatively retroductive one (albeit one arguably conducted in the light of the Forms). I shall spend most time discussing Plato's second and third periods, since they are most important for the argument of this book.

The early dialogues are dominated by ethical questions, and in particular by the search for real definitions of excellences of character (*aretē*) and their development. The basic presupposition here is that one must first know what a virtue such as courage or piety is before one can say anything about it, a quandary which we have already seen expressed in Meno's paradox. Besides ignoring the always presuppositional character of inquiry, the Socratic-Platonic presupposition seems to rest on a confusion between nominal and real definitions — we can use nominal definitions to acquire knowledge about their real designata as part of a process of arriving, via knowledge of natural necessities and kinds, at real definitions obtained empirically and fallibly. Plato expounds some positive ethical doctrines, with well-known paradoxical consequences — his cognitivism makes *akrasia* or weakness of the will impossible, while his centrism on the good makes the virtues inseparable, so it is impossible to be courageous but stupid. However, the real démarche of the early Plato is that while he is capable of expressing the inadequacies of various proposed definitions, he is not able to produce positive definitions and so defend the morality of Socratic reasoning against the charge of corrupting standards of behaviour — the very offence for which Socrates was put to death.

The theory of the Forms can be seen as one way of attempting to remedy this. In the early dialogues there is a distinction between knowledge and belief, but there is no suggestion that they possess different objects. Their forms, essences or ideas which would comprise real definitions are so to speak immanent. In the middle period they are transcendent. In his final period Plato may have been primarily concerned with showing how we can have immanent access to still transcendent forms. Much turns here on assumptions about Plato's consistency and the dating of particular dialogues like the *Timaeus*, normally assigned a late date but which embraces a full-blown theory of the Forms.

Socrates had searched for definitions of the 'good', the 'just', etc. Plato's theory of Forms attempted to specify what must be the case for knowledge (*epistēmē*) rather than mere opinion (*doxa*) to be possible. Already impressed by the apparent certainty of mathematics, Plato assumed that knowledge must be real, unitary and unchanging; whereas ordinary things were patently subject to decay, multiplicity and conflicting characterizations. He was thus led to posit an autonomous realm of abstract ideas or Forms, existing outside space and time and independently of their particular manifestations. Forms could not be apprehended by sense-perception, but grasped only by a process of dialectical abduction or assent, best conceived as a form of intellectual intuition and recollection (*anamnēsis*), encouraged by a long and elaborate education.

This doctrine leaves the relation between the two worlds unclear. Particular objects of experience are variously said to 'participate', 'imitate' and 'be made by' their transcendent forms. Moreover, as I have already argued in Chapter 2, any explanation or account of a particular instance of blueness in term of the Form 'blue' is homologous, i.e. not explanatory at all. Participation of the Form 'blue' in terms of the Form 'colour', which is perhaps what the later Plato was after, though not deep and itself question-begging (for one is only in a position to call something blue if one already knows it is coloured), would not be open to this objection. Furthermore, however the relation between particular objects of a sensate world and the Forms is to be understood, if the Forms are to discharge their explanatory burden, then unwelcome (e.g. lowly and self-contradictory) forms must be postulated. And this merely displaces — on to the transcendent realm itself — the very facts of diversity and change that it was designed to show were unreal. Aristotle additionally argued that Plato had committed a simple logical error in treating a property (such as 'beautiful') as if it were a substance (such as 'this vase'). But the most famous objection was formulated by the late Plato himself in the *Parmenides*: the so-called 'Third Man' argument. The Forms were necessary to explain both

(α) how the same thing can be called by different (and even contradictory) names; and
(β) how different (and even contradictory) things can be called by the same name.

Now the later 'one over many' motivation establishes a vicious regress. For if a plurality, n, of men are designated 'men' in virtue of their participation in the Form 'man', then, as the Form is itself a man, a further plurality, n + 1, of men is constructed. Such a plurality can itself only be designated a plurality of men inasmuch as its members participate in a further ideal 'man', generating a further plurality, n + 2, leading to a vicious regress.

So far I have argued that Plato could not sustain the determinacy or morality of Socratic dialectic without recourse to transcendent Forms nor the intelligibility of such Forms without homology, projective duplication and vicious regress. But it is in Plato's third period that his analytical achievements are, with good reason, most characteristically lauded. For he seemed to perform the considerable feat of showing how error without change (and hence the identification or correction of error) was possible, sacrificing the latter the better to preserve the spirit of Eleatic ontology. He did this in a series of five moves.

1. First he transposed statements about non-being (absence) into false statements.

2. Then he analysed statements about negation and substantial change (absenting) into statements about formal difference reversing the traditional analysis which, like Plato, confounded the different and mutually irreducible categories of difference and change.

3. Next he assumed that reference was always satisfied, so sequestering existential questions. (He is often congratulated for clarifying the Parmenidean confusion between the existential and predicative 'is'. But the generalized notions of reference, referent and existence, deny such an easy distinction, as do the categories of real [including subject] negation.)

4. He then boldly restated the 2E doctrine of ontological monovalence in declaring that 'knowledge is of what is', which, if the 'is' here is taken as (or as entailing) that of identity, commits him to the 1M epistemic fallacy; and, on the standard Greek assumption that knowledge is of what is universal (unchanging), adds to (2), the analysis of statements about difference into statements about generality, which, if Plato is still working within and for the theory of Forms (3L hypostatis and 4D dualism), are not only universal but necessary and certain.

5. Finally the Platonic theory of predication was completed by a 3L ontologically extensionalist theory of self-identity to the effect that everything is the same as itself and other than everything else. Plato thus laid down firmly the lineaments of what I called in Chapter 6 the 'analytic problematic'. But of course in doing so — in, for example, analysing change in terms of difference — he really negated or absented a pre-existing state of affairs; thus committing a performative contradiction, a theory/practice inconsistency. So in his third period he is no more successful than in his first two.

We can, however, begin to see why this book is called *Plato Etcetera*: (a) the Parmenidean concept of being Plato inherited; (b) the rationalist notion of knowledge as universal-and-necessarily-certain (note the tacit complicity of fundamentalism and irrealist dialectic in the genesis of the quest for an unhypothetical starting-point), and the corresponding differentiation of knowledge from belief; (c) the interdependence of Platonic transcendence and Aristotelian immanence, of strong and weak actualism (a completely achieved identity theory is as impossible in an open-systemic world as a totally unachieved one is useless and undemonstrable), exerting what I have called the primal squeeze between metaphysics and empiricism, in the absence of the mediating terms of natural necessity and empirically ascertainable alethic truth; (d) the Platonic analysis of negation and change in terms of difference and definition of the analytic problematic — these became the baseline for all subsequent philosophy. Thus it was empiricism v. rationalism, monism v. dualism, achieved v. non-achieved identity theory, being v. nothingness (rather than determinate non-being), presence without absence, being without change, knowledge without error, subject and object unmediated by intersubjectivity or spatio-temporality. The epistemological question of the nature of our access to reality gradually and, by the time of Hume and Kant completely, displaced the original ontological question of the nature of the reality accessed and it was not until Hegel and Marx that 'the problem of knowledge' was posed in geo-historical or practical terms. Superficially aporetic, deeply antinomial, philosophy was overtly riven by dichotomies and obsessed by hierarchized polarities, without concepts of mediation, constellationality, duality, co-inclusion, configurationality and emergence and lacking the kind of materialism which would not just challenge but metacritically explain this. Covertly it assumed the shape of one or other internally (because axiologically) inconsistent Tina compromise forms, manifesting its unhappy unconsciousness that its time was past and its place somewhere else — in Athens, in Plato's day.

(c) Aristotle

I will assume that the reader is familiar with the broad outlines of Aristotle's biography, take his massive contributions to biology and logic as read and deal with Aristotle for the most part in an Aristotelian way — starting from received opinions or endoxa and working through these to the aporiai in the Aristotelian corpus as we have it. It is now generally agreed that it is not the case that Aristotle started out as a loyal Platonist and moved to a progressively more materialist position. If anything, the inverse movement appears probable.

If there is a single philosophical question that dominated Aristotle's thought it is 'what is substance, *ousia* or above all real?' In the *Categories* the answer appears simple. What are unquestionably real are not super-sensible forms, as in Plato — for Aristotle, universals are immanent (on which more in a moment) — but particular concrete individual things such as men or oxen, of which so-called secondary substances (species and genera) could be predicated. The issue is complicated, however, by the Aristotelian analysis of change, which entails the co-relativity of matter and form, suggesting that a substance should be a composite of matter and form. However, Aristotle accepts Plato's epistemological criterion that what is knowable or definable must be eternal, universal-and-necessarily-certain, which fits form or essence, which is not perishable and common to many individuals, but not matter—form composites.[†] This raises two problems. First, how, after all, can particular individual things be known — the primary substances of the *Categories*? For, were they to be known there would have to be a form differentiating them. (This objection turns on the absence of the notion of the concrete universal = singular as a multiple quadruplicity.) Second, in what sense do Aristotelian forms differ from Platonic Forms? Are they not, as both universal and separable, liable to exactly the same objections that Aristotle advances against the latter, and which he reiterates in his discussion in *Metaphysics* Z of substance as form or definable reality. There are two ways in which Aristotle might wriggle out of this objection — to differentiate what is primarily real (the primary substances of the *Categories*) from what is

---

[†] Aristotle's not inconsiderable advance on Plato is to show how we could have unchanging knowledge of *changing* things. Thus the upshot of any process of knowledge was still a form expressing the essence of a thing susceptible to non-equivocal definition. But on Aristotle's dynamic cosmology, in which everything occurred in accordance with a tendency to its natural state (place, end or perfection), such things were nothing other than the actualization of their potentialities — in what we may term a kinetic actualism in contrast to Plato's eidetic actualism. And so the Aristotelian naturally came to ask four kinds of questions: what materials were involved?; what forms were actualized?; what end was being sought?; and what initiated the process? The answers gave the material, formal, final and efficient causes or components of the process. In the ideal Aristotelian explanation the last three all coincided. Any non-divine matter presupposes form, but matter can only be known as form, as actualized. Pure formless matter would be totally indeterminate potentiality. Causes of mundane objects may be internal or external but all terrestrial change presupposes a completely immaterial unmoved mover, pure form or God, whose self-thinking sustains the entire cosmos.

knowable, but this involves too big a break with Platonic metaphysical epistemology; or to distinguish from within the class of universals, species or essences those which are common to many individuals but may be uniquely defined from their genera or constituents and to regard the former, as participating in the life of the divine, as self-explanatory. In either case form is separated from matter, as it is, as pure actuality, in the case of the ultimate fount and object of knowledge, God = pure thought or 'thinking about thinking'.

Now, in this connection, it is worth reconsidering the conventional wisdom to which I have already paid lip service in Chapter 1, that Aristotle is a more 'materialist' thinker than Plato. There are several respects in which this is misleading. I have already argued for the intradependence of achieved and unachieved identity theory, immanent and transcendent universals, weak and strong actualism, monism and dualism. This can be brought out in Aristotle's case by considering the aporia of accident, the constitutive state of most outcomes in transcendentally real open systems, where the first great achieved identity theory must invoke a transcendent cause, posit an unknowable matter or appeal to a metaphysical λ ceteris paribus clause. Second, on the Platonic/ Aristotelian fault-line, Aristotle is caught in an epistemological squeeze or vice between Plato and Hume. Lacking a non-homological account of ontological stratification, Aristotle must supplement induction by *nous* or intellectual intuition. Third, directly related to this, is the inconsistency in Aristotle's psychology between the doctrine of the dependence of soul or psyche upon body, wherever an entity is on the ladder of nature ('if the eye were an animal, sight would be its soul'), prominent in *De Anima*, with the exception to this allowed in man in the case of abstract thought, his (sic) distinctive ergon or function, differentiating him from the other species. It is of course this particular ergon (a) in which Aristotle himself excelled, (b) as intellectual virtue, coupled with moral virtue and practical wisdom, in steering the golden mean between two opposed vices, which constituted for Aristotle the good life for man as such, (c) consisted in participation in the self-thinking thought of God, (d) completed the Aristotelian metaphysical circle via the theorem of the identity of pure form and shear actuality, reconciling, inter alia, Aristotle's two concepts of metaphysics (as theology and as the study of being as such), and (e) prefigured the Renaissance theme of man as *anima mundi*. Fourth, it is worth remembering that Aristotle not only accepted Plato's criteria for knowledge but also claimed, as

Plato did not, to have satisfied them. These criteria, achieved in Aristotle hylomorphically, enshrined the epistemic fallacy and its ontic dual, subject—object identity, actualism (in Aristotle's case of a kinetic sort), ontological monovalence (all entailing unchange at the level of identity and the actual), ontological extensionalism, anthropomorphism, hypostasis, intra-theoretical and theory/practice inconsistency and Tina compromise formation. And they entailed the unity of the sciences (contrary to the doctrine of the *Posterior Analytics*) and nature in metaphysics or first philosophy. Next it must be said that Aristotle is just as concerned as Plato with the quest for an unhypothetical starting-point and no more successful in obtaining it. This is manifest in the aporiai of *archai*. If dialectic produces, contra the Platonic aspirations for it as the supreme 'coping stone' of the sciences, as the *Topics* contends, only probabilistic knowledge dependent on the agreement of the interlocutors concerned, then it cannot furnish the premises which will license apodeictic conclusions for the syllogistic reasoning expounded in the *Prior Analytics*. This is manifest also in the alternative to dialectic — *nous*: the absence of any clear criterion for (the success of) intellectual intuition facilitated the dogmatic degeneration of Aristotelianism in the late Middle Ages.[†] Furthermore, just as Aristotle posited pure form and activity without matter, he posited prime matter as sheer potentiality without form. Accepting Empedocles' theory that the ordinary things of the world (oxen, stones) were compounds of the four basic elements — fire, air, earth and water (while adding a fifth — ether — as the element of the heavenly bodies) — he failed to provide any principle of composition (such as could have been provided by the development of Democritan atomism), resulting in a loss of explanatory power as great as that suffered by Platonic diarrhesis (division). Aristotelian 'quiddities' thus tended to proliferate in the wake of the identification of different and more kinds of matter (much to the ridicule of seventeenth-century atomists such as Boyle).

Early (and sometimes all) western philosophy is sometimes presented as if it were a case of Plato *or* Aristotle. Here I am suggesting we are dealing with a case of the tacit complicity of opposites (or dialectical counterparts) grounded in a common mistaken problematic (defined by Parmenidean monovalence,

---

[†] It is worthwhile recording here the strands of the critique of deductivism articulated in Chapter 2. At 1M open systems, at 2E change, at 3L totality (mediation, etc.) and at 4D the activity, conceptualized hot geo-historicized and social-relation-dependent character of human praxis.

Parmenidean/Platonic epistemic fallacy and the Platonic/Aristotelian
fault-line or primal squeeze [generating the oppositions of empiricism
v. rationalism, positivistic v. speculative illusion, immanence v.
transcendence, monism v. dualism, etc.]) — that is, Platonism and
Aristotelianism as necessary conditions of each other. Both Platonism
and Aristotelianism formed a lasting impact on subsequent
philosophy — and science. Thus to Galileo's post-Renaissance
Platonist physics one can counterpose Theodoric's pre-Renaissance
Aristotelian optics; but it is at best misleading to counterpose the
two as idealist and materialist. Instead what one has, as
Anaximander and Heraclitus[†] would have been the first to
appreciate, is the dialectical connection of opposites — a figure
which will emerge more than once in my tale and which helps to
explain the aporeticity or, as I called it in Chapter 1, the constitutive
problematicity, of philosophy. I have no space here to go further
into the structure of hylomorphism or to deal at greater length with
Aristotle's celebrated theory of the four causes, save to note the
teleology implicit in the ideal Aristotelian explanation, where final,
formal and efficient causes all coincided.

This is not a history of philosophy but an excursus into passages in
it, so I take a giant leap forward to the seventeenth century and the
figure of René Descartes.

§ 2 The Consolidation of Epistemology

We have seen how the transition to epistemology began with Plato,
following Parmenides. But it is with Descartes (1596–1650) that the
question of our access to reality takes definitive precedence over —
and indeed determines — the question of the nature of reality (at least
overtly). It is Descartes who sets the cast of the representationalist
view of knowledge and what I am going to call the Cartesian-Lockian-
Humean-Kantian paradigm. It is Descartes who first asked the
question ' how do I know?'; and who assumes that the only way to
answer the question is to begin from the immediate data of
consciousness, so sowing the seeds for the scepticism, subjective
idealism, classical empiricism and solipsism to come. Indeed it is
Descartes who, by inwardizing and subjectivizing (as well as
commencing the secularization of) rationalist criteria for knowledge,
ensures the eventual triumph of empiricism; so that, as I have argued

---

[†] As materialist a figure as one can get in philosophy until Hobbes's mechanical
materialism.

elsewhere, we could characterize the history of western philosophy in terms of the coordinates: historical determination by rational epistemology; structural domination by empiricist ontology.

At the age of twenty-three Descartes had a dream of his mission, which was probably

(a) to establish the unity of science and mathematics (so resuming a Platonic project);

(b) to reconcile the findings of the new physics, for which Giordano Bruno had been, and Galileo was to be, tried before the Inquisition (the former perishing, the latter recanting), with the requirements of the Christian faith (so anticipating Kant's project).

Descartes held mathematics to be a paradigm of *certain* knowledge, and, setting himself to accept only those beliefs of his which were 'clearly and distinctly true', he asked himself, exploring the procedure of methodical doubt, what it was that he could not possibly doubt, that is, which would yield incorrigibility and with it permanence and insusceptibility to future falsification. The sceptic could doubt, or so it seemed to Descartes, the existence of an external world, or his body, or past beliefs (dependent upon fallible memory). But what he could not doubt was that he himself was doubting, and that therefore he himself exists, together with all the other immediate items of his conscious existence, as a thinking substance or *res cogitans*. (This is the famous 'cogito, ergo sum'.) Actually all that Descartes had proved, on his premises, was that a thought exists; the link between thought and thinker must remain contingent, but let that pass. Next Descartes, searching through the contents of his consciousness, found that he had the idea of a perfect being, God. Descartes did not consider what if his idea of perfection was imperfect, or what if what was 'clear and distinctly true' to him was not to God or another thinker. But again, let that pass. For Descartes such a perfect being would not be a deceiver, so he assumed that he was warranted in his belief in the permanence of the soul, and of mathematical truths, the validity of deduction and the existence of body and indivisibly extended bodily substance subject to the mathematical laws of mechanics.

As has frequently been remarked, Descartes's whole argument is viciously circular. Methodical doubt is motivated by the consideration that the senses do sometimes deceive and so Descartes was forced into the corner of distinguishing between systematic and occasional doubt and ascribing the latter to the abuse of man's free-will. But then

Descartes's entire system is grounded in a kind of mental self-abuse or onanism. Moreover, the argument for the existence of doubt is formulated in a language which is already known and, like the criterion of 'clarity and distinctiveness', presupposes interlocutors (such as the set of Objectors to the *Meditations*) arguing intersubjectively (dialogically) in and about and by means of a world of referentially detached objects. His argument relies on memory and presupposes the validity of deduction in addition to a particular conception of the self (as a composite of two distinct substances) and of God (which arguably on a conception of an omni-possible god should contain all the imperfections as well as the perfections). In short, Descartes *fideistically* presupposes what he has to prove, is guilty of an unserious scepticism (a charge implicitly made against him by Hegel in the *Introduction*, in contrast to its allegedly self-perficient scepticism, of the *Phenomenology*) and adopts the endemic stance of first philosophy of neglecting the non-presuppositionless character of all inquiry.

There is a direct line between the Cartesian demand for incorrigibility (albeit made in the interests of a mathematized science), the Platonic/Aristotelian quest for an unhypothetical starting-point, the postulate of Parmenidean monism and the primordial search by Thales for a unitary originating material one. We have already seen how Parmenidean monism must reduce to the performative contradiction of Cratylan silence. In virtue of his subjective/quasi-solipsistic starting-point, Cartesian incorrigibility will end in the performative contradiction of punctualist ego-present-centric Humean solipsism. In a letter to Princess Elizabeth of Bohemia, Descartes, committed to mind–body dualism (which will curiously re-emerge in the noumenal–phenomenal contrasts of transcendental idealism and the two language theories of Waismann, Winch and Davidson under the auspices of the late Wittgenstein), argues that there are three unanalysable notions — the soul, the body and the union between them. But elsewhere he espoused a physical seat for mind–body interaction in the pineal gland, leaving himself open to the scorn of Malebranche in his occasionalism, Leibniz in his pre-established harmony of monads and Spinoza in his double-aspect parallelism (theories no less objectionable in the absence of an emergent powers materialism). But the chief objection to it is more basic. It turns on Descartes's conception of a perfect closed actualist — and physically monovalent — deductivist science of body, taken in conjunction with his postulate that the sole exception to such a science was the free-will of the human soul. For if free-will can intervene in the allegedly actualist-deductivist-fully determined sphere of body, then either (α) the system cannot be closed after all, or (β) the will cannot really be free, but must be, as Spinoza held, determined.[†] It is worth saying a word on another curious reprise of antiquity. Like Parmenides, Descartes accepted neither vacua nor voids. His paradigm of action by contiguous contact was immensely influential. It underpinned Newtonian classical mechanics and classical theory generally. Newton continued to search for a Cartesian theory which would explain the phenomenon of gravity. And the Michelson–Morley experiment, which was to retrospectively vindicate special relativity, was designed specifically to establish the existence, and ascertain the velocity, of the ether.

Descartes is no more satisfactory when it comes to the details of his philosophy of science. For having denigrated the value of sensation (as consisting merely in confused ideas) in favour of his ideal of a unified deductive system derivable from true a priori first principles, to be yielded by metaphysics (the trunk of the tree of knowledge), he nevertheless performed a posteriori experiments of not inconsiderable value, rendering himself vulnerable to a charge, once more, of theory/practice inconsistency in the medium of immanent critique. Rationalists have always had difficulties in explaining the following:

(α) How contingency is possible. This is especially evident in Leibniz, who wanted to sustain the true contingency of matters of facts, which, anticipating Hume, he rigorously distinguished from analytic truths, and his life-long search for the principles of such a complete system of simple substances or monads that the concept of every individual would contain all that it ever was or would become, so that every proposition about it would be necessary and rational agreement in philosophy and science would reign.

(β) Why experiments should be necessary.

(γ) How scientific change is possible.

Before describing the genealogy from Locke to Hume, it is worth noting the comparable aporiai that the great line of British empiricists from Francis Bacon, who, like his slightly younger contemporary Descartes, stressed the practical value of the new science, through Hobbes, Locke, Berkeley, Hume, Mill and Russell have typically faced.

[†] Although Spinoza cannot be completely let off the hook, for what explains the emotions of joy and sorrow?

(α) The aporiai of the doctrine that all ideas derive from experience. The notion of a tabula rasa at birth must be rejected in favour of innate capacities; and the notion of autonomized mind in experimental science correspondingly dismissed to make way for the idea of conceptual preformation as the result of a long, arduous process of socialization which enables a biologist, for instance, to see chromosomes. But there is a fatal equivocation in this basic postulate of empiricism. For if all ideas are derived from experience, this means that false ones are too. So we must distinguish a theory of explanation where 'experience' means something like 'social practice' and a theory of evaluation where we are to confirm or falsify ideas by recourse to experimentally designed test situations. This analysis is of course at variance with the rationalist, and specifically deductivist, criteria of knowledge that empiricists take over from Descartes and Aristotle (for the necessity for experiment presupposes the contingency of closed systems), in addition to generating an internal antinomy between the deductivist analysis of knowledge and the inductivist analysis of its acquisition. Once more we see the effects of primal squeeze and the results of the absence of the concepts of ontological stratification (grounding natural necessity) and alethic truth.

(β) The aporiai of the status of apparently synthetic a priori propositions such as arguably those of (a) mathematics and (b) philosophy. In respect of (a), the most extreme position was taken up by J.S. Mill, who argued that mathematical propositions were empirical (this resonates with the primal confusion in empiricism between theories of explanation in the extrinsic and justification in the intrinsic aspect). For us, the former constellationally embraces the latter, so that reasons can be causes. In respect of (b), the most pressing problem has been the epistemic status of empiricism itself. Is it analytic, and so merely 'trifling', as Locke was prepared to accept, or empirical, and so subject to inductive doubt, as William James conceded; or neither, but mysteriously ineffable and so 'consignable to the flames', as Hume should have admitted, or jettisoned, as of no further use, a position the early Wittgenstein seriously adopted?

(γ) The aporiai of how Humean conclusions are to be avoided (on to which I shall shortly come) and practical dogmatism not be the inexorable effect of theoretical scepticism.

Locke (1632–1704), like Descartes, conceived himself as a propagandist for the new science. Moreover, he was, especially in his major work, *An Essay Concerning Human Understanding*, highly influenced by Descartes. He starts from the egocentric standpoint, whose inevitable outcome is solipsism, and assumes that we must begin with the immediate data of consciousness. Moreover, in close contact with Boyle, he understood the nature of reality in terms of the corpuscularian conceptual scheme, distinguishing, like Descartes, between primary and secondary qualities, the former ingredient in reality, the latter merely modes of our perception of it. Accepting Cartesian premisses and rationalist criteria, but lacking Descartes's a priorism and more or less immediate recourse to God, Locke argued that we could only have knowledge of our ideas — of sensation and reflection — all of which derive ultimately from experience. It is not clear how he felt entitled to assert this. In any event this meant that, since the (at least immediate) objects of knowledge were in our minds, we, unlike God, could not have knowledge (or at least certain knowledge) of the real essences of things, but only of their nominal essences, which were comprised by the properties under which they were known for human convenience and practical interest. Undoubtedly in forming this opinion he was influenced by the 'sad experience' of the chemists of his day who 'sometimes in vain searched for the same qualities in one parcel of sulphur, antinomy or vitriol, which have been found in others'.[1] But how can we even know their nominal essences, or that, as Berkeley was to charge, that there is a distinction between primary and secondary qualities? Locke's way of ideas is intrinsically aporetic and, starting from Cartesian presuppositions, paves the way for Berkelian scepticism about matter and Humean scepticism about everything. If we have true knowledge only of the contents of our minds, how can we know which are true and which are false? This is a problem inherent in any representationalist theory of perception, but it is already implicit in Aristotelian hylomorphism. Even more seriously, how can we know that things do indeed have real essences, or that there are primary qualities or indeed that anything exists independently of us at all? Here again, the absence of the key notions of primary polyadization, the transcendentally necessary pre-existence of social structure, referential detachment and alethic truth take their toll. Indeed when, with Ryle, the reaction to the Cartesian ghost in the machine and the Lockian way of ideas sets in, philosophers even went so far (under such slogans as 'concepts are abilities or capacities') as to deny the existence of mentalistic states at all, depositing the ghost of a thoroughly autonomized mind in the dustbin of geo-history.

It is the argument of this section that Cartesian premisses lead to Humean conclusions. So let us turn without further ado to Hume. The avowed aim of Hume's *Treatise* (1739) was to establish a para-

Newtonian 'mental mechanics', a genuinely empirical science of human nature, in which it could be seen that 'there is no question of importance, whose decision is not comprised in the sciences of man'. One aim of his humanism (and in which Hume was paradoxically successful) was to effect an anti-Copernican counter-revolution. Indeed, Hume himself, as the anonymous author of the *Abstract to the Treatise*, went out of his way to stress the importance to be attached to the principle of the association of ideas: '[though] these are only ties of our thought, they are really *to us* the cement of the universe'. In fact, he draws to the limit the subjective idealist implications of the Cartesian turn. Moreover, he is the permanent attractor point of the representationalist paradigm (not least, as we shall see, because of his antinomies). The fundamental aporiai of his system derive straight from Cartesianism, viz. acceptance of (1) the doctrine of the veil of ideas and of (2) a fundamental distinction between consciousness and other kinds of stuff. All we are aware of are our perceptions, which (because there are no innate ideas) derive ultimately from primary impressions of sense — or, as later phenomenalists would put it, sense-data — which are, like physical corpuscles, simple and unchanging, whence simple and complex ideas and secondary impressions of reflexion arise. Anticipating the doctrine of the 'Transcendental Aesthetic', Hume argued that space and time were merely the modes in which perceptions occur. All reasoning consisted in relations between ideas, which were ultimately tautologies, or relations of fact, all of which were founded on the principle of cause and effect. Anything that did not conform to this fork (e.g. metaphysics, theology, morality, mental mechanics[?]) was sophistry and illusion and should be 'consigned to the flames' (so much for the *Treatise* and the *Enquiry*).[†]

Hume was concerned in his discussion of causality both to establish the negative thesis, contra the rationalists, that such propositions as everything had a cause or that any particular cause could be attributed to any particular effect could not be known;[‡] and to assert a positive doctrine of his own to the effect that we say 'x causes y' when there is precedence in time, contiguity in space (NB

[†] In this respect, Hume lacked the subtlety of the Kantian characterization of the transcendent realm, which can be 'thought but not known', or of the early Wittgenstein's *Tractatus* (1922), of that which can be 'shown but not said'.

[‡] Hume would have been the first to realize that on his epistemology his paradigm of Newtonian mechanics (let alone his own mental mechanics) would turn out to be impossible, for which, as with all sceptical quandaries (which inevitably lead to theory/ practice inconsistency and susceptibility to immanent critique), 'carelessness and inattention' were the only remedies.

monovalence again) and the idea of necessary connection. This he analysed as a projection based on our experience, which, with vivacity and custom, would approximate certainty. Here, then, is the basis of the 'constant conjunction of events plus subjective contribution of mind' analysis of causal laws. Unfortunately for Hume but fortunately for science, no sooner had Hume formulated this famous analysis than he reached the conclusion that custom and vivacity could not do what Aristotelian *nous* had been unable to do, viz. convert the proposition 'all my (or currently known) experiences of x are accompanied by experiences of y' to the actualist desideratum 'all x's are y's' (the aporia of causality). (Even the later Wittgenstein was entrapped in this problem, being unable to give criteria whereby we know that the rules of the language game we are playing would carry on under the prescriptions/descriptions we give them.) Moroever, it is clear that on Hume's premisses we cannot know that we have any knowledge of objects or matters of fact (so, para- doxically, shades of Leibniz, the only knowledge we can have is of relations between ideas!). For we are imprisoned inside the veil of ideas (the aporia of perception). Nor, just as events appear 'loose and separate', 'conjoined but never connected', can we have knowledge of our own self-identity. For this upon Humean exegesis reveals itself as a mere bundle of perceptions (the aporia of self-identity). Nor is it clear how I am entitled to rely on memory (the source of regularity and association) or draw any inference, e.g. from seemingly past states, as to the existence of my body or another mind from my ego- present-centric impression(s) of a punctualist atomist self disengaged from practice.

But Hume abounds in interpretive antinomies. He is the founding father of modern positivism. (a) As the archetypal positivist, virtually the whole of post-Humean philosophy has taken over his empirical realism, his actualism and his reductionist (constant conjunction) analysis of laws. No matter that he combines the contingency and the actuality of laws (instead of their necessity and transfactuality) at the price of the problem of induction. (b) He is the all-purpose sceptic who woke Kant from his dogmatic slumbers and, thinking reason to be the slave of the passions, could announce that it is 'not contrary to reason to prefer the destruction of the whole world to the scratching of my finger'. (c) He is the fideist who invokes 'carelessness and inattention' as the cure to scepticism. Carelessness and inattention mean of course the same as before. (d) Thus he is the conventionalist who upholds law and order and the existing order of things. (e) He is the ironist who fails to find in his a-historical philosophy the satisfaction of his 'ruling passion', to wit, his search for literary fame, but finds it instead in a history, which, on his philosophical premisses, should be impossible to write. (f) He is the amoralist who declares no 'ought' from an 'is', becomes the paradigm emotivist and paves the way for cynicism and nihilism but dies content in his humanistic atheism. Hume is a revolving turntable, in which those who seek will locate a multiplicity of philosophical options. At the price of some arbitrariness I am going to divide Chapter 10.1 into the critical tradition which reacted against him and §3 of this chapter into the positivist, perspectivist and hermeneutical traditions which accepted different, but in crucial respects, aspects of Humeanism. We have seen how Descartes, by inwardizing and subjectivizing the primordial philosophical quest, inaugurated a historical reprise of the Parmenidean reductio ad Cratylus in the solipsistic punctualist ego-present-centrism of a Hume who could not take his unserious scepticism seriously, but paradoxically formed the backbone, or a substantial part of it, of philosophy after him. Before turning to the turntable, I want to discuss the tacit complicity of dialectical counterparts, such as empiricism and rationalism, explained by their stemming from a common mistaken ground. In this case the ground is provided by the unholy trinity of ontological monovalence, which makes negation, absence and change impossible, the epistemic fallacy, which makes a non-anthropic ontology impossible, and primal squeeze, which accounts for the immediate opposition between empiricism and rationalism, and of the positivistic and speculative illusions, in virtue of the absence of the mediating terms of, in the transitive dimension, empirically controlled scientific theory and, in the intransitive dimension, ontological stratification and alethic truth. Notice that, on the epistemic fallacy, both empiricism and rationalism define the objects of knowledge in terms of an essentially human attribute, viz. experience (generating empirical realism) and reason (producing conceptual realism). What the Cartesian problematic does, when carried to its Humean limits, is to make referential detachment impossible.

Let us step back a bit. Among the problems of epistemology are (1) the question of the possibility of knowledge. Now scepticism and dogmatism are mutually complicit dialectical counterparts. Thus Hume dogmatically presupposes the transcendentally refutable analysis of causal laws in terms of a constant conjunction of subjectively apprehended events or states of affairs. His actualist analysis is mirrored in Leibniz's pre-established harmony of monads and Spinoza's co-occurrence or universal parallelism of modes, but it is already implicit in the Aristotelian-Cartesian ideal of a deductive science. Hume now finds, mired in the aporiai of the transdictive complex, that to sustain the possibility of this analysis he has to rely on custom, i.e. fideistically upon convention, whereas Leibniz and Spinoza make appeals respectively to an actual transcendent and an immanent natural God, once again fideistically.

2. If knowledge is possible, the question comes as to whether its objects are, from the standpoint of the epistemological materialism articulated in Chapter 5.2, real or ideal. Here we have already noted the tacit complicity of immanent and transcendent theories, achieved and unachieved identity theory, weak and strong actualism, epistemological monism and dualism in the irrealist ensemble and the defensive shield and Tina compromise form this inconsistent ensemble necessitates as the reality principle takes its toll. In respect of ontological materialism, we have the tacit complicity of dualistic disembodiment, which flows inevitably from Cartesian premises, and physicalistic reductionism, which, so long as it is given an actualist interpretation, is the only plausible interpretation of the new science. Turning to practical materialism, we can ask whether knowledge is an individual or social phenomenon. Cartesianism points inexorably in the first direction. Yet Descartes withholds *Le Monde* from publication when he hears of Galileo's inquisition; Locke declares himself an under-labourer to such masters as a Boyle or a Sydenham, 'the great Huygenius' and 'the incomparable Mr Newton'. And it was Hume's declared intention to emulate Newton. I abstain from further pressing the obvious charge of performative contradiction.

3. If knowledge is possible, is it source, experience or reason? I have already commented on some of the aporiai of both empiricism and rationalism individually considered. Let us take them together. Empiricists back induction but cannot account for natural necessity without tacit recourse to an (unknowable) actualist analysis of laws. Rationalists back deduction but perform experiments. Both testify to the effects of primal squeeze. Thus what are, ontologically, the reified facts of empiricism but the flotsam of rationalisms's hypostatized ideas; and whence come such ideas, epistemologically, but as at least the co-product of experience in the sense of social practices and the ideologies which englobe it? At the particular pole of knowledge, solipsistic atomistic punctualist ego-present-centrism necessitates at the general pole of knowledge an actualist blockist closure as its dual and vice versa. The aporiai which enmesh both require a new transcendent, most usually social convention or God. There is an internal antinomy here. For reason, or enlightenment, requires mediation by faith, and faith, after the Cartesian turn, demands the support of reason, or enlightenment, as Hume, Kant, Hegel and Nietzsche in their different ways show.

4. Let us go through some of the assumptions shared between empiricism and rationalism. Ontological actualism at 1M makes impossible experiment and applied scientific knowledge, stratification or epistemic without ontic change. Ontological monovalence at 2E fixes the terms of a sceptical/solipsistic/fundamentalist/fideist problematic, making change in theory or its objects impossible. Ontologial extensionalism at 3L renders impossible systematic intra-activity or totality, including emergence and the constellationality necessary to prevent detotalization of knowledge from its objects, which is an inexorable effect of Cartesianism. At 4D dualistic disembodiment is tacitly complicit with physicalistic reductionism. At 5C an individualist market society is growing in the humus of an absolutist or authoritarian state.

Cartesian and Humeanism represent decisive breaks. But we should not forget the continuities — of the arch of knowledge tradition (cf. Chapter 2), of the analytic problematic (cf. Chapter 6)[†] and of the unholy trinity of Parmenidean/Platonic/Aristotelian provenance.

§ 3 The Humean Turntable I: The Positivist, Perspectivist and Hermeneutical Traditions

Santayana remarked that to be ignorant of the history of philosophy is to be doomed to repeat it. And Marx famously observed that history occurs twice: the first time as tragedy, the second time as farce. These could be taken as epigraphs for this section.

A century on, Mill and Comte formed from Hume the (dogmatic, so it must appear) positivist backbone of the orthodox view of science until *c.* 1970, mediated by Mach, the early Wittgenstein and the Vienna Circle. The last two wedded Machian epistemology — 'the communication of scientific knowledge involves description: that is, the mimetic reproduction of facts in thought, the object of which is to replace and save the trouble of new experience: that is all that natural laws are' — with the powerful new logical tools of Frege and Russell. I

---

† Thus what is Leibniz's principle of the identity of indiscernibles but a restatement of the principle of self-identity which Plato laid down. In fact, both forms of Leibniz's principle are false. At 1M d_a non-identicals may be d_i identicals (or science would never get off the ground) and vice versa; and a difference which is indiscernible at one level or in some system may turn out to be discernible at or in another. At 2E the dispositional identity of a thing with its changing causal powers allows us to posit changing identicals whether they are discernible or not. At 3L holistic causality allows us to posit different identities, while changing reflections and perspectival switches permit changing and differing discernibilities. And the list could be continued.

will for the present restrict myself to some remarks about Frege. For Frege, mathematics was neither empirical (contra J.S. Mill) nor synthetic a priori (contra Kant), but was derivable from the meaning of the terms used to express it, i.e. analytic. (Thus numbers could be defined in terms of the concept of equinumerocity.) His foundational-ist programme to reduce the whole of mathematics to logic broke down under the combined impact of Russell's discovery of the set-theoretic paradoxes, which greatly disheartened him, and Gödel's theorem (both already discussed). What is perhaps pertinent to stress here is Frege's theory of existence. Accepting the Kantian doctrine that existence is not a predicate, he argued that it is a second-order predicate: that is, to say that a red thing exists is to say that redness has instances. Closely associated to this is his pivotal distinction between sense and reference and his analysis of the subject—predicate structure of sentences such as 'Meno is circular'. Subject, predicate and sentence all have both sense and reference. Thus Frege has a generalized notion of reference, but it turns out both to presuppose existence and to denote its truth-value, allowing the formulation of the truth-table semantics crucial to twentieth-century logic. The sense of Meno is given by his description, the reference by the object the description picks out. The sense of 'is circular' is a concept, while 'this is x' refers to a function which yields a value for each object that is referred to by the name substituted for x (predicates thus have unsaturated reference). The sense of a whole sentence is its thought and the reference of a sentence is its truth-value. Now if, as I have already suggested in Chapter 3.1, Frege had said not that the reference of a sentence is its truth-value, paving the way for extensionalist truth semantics, but that the referent of a sentence may be detachable from it (and not just the reference of its subject), in which event it may have the ontological value 'true', this would have paved the way to consider the alethic truth *grounds* of, and grounding of, its ontological truth. This would have opened an avenue to the semantic stratification of truth grounds (alethic truth qua ontological stratification) avoiding the homology of truth-value or truth-conditional semantics. Philosophy would then have had the concept of truth independently of our access to it (in the intransitive dimension), and assertion as a function of our epistemological powers (in the transitive dimension).

The purist form of empiricism which made use of the new logic was Wittgenstein's *Tractatus*. According to the picture theory expounded there, the world consisted entirely of simple facts and the only significant use of language is to mirror these facts in a scientific language which is structurally isomorphic with the facts (as near a statement of subject – object identity theory and the epistemic fallacy as in Plato). Logic and mathematics were empty tautologies; all else, including metaphysics and ethics, is nonsense and Wittgenstein accepted the force of his argument — how was the *Tractatus* itself possible: it shows what cannot be said.

The later Wittgenstein was the early Wittgenstein's fiercest critic. Language is tied to differentiated social practices, oriented to human purposes. The transcendental solipsism of the *Tractatus* is rejected: no purely private language is possible. Moreover, languages are governed by rules which are specific to particular language games, between which only relations of family resemblance at best hold. Philosophy is a battle against the bewitchment of our intelligence by language. The dissolution of this bewitchment lies in a return to the practical consciousness embodied in life-forms, rather than in abstract theories such as those which model words on names. To know a form of life is to know the rules that govern it, and the condition for this is to know how to carry on in that form of life. But how do we know that we are carrying on in the right way? For any rule there will be a potential infinity consistent with it. So the problem of induction returns and to this the late Wittgenstein can only give a fideistic-conventionalist response. Similarly the absence of ontological stratification and the concept of alethic truth make impossible a concept of depth which would ground our attributions of resemblance. Wittgenstein then becomes a weak actualist concerned to save the phenomenology of everyday life. His great insight was to see social practice as a necessary condition for language-acquisition and use. But to the general aporiai of the transdictive complex he is no better off than Hume.

Contemporary analytic philosophy is characterized by paradox. There is (a) the co-existence of a holistic view of language and ontological and logical extensionalism (which in the case of both Quine and Davidson can only be saved by tacit recourse to implicitly intensional concepts such as that of logical truth or the same); (b) the combination of the concept of a rigid word(signifier) – object(world) relationship with the notion of the mutability of sense (signified) and the open-textured nature of use; (c) the idea of the impossibility of alternative conceptual schemes, a new ethnocentric fundamentalism (in which charity of interpretation begins at home), associated with Davidson — or the other new fundamentalism associated with Dummet's attack on metaphysical realism on the grounds that it would be impossible to grasp the meaning of sentences about the world if the world in itself was different from the way we found it to be — combined typically, in the case of Rorty, with the Kuhnian emphasis on the multiplicity of paradigms, or, in other words, conceptual schemes;[†] (d) stress on the purity of extensionalist concepts combined with emphasis on the metaphoricity of effects; (e) acceptance of ontological causality combined with rejection of or agnosticism about ontological realism; (f) commitment to a double language thesis, as in Davidsonian anomalous monism or Rorty's eliminative materialism and hermeneutics, producing the familiar incoherent matrix of dualistic disembodiment in the intrinsic aspect and physicalistic reductionism in the extrinsic one. Most of the twentieth century has been dominated by an emphasis on language, ideal or actual. But there has recently been a shift of emphasis to the philosophy of mind. Here representationalism is once again at work, even if it is generally accepted that mental states are not self-intimating and so cannot provide incorrigible foundations for knowledge. However, even accepting a representationalist framework, with its characteristic difficulties in sustaining existential intransitivity,[‡] its tending to disengage the percipient from material practice and its atomist/punctualist conception of self, we can hold that beliefs may be better or worse representations (in the intrinsic aspect) of their object, while conceding them to be naturalistically emergent powers of the brain (in the extrinsic aspect).

It is time to turn more briefly to look at the perspectivist positions which derive from Nietzsche. First, there is the perspectivist thesis itself. There are no facts, only interpretations. And this is a fact we have to forget. But a stratified conception of the self over distanciated space-time allows us to situate the social production of knowledge (in the transitive dimension) as distinct from things (in the intransitive dimension) as itself an item of knowledge to savour and remember. Second, we find in Nietzsche a rejection of the metaphysical in favour of the empirical world of actuality. But what is this rejection but a metaphysical posture? And one which prioritizes uncriticized notions of the actual and the empirical over the possibility of deeper, negative, fuller or more practical (cf. 1M – 4D) realities. Third, there is the doctrine that what matters about a belief is its life-affirming character. But it is certainly arguable that a belief will be life-affirming

---

[†] Davidson's attack against alternative conceptual schemes turns on the fact that while knowing what a sentence means is a matter of knowing its truth conditions, we can only identify its truth conditions by considering what can intelligibly be attributed to the speaker by *us*. This is best styled a hermeneutic verificationism.

[‡] Gibsonian ecological perception theory with its emphasis on an organism's environment in yielding in perception the possibility of various affordances allows us to sustain both the objectivity of its environment and the organism's engagement in activity.

to the extent that it is true. This is not to disagree with the Nietzschean aphorism that among the conditions of life there may be errors. Completeness and total consistency are unattainable in science so we should be aware that we are unlikely to get them in ordinary life. Closely connected with this theme is the Nietzschean injunction to become (or, in a Foucauldian inversion, refuse) what you are (e.g. encapsulated in the *amour fati* of eternal recurrence). But this is to be taken in the sense of self-overcoming and in the aesthetic frame of the creation of something new. Then there is Nietzsche's doctrine, reminiscent of Bergson, that language necessarily falsifies reality in the interests of biological survival. If this means that the world is always going to appear to us too multi-faceted, complex and differentiated to allow time, in virtue of what I have called the 'axiological imperative', for a complete description, then this thesis is unobjectionable. But not all of reality is equally significant, either theoretically or practically. In pure science, in virtue of ontological stratification, we are interested only in those aspects of reality which cast light on the generative mechanisms of nature. This is not to falsify, but to taxonomize reality. And when it comes to the applied sciences, biological survival provides surely the best possible grounds for our classifications. But it is on morality that Nietzsche is perhaps most thought-provoking. Moralities, he declares, are 'baroque and unreasonable in form — because they are addressed to "all" and generalize where generalizations are impossible'. This is a powerful critique of personalism. But in elaborating his emotivism, he abandoned the concretely singularized ethics that this last quote shows was theoretically available to him, and which I have attempted to substantiate in Chapter 7.

Heidegger sits at the crossroads of the perspectivist and hermeneutical traditions. I will treat him and Derrida only briefly here. Heidegger elaborated in *Being and Time* (1927) a unique ontology which would recapture the most pertinent features of our existence. But for him being was always mediated by *Dasein*, human being, and ontology was unstratified, so that he did not break with the anthropism and actualism characteristic of the western philosophical tradition. In his later work he elaborated a meta-ontology, once more mediated by human being and nostalgic in temper and effect. In Derridean deconstruction, philosophy (and literature) is seen as characterized by hierarchicized pairs in which the privileged term is shown to be constituted by what it suppresses, marginalizes or excludes, which will later return to haunt it. Inversion, chiasmus and erasure are the features of this method. But Derrida has an unfortunate tendency to elide the referent in the semiotic triangle of

Chapter 3, which self-deconstructs his own practice which cannot thereby be theoretically sustained, as well as (until very recently[2]) to neglect the material and cultural structures whence texts derive their meaning. And in his critique of logocentricity he underplays both the importance of the mutuality of hermeneutic interpretation and the necessity for the duality of immediate and mediate knowledge if sentences and actions are both to be understood and to have their understanding understood.

We have already discussed hermeneutics in Chapter 5, but a brief recapitulation is in order here. Hermeneutics had an early precursor in the seventeenth-century Italian Vico, who argued, contra Descartes, that the human sciences were better placed than the natural sciences because man could understand what he himself had made. But the immediate philosophical ancestry of modern hermeneutics comes from Weber, Dilthey, Simmel and Rickert. They modified Kantian dichotomies to produce contrasts between the phenomenal world of nature and the intelligible world of human beings, grounding distinctions between causal explanation (*Erklären*) and interpretive understanding (*Verstehen*), the nomothetic and the idiographic, the repeatable and unique, the realms of physics and society. Within this tradition a discrimination must be made between neo-Kantians, such as Weber and Habermas, who seek to synthesize positivist and hermeneutical principles, and dualists (or Vichians), such as the Wittgensteinian Winch and the Heideggerian Gadamer, who deny positivism any applicability in the human domain. What unites most hermeneuticists is that they have accepted as the backdrop to their anti-naturalism fundamental features of the positivist account of natural science, most notably the Humean theory of causal laws and perceptual criteria for ascribing reality. If these theories are rejected, then the possibility of a qualified discriminated naturalism which would do justice to the specificities of the social domain within a generic concept of science (such as I have argued for in Chapter 5) re-arises. Second, hermeneuticists often display the legacy of positivism in their search for an interpretive fundamentalism or a view of conceptuality as exhausting rather than being essential to the constitution (reproduction or transformation) of social life. Thus although social life is indeed irreducibly concept-dependent, it does not follow either (a) that such conceptualizations exhaust the subject matter of social science (consider the social states of hunger, war or imprisonment or the psychological ones of anger, courage or isolation) or (b) that such conceptualizations are incorrigible (rather we know, since Marx, Nietzsche and Freud, that they may mask, repress, mystify, rationalize or otherwise occlude the nature of the activities in which they are implicated) or (c) that recognition of the conceptuality of social existence rules out its scientific comprehension. None of this is to deny that hermeneutics plays an essential role in social science, and indeed everyday social existence. But underneath the positivist legacy to the hermeneutical tradition lies the dead hand of the unholy trinity, the epistemic fallacy, ontological monovalence and primal squeeze, in the form of an ontologically conceptual actualism.

10

Philosophy and the Dialectic of Emancipation

The philosophers have only *interpreted* the world in various ways;
the point is to *change* it.

MARX

§ 1 The Humean Turntable II: The Critical Tradition

In this section I am going to attempt the rather ambitious project of
tracing the genealogy of the fall of actually existing socialism from
Hume. So let me start with an overview of the situation as I see it.
Hume sets the sceptical challenge to Kant, whom he awakes from his
Wolffian slumbers. But Kant accepts Hume's empirical realism,
crystallized in the Second Analogy, and it is this which necessitates
the noumenal/phenomenal split epitomized in the Third Antinomy.
As transcendental idealism develops, dichotomies proliferate. Hegel
attempts to repair these dichotomies in a transfigurative actualism.
The three keys to his system already discussed in Chapter 6 are (α)
realized idealism, (β) spiritual constellational monism and (γ)
preservative dialectical sublation (Hegel's immanent teleology),
which are marred by centrism-expressivism and actualism, the
speculative illusion and triumphalism, and monovalence and endism
respectively. Marx is unable to shed the actualist, constellationally
monist and endist features of absolute idealism — because, although
an untheorized scientific realism is the true methodological fulcrum of
his work, he never engages in the necessary critique of empirical
realism. Marx displaces (α) *Geist* on to labour, (β) cognitive
triumphalism into practical Prometheanism and (γ) endism into
communism (all as aspects of a materialist inversion). Subsequently
actualism becomes the attempt to build socialism in one country on
the basis of an expressivist-centrist ideology. Monism becomes the
Stalinist planning which informed industrialization at the expense of
the peasant majority. Endism becomes the supposed achievement of

socialism, the abandonment of human and civic rights, the demise of the negation of the negation and the eclipse of all opposition and critique. Together these three yield the homuncular commandist party-state built on 1M neglect of alterity, of the differentiation necessary for a true totality on the basis of a huge illicit fusion, whereby bureaucratic and at times Machiavellian sectional interests were represented as universal on the basis of an expressivist national unity and a centrist actualist monism, reflected most obviously in the absence of a sector corresponding to civil society (cf. my Chapter 7, (β) the realm of social virtue). This was coupled with the manipulative and mechanistic use of instrumental reason on subjects$_2$ modelled on Humean bourgeois-individualist man, and informed by sociological reductionism in ethics and neglect of the dispositional (including agonistic) and expressive components of action, as legitimation crises were reinforced by motivational ones. All this ideologically reflected the most primitive Hegelian logic of being (at 1M scouting non-identity), with the logic of essence typified by coupled pairs of oppositions, epitomized by the west or the necessary (erstwhile Trotskyist) enemy within (in Hegel essence does not transcend the standpoint of transcendental subjectivity, here represented by the party-state), while the place of the realm of totality was exported to the western colonies as an ideology of national liberation. At 2E the party-state neglected existentially constitutive process and the presence of the past (and outside) generally; the concept of transformative negation and the non-monovalent geo-historicity of social forms. At 3L it neglected global intra-dependence, the necessity for constitutional mediations and the concept of radical negation. At 4D the typical intrinsic aspect/extrinsic aspect split was represented in the division between a characteristically disembodied party apparatus and a reified populace. Here also was shown a shallow disregard for freedoms (including rights, democracies and other liberties) and no sense of a dialectic of emancipation dependent on absenting, assertorically sensitized and dialectically universalizable agency.

How did all this come to pass? We could picture (a)–(f) on pp. 192–3 above as a Humean wheel making possible the Humean turntable which is the basis of the antinomial critique of Hume. The omissive critique of Hume pinpoints his failure to sustain a non-anthropic ontology, his ontological actualism, monovalence and extensionalism (at 1M–3L) and his mechanistic reifying conception of man (at 4D). We have already posted in Chapter 9.2 the immanent critique of Hume, which culminates in the lack of seriousness or theory/practice inconsistency involved in his repair to 'carelessness and inattention'.

Kant's aim, like Descartes's, is to reconcile science, specifically

Newtonian science, and rational faith in the fundaments of Christianity, specifically the freedom of the will, the immortality of the soul and the existence of God. More directly, in response to Humean scepticism, it was to 'sever the root of *materialism, fatalism, atheism, free-thinking*, and fanaticism and superstition'.[1] I will coordinate my discussion of Kant around Kant's three 'Critiques' — of pure reason, practical reason and judgement — which there are some grounds for seeing as laying (in the first case consciously) a reactive base for Hegel's principles of (β) constellational monism, (α) realized idealism and (γ) immanent teleology.

In Kant's First Critique he displaced the performative contradiction or self-referential paradox of empiricism, manifest, for example, in the unverifiability of the principle of verification, by failing to show how we can have direct encounter or *Anschauung* with the synthetic a priori propositions of the critical philosophy, that is, how they can be known and not just thought; or how we can have knowledge of the understanding-in-itself as distinct from an appearance of it; or how we can know that knowledge is indeed two-sourced (ectypal), that is, of the grounds for Kant's celebrated synthesis of the principles of rationalism and of empiricism. In particular, Kant must resort to faith, long before the Second Critique, to save the empirical character of our knowledge. What happens in transcendental idealism is that to sustain the concepts of the necessity and universality of laws (ontological) structure is *involuted* within the transcendental subjectivity of mind, in a radical de-ontologization of the world which is the price Kant pays for resurrecting structure within a fundamentally Cartesian model of man. Although, if we waive the objection as to its knowability, the necessity of causal laws is saved, that of their universality is not. For Kant accepts Humean empirical realism, particularly as embodied in the 'constant conjunction plus subjective contribution of mind' analysis of causal laws, that is to say, Hume's actualism. This is spelled out in the 'Postulates of Empirical Thought', where the domains of the real and the possible are reduced to the domain of the actual. In virtue of this he is unable to maintain the conditions of possibility of either experimental or applied knowledge in science. For actualism presupposes closed systems, which are a condition, normally socially produced and maintained, of the alignment of the realms of the real, the actual and the subjective, whether the subjective be conceptual (as in Leibniz) or empirical (as in Hume and Kant). And the fallacious reduction involved in empirical anthroporealism, overseen by the epistemic fallacy, presupposes in turn the reification of facts and the fetishism of closed systems, expressed in the reciprocating ontic fallacy. So Kant is unable to sustain the discursivity of the intellect or the intelligibility of Newtonian science.[†]

But worse is to come. For his actualism, as manifest in the Second Analogy, makes impossible the causal agency necessary for science and morality alike (and allegedly reconciled in the resolution of the Third Antinomy). Here we detect the effects of ontological mono-valence. There is a direct line between the Parmenidean one, Platonic mind−body dualism and the analysis of negation in terms of difference to be followed by the subsumption of difference under generality, Cartesian mind−body dualism and deductivism and the Kantian split between the noumenal and phenomenal realms,[‡] the hermeneutical dichotomous contrasts discussed in the last section and Davidsonian anomalous monism given the imprimatur of late Wittgenstein's supposedly two 'language games theory'. Paradoxical consequences flow from this. Morality loses its agent-directing power. We are each, because of the systematic interconnection of the world, established by the Third Analogy, individually responsible for everything that has ever happened and will ever happen in virtue of a primordial choice made in the noumenal realm (which necessitates the duplicitous replication of the phenomenal world within it) prior to our birth and outside time. There is no ground here for the assignment of elected, legal responsibility (which depends upon the imputation of causal responsibility) for any particular act and hence no ground for sanction or punishment for, say, an individual act of theft; no grounds for Pietist morality; and no grounds for distin-guishing between the supreme good, established by the categorical imperative, and the highest good, in which happiness will be proportioned to virtue — for the ethical consequence of Kantian (implicitly ontological) actualism is a radical egalitarianism of virtue (since we are all responsible for everything, we must all be equally so). And hence neither reason nor ground for rational faith in the immortality of the soul or the existence of a beneficent God. What we have instead is a fideist *Jenseits*, to become in Hegel the constellational closure of geo-history and in Marx communism. Like Hegel, Kant also has a this-worldly response to a problem of how a perfect God could have produced an imperfect world and this turns — in an echo of Adam Smith, whom Hume read approvingly on his death-bed — on a

---

[†] Moreover, in his deduction of the schemata, he resorts to the palpably antiquated notion of a unitary time-consciousness.

[‡] It is worth stressing that it is Kant's empirical realism, i.e. his conception of an actualist-regularity-determinist-Laplacean realm conforming to the three analogies, which necessitates his resolution to the Third Antinomy, i.e. the placing of 'free man' outside it.

dialectic of the 'unsocial sociability of man', which would usher in an enlightened universal cosmopolitan order, the ground for rational history.[2] What is of immediate interest to us here is his Cartesian bourgeois individualist model of man, free in his subjective preferences (in the intrinsic aspect), determined as part of the natural order (in the extrinsic aspect); the former encouraging a voluntarism at 5C, the latter reification in the tacit duplicity of dialectical counterparts.

The Third Critique is in part an attempt to resolve the contradictions within and between the first two. Thus Kant resorts, again fideistically, to a theo-teleo-logically motivated 'as if', to make nature mind-like to effect a correspondence between the empirical manifold we apprehend and the transcendental object; to sustain in aesthetic judgement that intra-subjectivity which is absent from the Cartesian bourgeois individualist model of man, determining the ideological function of the aesthetic I discussed in Chapter 7; to repair, in reflective judgement, the problems of the transdictive complex, most notably the problem of induction, that the Second Analogy, no more than Aristotelian *nous* or Humean 'carelessness and inattention', cannot resolve (for even if it be accepted that the transcendental deduction of the Second Analogy establishes the principle 'given y, something must have caused it', it does not license the substantive proposition 'x causes y' — in the absence of the concepts of ontological stratification and alethic truth — no matter how many x's have been conjoined with y's).

I have already discussed Hegel in some detail in Chapter 6, but it is worth engaging in some recapitulation here. I am going to relate the three motivations for absolute idealism to the three principal keys to his philosophy, lines of materialist critique, his immediate historical predecessors and the historical pediment of his dialectic. And I am going to use his criteria of seriousness, clarity and totality or rationality to yield immanent, antinomic and omissive critiques respectively, though, given the claims of his system, all criteria will fall under the category of immanent critique, of which antinomial and omissive critiques are also forms. Thus (α) his claim to realize the traditional goals of philosophy within an immanent metaphysics of experience (the legacy of Kant) yields his principle of realized idealism, encapsulating the epistemic fallacy, his postulate of subject–object identity, his centrist-expressivist totality, and is liable to the critique of epistemological materialism and, in particular, like Kant, his failure to sustain the autonomy of nature. His failure to achieve rationalist criteria of knowledge, an absolute absolute (the outcome of the Eleatic strand and the vindication of the primeval

Parmenidean one) is reflected in the exoteric split between the this-wordly left Hegelian Mark I and the *Geist*-centric right Hegelian Mark II and esoterically in the splitting of the actual at 1M, the positive at 2E, the extensional at 3L (which is coated with an intensional gloss), the agentive at 4D and the social at 5C, and this mimics the dichotomous dualisms reflecting the dirempt world of early modernity and expressed in the philosophy of Kant. This makes Hegel vulnerable to the charge of lack of seriousness, the nub of his critique of Kant, and so to a straightforward immanent critique. These splits are of course also at once the source of interpretive antinomies and the site of metacritical voids.

Next (β) comes Hegel's quest for a differentiated totality or a unity-in-diversity in which differentiation would be a necessary condition for unity, reflecting the descending movement of the Ionian strand, resumed in neo-Platonic and Christian eschatology and manifest in Schillerian dialectics of diremption, which would also be opposed to Spinozan monism and Schelling's point of indifference, later to be likened to a 'cow in the night'. This generates Hegel's spiritual constellational monism, the logical mysticism of the speculative illusion, product of the primal squeeze on the Platonic/Aristotelian fault-line, his cognitive triumphalism and renders him vulnerable to the critique of ontological materialism and Marx's charge that he knows only 'abstract mental labour'. His constellational monism produces in turn a host of recrudescent surds like the return of Aristotelian matter or non-being or the Kantian unknowable thing-in-itself. Moreover, it is here that the interpretive antinomies are sharpest. For left with the irrational or demi-actual portion of reality Hegel is no better off than Kant, on which it would appear precisely as an unknowable thing-in-itself (cf. the criterion of seriousness), a Fichte, on which it would appear as a potentially endless task (for transfigurative redescription [cf. the criterion of completeness implicit in Hegelian totality]) or a Schelling, on which it would appear as an opaque obscurity (cf. the criterion of clarity). Hegel is thus forced to fudge this issue, trapped in an antinomy between rational philosophy and empirical science. The hyperintuitionism he proclaims and the transformationalism he practises render him vulnerable to the charge of theory/practice inconsistency and heterology, symptomatic of the absences the omissive critique or metacritique$_1$ will pinpoint, with his fudging perfectly reflecting the lack of distinguishing clarity with which he taxed Shelling.

Finally, (γ), there is the desire to avoid the fate of the Beautiful Soul without an Unhappy Consciousness which gives us his principle of preservative dialectical sublation. This may be related to his immanent teleology, his endism or constellational closure of geo-history and his failure to sustain the geo-historicity of social forms, to which we may oppose practical materialism and the critique of ontological monovalence (the third and primal member of the unholy trinity of Parmenidean/Platonic provenance). Now transformative practice can only negate or absent the given. There is an injunctive paradox in the Plateaunic theory of objective spirit as there is self-referential paradox or performative contradiction in the primordial Parmenidean poem, the Platonic *act* of the negation in terms of difference and, at least arguably, in the Hegelian announcement of the end of geo-history. It is here that Hegel expresses most translucently irrealist philosophy's characteristic denegation of change. Less macroscopically, we may see his failure to save the constellational closure of geo-history as an index of his failure both to complete the ascending movement of the Ionian strand and to make good his claim to achieve a complete totality or to have avoided a Fichtean endless task. Because transformative praxis can only absent the given, there remains the permanent possibility that it may absent the (conceptual and conceptualized) conditions of possibility of that praxis and/or the given in what I have called 'endosmotic refutation', that is to say, the seepage back into Hegel's categorial system (e.g. with respect to the concepts of space, time or causality, or class, or women) of real-world change, so that there is always a chance, contrary to Rorty and Fukuyama, that the last conceptual revolution has not occurred.[†] It is here that we see the apologetic effect of Hegel's analytical reinstatement in dialectical transfigurative connection designed to reconcile himself to actuality (to overcome his self-diagnosed 'hypochrondia') and to flatter the vanity and comfort the troubles of his contemporaries by portraying them as the constellational realization of absolute spirit. But he escapes the fate of Jesus, of the Beautiful Soul, only at the price of an Unhappy

---

[†] In *Philosophy and the Idea of Freedom* I argued that Rorty conjures up an ideology for a leisured elite. There is no incompatibility, as Michael Billig seems to think, between my universalizing description of Rorty's rhetoric and Billig's particularizing characterization of his text as symbolic, in the register of the syntax of hegemony of the *Pax Americana* of the 'New World Order'. For this is a classic instance of the representation of ideologically expandable/contractable/displaceable/recondensable sectional interests as universal. For Rorty, on the new quasi-Davidsonian foundationalism, interpretive charity begins ego-present-centrically at home and totalizes ethnocentrically outwards in a combination of what Rom Harré and Peter Mulhauser have labelled the 'interpretive' and 'directive' uses of the pronoun 'we'.[3] Genealogically speaking, the Humean turntable transports us as readily to the politics and ideology of a Bush or a Clinton as to the demise of the commandist actually existing 'socialist' party-states.

Consciousness, the acceptance of positivity, of rationalization rather than reason, of fate instead of freedom. It is here that the omissive critique signposting the voids at the heart of absolute idealism is most apposite: of a non-actual real, a real negativity not undone and contradiction uncancelled, an open totality, an ongoing absenting absentive transformative praxis which cannot merely reproduce the status quo, but always contains (via the theorem of the [dislocated] duality of structure and praxis) the possibility of the transformation of its transcendental presuppositions, and hence of endosmotic refutation (cf. 1M−5C). To the omissive critique and Hegel's shortfall I shall briefly return.

In relation to (α) we can align, mainly as residues as I explained elsewhere,[4] Marx's actualism, manifest most starkly in the problem of abstraction. To (β) we can match Marx's constellational unidimensionality on one (albeit arguably the explanatorily most important) of the totality of master−slave-type relations and his displacement of Hegel's cognitive triumphalism onto practical Prometheanism. In respect of (γ) we can set Marx's post-dated endism and the consequential functionalist, evolutionary and teleological strains of much Marxism after Marx, as well as the failure of subsequent Marxists to complete his unfinished business, i.e. to realize that geohistorical materialism is a research programme which has only just begun (far from being post-ed). But another matrix is possible too. If to (α) we relate the *Critique of Pure Reason*, to (β) the *Critique of Practical Reason* and to (γ) the *Critique of Judgement*, we can then see in (α) Marx's *epistemological* actualism, which gives us tendentially (via the epistemic fallacy) monism and reductionism and, via ontological monovalence, a projected endism. Then we can find in (β) Marx's sociological reductionism in *ethics* and locate in (γ) Marx's *quasiaesthetic* teleological tendencies.

I promised to return to the omissive critique. We can see Kant as engaged in the metacritique₁ of the Cartesian ego from which modern philosophy starts — arguing that an objective manifold is a condition of possibility of the transcendental unity of perception which allows us to synthesize the empirical manifold presented by a world unknowable-in-itself. Hegel in his metacritique₁ of Kant's sees the transcendental unity of self-consciousness as a social achievement ultimately grounded in a public world of moral order, enshrined in the constitutional structures of his rational state. Marx in his metacritique₁ of Hegel identifies the real basis of the Hegelian state in civil society (later, modes of production) founded on the alienation and exploitation of labour-power, radically generalizes Hegel's dialectic of mutual reconcilation into a dialectic of de-alienation and

shows capitalism to be a geo-historical product, destined to make way
for one in which 'the free development of each is a condition for the
free development of all'. Dialectical critical realism argues that this
goal can only be achieved by a radicalization of Marx's dialectic of de-
alienation into a dialectic of liberation from the totality of
master – slave relations, and that this moral goal of universal human
autonomy is a presupposition of the most elemental desire, the first
initiating act of referential detachment, induced by negativity in the
guise of absence. It further argues that the critique of ontological
monovalence, and the epistemic fallacy and hence actualism
involving, inter alia, critiques of the Parmenidean one and the
Platonic normalization of Parmenidean monism in the analysis of
negation and change in terms of difference and eidetic (to be followed
by hylomorphic) identity generalized into a critique of the full
ensemble of categorially flawed and Tina compromised irrealisms, is a
necessary condition for that totalizing depth praxis which would
produce a plausible concretely utopian model of flourishing under the
eudaimonistic society, necessary for the actionability of the project of
universal human emancipation.

§ 2 Counter-Conduct

The story as I have told it is a critical one, but, although, as far as I
know, in its main thrust it is original, clearly other dimensions of
criticism are possible. We have thus to ask the general question,
which will be given one specific elaboration, of the history of
philosophy: to what extent are alternative narratives possible? This
question can be broached from the side of

(a)   vantage-point;
(b)   topic;
(c)   ideological distortion or bias;
(d)   lack of reflexivity.

In general the history of philosophy has been progressivist and
unilinear. This has been its general tendency since Hegel. But there
have been no shortages of critics of the post-Hegelian problematic
from within the tradition of the story I have told — from
Kierkegaardian existentialism, with its emphasis on the radical
autonomy and contingency of individuals, to Heideggerian nostaliga,
with its tale of the successive occlusions of being from the pre-
Socratics to the contemporary age of technology and nihilism. To the

progressivist view of philosophy one could well counterpose a history of it as composed of constitutive antagonisms, of dialectical counterparts in tacit complicity, of curious reprises, of deep continuities and a multiplicity of traditions, such as the tradition of neo-Platonism or of Thomism for which I have had no time here. As for its unilinearity, there are almost always a multiplicity of traditions, currents and paradigms, though how much these differ and whether one is hegemonic (and if so, how it exercises its hegemony) are highly contingent affairs. My story is obviously only a story of western philosophy, so we have to ask to what extent the history of philosophy, indeed philosophy itself, is Eurocentric. For, on the one hand, there is evidence, most dramatically portrayed in Martin Bernal's *Black Athena,*[5] of the African and Asian roots of Greek culture, including its mythyology and poetry out of which the origins of Greek philosophy, as I indicated in Chapter 9.1, arose. Then, on the other, there are traditions, such as that of Indian philosophy, of remarkable power and subtlety with striking affinities and parallels to those in western philosophy. Then again it could be asked why should we take western thought as our point of reference. What of African philosophy? Or Confucianism? Lurking around here are questions of criteria of rationality. It seems we only take 'western' criteria of rationality for granted because global geo-history has turned up with certain cultural milieux causally related to dominant power$_2$ relations. Is this necessity? Or accident? Or a combination of both? In any event, globalization and action at a distance has produced tendencies which are homogenizing with pockets of local ethnocentricity.

What has been marginalized, subordinated, fragmented, omitted or occluded in a philosophical account? Does it thematize relations of production, the oppression of women, ethnic minorities? Does it broach the topics of education, sexuality, the division of labour? If not, why not? What are its characteristic biases, blindspots, voids? All this is matter that raises questions of metacrique$_2$ which I will treat in my forthcoming *Philosophical Ideologies.*

Then who are the writers? Why are there so few working-class philosophers? Is to be a philosopher to be 'middle class'? Why were there no women philosphers until very recently? Can an account account for itself?[6] Does it practise immanent critique on itself? I have talked of philosophy's substantive analogical grammars, but what exactly are the shifting relations between science, politics, economy, culture, religion and philosophy? What are the power$_2$ relations at work inside philosophy? And should one talk of philosophy in such a hypostatized way, as if there were not many different philosophies and philosophical ensembles with differentiated and putatively discordant rhythmics of their own? It is time to concretize the discussion.

It is only possible to deal explicitly here with one example of a group systematically subalternized in the history of philosophy, namely that provided by feminist philosophers and historians, viz. women.[†] Here one is dealing with at least five aspects of domination, viz.:

(a) domination by suppression;
(b) domination by exclusion;
(c) domination by marginalization and/or fragmentation;
(d) domination by idealization;
(e) domination by tacit complicity.

In the tradition woman is typically there for the sake of, or requires completion by (i.e. only achieves her full individuation in and through), men. Thus we have already seen how women in Hegel, confined to the family in the triad of family, civil society and state, are consigned to the status of the demi-actual (cf. 1M splitting), although treated especially in *The Phenomenology of Mind* as representative of divine law. The process of domination by idealization is perhaps carried to the limit in Rousseau, where woman is both symbolic of a lost past and emblematic of the projected future, but not an agent in the present in the process of her own self-emancipation (cf. 2E splitting). Descartes's procedure of radical doubt made, quasi-solipsistically, education open to women in the home, excluded as they were from Latin and the classroom. Yet of course science remained a collective endeavour. This is domination by exclusion. Arguably in stereotyping the domination of women in terms of the 'looked at', Simone de Beauvoir helped to perpetuate the form of domination by tacit complicity.

But in thematizing the subjugation of women we have to treat of allegory and myth, analogy, metaphor and metonymy as well as the underlying power$_2$ relations to which philosophical ideological discourse offers diagnostic clues. Thus we have woman as temptress in the Genesis story, as incapable of full morality,[‡] as the unbounded (Pythagoras), as matter, as non-being, as body, the

---

[†] I should make it explicit here that I am deeply indebted in what follows to Genevieve Lloyd's classic *Man of Reason*.

[‡] Notoriously Freud did not stop to consider that women might possess a superior morality, viz. one based on solidarity, trust and care, to that which pitted super-ego against id, or, in the Kantian story, duty against desire.

irrational or the demi-actual, as helpmate to man (Aquinas), as nature (Bacon) to be penetrated by science, and, most typically, on 'divided soul' models, as representing either the split (in Plato) or the lesser of the two (or more) divisions. Thus Hume, for whom reason was the slave of the passions, nevertheless distinguished between calm and violent passions and argued that the former, in the public sphere of civic society as distinct from the private realm of the family and/or, depending upon circumstances, paid work, could exercise a curbing and thereby socializing influence on the natural acquisitiveness of human beings. But of course women were *excluded* from the public sphere and hence by association tainted with the less rational.

The subjugation of women cannot be overcome by such philosophical exposure. In particular, vexed questions of sexuality and gender, not to mention relations on all four planes of society, remain. The idea that sexuality is biologically given, whereas gender is socially constructed, seems too simplistic for many feminists now. But does this mean that there is a distinct female rationality, as is compatible with Spinoza's definition of the mind as the idea of the body? Or do we stick with the Kantian ideal (despite his notorious misogyny) of a reason that transcends sexual difference?

§ 3 Philosophy and the Dialectic of Emancipation

Insofar as *Plato Etcetera* pivots on dialectical critical realism, it is vital for us to have vindicated a robust ontology and concept of negativity. The former has not been sustained since Hume and Kant in a process inexorably initiated by Cartesianism, and has been historically subordinated to epistemology since Plato, following Parmenides. I have tried to sustain negativity both in the sense of (a) absent being (real determinate non-being) and in the sense of (b) ill-being, and to wield them and to unite them in the dialectic of freedom sketched in Chapter 7. I have located in the fourfold polysemy of absence (as product, as process, as process-in-product and as product-in-process) the hub of both existence, through the critique of ontological monovalence and the transcendental reduction of real negation, and causality. Real negation is consistent with distanciation without transformation; transformative negation is consistent with exogenous sources of change; and radical negation is consistent with multiple determination within a totality. Therefore we have the theorem: real negation $\geq$ transformative negation $\geq$ radical negation $\geq$ linear negation. Epistemologically, I have subsumed causality under a generalized notion of existence. Ontologically, I have prioritized the triunity of space, time and causality; stressed the fivefold causal chain consisting, typically, in the transfactual efficacy of the generative mechanism of structures, the rhythmic (viz. irreducibly tensed A-serial spatializing processual) exercise of their causal powers, potentially mediated by the holistic causality and intra-activity of an (in general) partial totality, dependent in the human sphere upon the embodied intentional causal agency of emergent structurata, codetermining a concretely singularized conjunctural outcome. *Causality is fundamentally absenting* in the human realm by potentially rational praxis. In respect of (b), I have negatively generalized the concept of constraint to include any kind of ill, which can always be seen in the key of absence. The unity of (a) and (b) is most simply captured in the dialectic of agency. In seeking to absent an ill, I am logically committed to absenting all dialectically similar ills (constraints); and thence to absenting all ills in virtue of their dialectical similarity as ills; whence to the totalizing depth praxis oriented to the principle of universal concretely singularized human flourishing (a positive generalization of the concept of freedom) in nature. Remedial absence implied in elemental desire, mediated via the discursive presuppositions of praxis, or referential detachment, mediated via the practical presuppositions of discourse, entails, by the logic of dialectical universalizability, the goal of universal human emancipation. This most ontologically negative philosophy therefore produces the most ethically positive results.

What are the components of an adequate practice of philosophy? First, *Lockian under-labouring* (which will include ideology-critique) for science, social science and the project of human emancipation. This will incorporate the Baconian, Kantian, Marxian and Nietzschean critiques of illusion (with the Marxian critique taking the triple form of a critical hermeneutic of agents' conceptions, organized around counter-hegemonic struggle over discursively moralized power$_2$ relations, ideological categories and their theoretical legitimations and the explanatory structures which account for both). It will entail the defence of reason and freedom, both progressively generalized, and practical solidarity with and engagement in the dialectic of human self-emancipation. Second, what I have elsewhere described as *Leibnizian metaphysics$_b$*,[7] involving the critical assessment of the conceptual and moral hard-cores of research and practical pro-grammes. This will necessitate both that Aristotelian propaedeutics, the continual circulation in and out of the sphere of formal reasoning, in which meanings remain stable, vital for the dialectic of dialectical and analytical reasoning in science; and William Morris-style concrete utopianism, counterbalancing actualism and informing neo-Blochian hope. Third, *Kantian transcendental argument*. First, metacritically$_1$ extended to include Hegelian dialectical phenomenology and then materially circumscribed to take in Marxian explanatory meta-critique$_2$. A metacritique$_1$, it will be remembered, isolates a transcendentally or otherwise significant absence; a metacritique$_2$ additionally explains it. Fourth, it is part of the job of philosophy to be a *Socratic/ Nietzschean gadfly* on the neck of the powers that be, a role that must be envisaged to incorporate both Bachelardian value-commitment and Gramscian optimism of the will and *realism*, informed by concrete utopianism, not pessimism, of the intellect. Fifth, a medley consisting of Derridean critique of the philosophy of presence, entailing a perspectival switch from every centrism to its periphery, every figure to its dialectical ground; Foucauldian counter-conduct, entailing resistance to every repression; and Habermasian dialogicality, entailing a willingness to communicate with and listen to all.

Indeed dialectical critical realism may be seen under the aspect of Foucauldian strategic reversal — of the unholy trinity of Parmenidean/Platonic/Aristotelian provenance; of the Cartesian-Lockean-Humean-Kantian paradigm; of foundationalisms (in practice, fideistic foundationalisms) and irrationalisms (in practice, capricious exercises of the will-to-power or some other ideologically and/or psycho-somatically buried source) new and old alike; of the primordial failing of western philosophy, ontololgical monovalence, and its close ally, the epistemic fallacy with its ontic dual; of the analytic problematic laid down by Plato, which Hegel served only to replicate in his actualist monovalent analytic reinstatement in transfigurative reconciling dialectical connection, while in his hubristic claims for absolute idealism he inaugurated the Comtean, Kierkegaardian and Nietzschean eclipses of reason, replicating the fundaments of positivism through its transmutation route to the superidealism of a Baudrillard.

Second, dialectical critical realism may be seen as counter-conduct insofar as through its (a) longitudinal (1M−4D/5C), (b) lateral (topical), (c) scalar and (d) metacritical realism it reverses the primordial and enduring historical idealism of philosophy; and insofar as it is practically oriented to the abolition of the totality of master−slave-type relations in the context of the unfinished moral evolution of the species. And most generally insofar as it is committed to the absenting of constraints on absenting absences or ills, i.e. to dialectic as the pulse of freedom. We have seen that the proximate basis of the problems (really the problem-field solution sets) of philosophy is alienation and reification, which expresses itself as the fear of change, and especially change at 4D/5C in the power$_2$

relations at work in four-planar social being. But the problems of philosophy, not to be resolved but ultimately to be explained by their ideological effects, as I shall relate in some detail in *Philosophical Ideologies*, will not be remedied by intellectual critique alone. I have attempted a 2E unification of the problematic of 'the problems of philosophy', while affirming rational resolutions to them; and essayed a real definition of philosophy as the Janus-faced aporetic and generally unconscious normalization of the status quo ante. It is the epistemological naturalization of the status quo which explains the fact that changes but not differences have to be justified. It is this reification which explains the ethical projection of the negative and the role of the aesthetic as a false mediator between genuine sympathy at the plane of intersubjectivity and systematic social divisiveness at the plane of social relations, and more generally as a surrogate reconciler to the real problems at 4D/5C. And it is the same reification which explains the detotalization of the local present from (in reality, existentially constitutive) geo-historical process (and thus the tacit complicity of indexicalism and blockism, punctualist atomism and closure). It is important to stress the Janus-faced character of philosophy. For Plato makes the world safe for Euclidean geometry, Descartes for the new mechanics. Hegel paves the way for Marx and self-reflexive geo-historicized social science, Nietzsche for Freud, Frege for the new information-based technololgies. All this is to say that the local present contains new beginnings and possibilities for development as well as continuities and the debris of the dead.

The history of philosophy can be reviewed as a series of Achilles' Heel critiques, on which an Achilles' Heel critique seeks to show that it is where precisely a position seems strongest that it is really most weak, and considered under the figure of the tacit complicity of dialectical counterparts, declaring at once the constitutively antagonistic and dilemmatic character of philosophy. Let us consider the former aspect first. Parmenides cannot sustain the primal one and must resort to Cratylan silence and ultimately ego-present-centric solipsism. Plato cannot sustain the morality of Socratic reasoning without recourse to the Forms. But the Forms cannot be upheld without self-predicative paradox and tacit appeal to the transient sensate world. Furthermore, the transience of this world is only further confirmed by the Platonic act (a negation) of the analysis of negation and change in terms of difference (the diachronic counterpart to the synchronic naturalization of the status quo noted in the previous paragraph). Aristotle mires himself in the aporiai of substance and cannot, without appeal to a transcendent God, account for his own scientific practice. Descartes cannot sustain the *cogito* and must bow to an antinomy between doubt and himself. Hume cannot maintain the principle of the association of ideas on which he flatters himself or the theory of causality for which posterity has credited him. Kant cannot sustain the discursivity of our intellection or an intelligible concept of freedom, so that neither Newtonian science nor Pietist morality are upheld. Hegel negated negativity and geo-historicity alike, announcing himself as the supreme undialectical dialectician, and he produces merely a demi-absolute, yielding antinomies which force him back into the positions of a Kant, Fichte or Schelling. Empiricists have not yielded a coherent concept of experience, nor rationalists of a (non a posteriori) concept of reason. Marx never engages in the critique of empirical realism necessary to sustain the intelligibility of his own scientific practice or produces a plausible vision of flourishing under socialism. Nietzsche cannot sustain the truth about truth. Heidegger produces an ontology mediated by human being (i.e. an anthroporealism) and dependent on the despised ontic realm. Derrida, lacking the concept of referential detachment, cannot maintain the coherence of textual deconstruction. Positivists cannot sustain their own metaphysical critique of metaphysics without performative contradiction, and Rorty asks us to believe in reductionist materialism but engages (with causal effect) in the practice of conversational hermeneutics.

I have already noted the systematic illicit intra-dependence of anthroporealism and transcendent realism — manifest in, for example, the actualist split in reality, revealing the metacritical void of the concept of the non-actual real — as a result of the primal squeeze on the Platonic/Aristotelian fault-line (extrajecting the concepts of ontological stratification and alethic truth). This internally inconsistent ensemble requires a defensive shield and produces a Tina compromise form as axiological necessities press about it. It is susceptible to metacritique$_1$. The illicit intra-dependence must be explained in terms of the epistemic fallacy, revealing the profound anthropism (coupled with reificatory anti-humanism) of western philosophical thought. This in turn must be accounted for in terms of the dogma of ontological monovalence (historically traceable to Parmenidean monism with its reductio ad Cratylus). This in turn was curiously reprised in the subjectivism, scepticism and solipsism of the transition from Descartes (committed like Parmenides to physical monovalence) to Hume. The ground was thus laid for the eventual triumph of a dogmatic empiricism, untempered by the scepticism of the Enlightenment, as the hard-core of at first a representationalist-monological problematic of presence, and then, when the scientific and political upheavals of the twentieth century seeped through into the temporarily lagged consciousness of philosophy, for the irrationalist collapse of criteria of truth, objectivity and human need.

How do we remedy this state of affairs? The first step is to think the constellational identity of the possibility of judgemental rationality (in the intrinsic aspect) within the actuality of epistemic relativity (in the transitive dimension) within the necessity for ontological realism in the intransitive dimension. The second step is to absent the absence of the concept of absence, and the categories of ontological stratification, negativity, totality and agentive agency in the ontological—axiological chain provided by dialectical critical realism. Let me briefly rehearse this. We start with the concept of absence (e.g. manifest in desire), which immediately gives us the concept of referential detachment and existential intransitivity; whence we proceed to classification and causality. With the first glimpse of ontological structure we have alethic truth and the transfactual efficacy it affords. But to cause is to negate, and all negation is in space-time and so we have the whole gamut of 2E categories from constraint to dialectical contradiction to rhythmic spatio-temporal efficacy. The contradictions within and between entities yield emergence, and thence it is a short route to the 3L categories of totality, holistic causality, the concrete universal ↔ singular. Totality is inwardized as, inter alia, the reflexivity shown in judgement and the monitoring of practice. Now in the realm of 4D, in virtue of the transcendental necessity of social structure for practice, we can derive from the sole premiss of the activity-dependence of social structure, the transformational model of social activity, the relational social paradigm and the epistemological, ontological, relational and critical limits on naturalism, including the derivation of value from facts, that is, the whole circle of 5C concepts. In virtue of our intentional embodied agency, to act is to absent, and in desire or the solidarity implicit in the fiduciariness of the judgement form, the object of our absenting agency is constraint. Then, by the logic of dialectical universalizability, we are driven to absent all dialectically similar constraints, and then to absent constraints as such in virtue of their being dialectically similar; and finally to engage, on the basis of the progressive generalization of the concept of freedom to incorporate flourishing and potentialities for development, and the negative generalization of constraint to include ills and remediable absences generally, in the totalizing depth praxis that will usher in the eudaimonistic or good society. I do not believe that such a society will be free of problems, including pressing philosophical ones, but one might hope that they will be of a different order to those I have attempted to resolve in this book.

Appendix: Explaining Philosophies

What is your aim in philosophy? — To show the fly the way out of the
fly-bottle.

WITTGENSTEIN

All social life is essentially practical. All mysteries which lead theory to
mysticism find their rational solution in human practice and in the
comprehension of that practice.

MARX

§ 1 Philosophies as Social Ideologies

Ideologies are:

(a) (communicative) discursive/(moral) normative/power (and
   especially power$_2$) *intersects* of the social cube, as depicted in
   Figure 5.10, Chapter 5.1;

(b) as such they are potentially or actually sites of *struggle*, especially
   hermeneutic hegemonic/counter-hegemonic struggles over
   discursively moralized power$_2$ or master—slave-type relations;

(c) in a strong sense — which I shall write as ideology*, when it is
   necessary to disambiguate it from the more general sense —
   embodying *categorial error*.

Thus we shall see how illicit fusions can be used to represent
particular and sectional interests as general or universal and
conversely how illicit fissions can be used to present universal
interests as partisan; how ideologies act so as to screen social conflict
and contradiction and connections alike as well as to legitimate the
existing order of things. I shall show how philosophical ideologies in
particular exploit extra-philosophical material, usually drawn from
the past, as analogical grammars, either imbuing their form with
content or illustrating the latter.

In general one is only justified in designating a system of ideas, I, as 'ideological*' if one is in a position to *explain* them. Indeed three sets of conditions should be satisfied, which I shall call (α) *critical*, (β) *categorial* and (γ) *explanatory*, viz.:

(α)   one should possess a theory or set of theories, T, that can explain most, or most of the significant, phenomena that I can explain plus some significant phenomena that I cannot, and explain in immanent or metacritical$_1$ terms why this is so, i.e. $T>I$;.

(β)   one should be able to demonstrate that I embodies categorial error, that it offends against a necessary condition for our adequate understanding of being, or of some relevant domain of being (e.g. that a theory of science cannot sustain the transfactuality of its subject matter), which we could write as T dem.CE(I), although in some cases it may not be possible to isolate the relevant category mistake independently of the role that I plays in reproducing or reinforcing oppressive power$_2$ relations;

(γ)   one should be able to explain the reproduction of I, including its limits of possibility, for example in terms of a level of structure or degree of totality that T but not I describes, i.e. Texp(I) *and* be able to self-reflexively situate one's own theory, when one will be able to claim a metacritique$_2$ or explanatory critique of I, which will automatically issue in a negative evaluation of the explanans of I and, ceteris paribus, motivate action oriented to transforming it.

($\alpha - \gamma$) may take the form of a dialectically explanatory argument, showing the alethic truth of the falsity or partiality of a phenomenon.

I will exemplify the categorial condition by considering Marx's celebrated analysis of the value and wage forms and then use it analogously to cast light on the ideology-critique of positivism, the dominant modern theory of science, before setting out a general schema for the understanding of philosophical and social ideologies and exemplifying it by other ideological configurations. For Marx, fetishism anthropomorphically invests commodities with magical powers of their own independently of the social relations which reproduce them. Naturalizing value relations in this way desocializes and de-spatio-temporalizes them. Despite this they are real but geo-historically specific relations for Marx. They act so as to conceal the geo-historically specific class relationships which underlie the surface phenomena of circulation and exchange. One might call this a second-order critique, insofar as it demonstrates the conditions of possibility

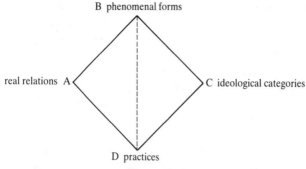

Figure A.1

of a social form. But Marx gives a first-order critique of the wage form, turning on the category mistake of confounding powers and their exercise, in which the value of labour-power is transformed into the value of labour, which he declares to be an expression 'as imaginary as the value of the earth', 'as irrational as a yellow logarithm'; that is to say, he identifies the phenomenon itself as false (or, to put it in more Kantian language, that the category is not properly applicable to experience at all). Its social effect is clearly to conceal the reality, in the process of capitalist production, of unpaid labour, the source of surplus value. And as Marx says, 'if history took a long time to get to the bottom of the mystery of wages, nothing is easier than to understand the necessity, the raison d'être of this phenomenon'.

Accepting that phenomenal forms, such as the value and the wage form, are necessary for the operation of a capitalist, one could set out the schema depicted in Figure A.1. Real relations, A, typically located by Marx in the sphere of production, generate phenomenal forms, B, characteristic of the spheres of circulation and exchange, which in turn are reflected in the categories of ideological* discourse, C, which sustain such ordinary commercial practices as buying and selling, wage-negotiating, etc. at D. These are of course in turn necessary for the reproduction of A. The dotted line BD denotes, as it were, the texture of everyday life. Marx's analysis moves retroductively (transcendentally [dialectically]) from B to A, enabling immanent critiques, omissive critiques and metacritiques$_2$ at C informing counter-hegemonic praxis at D. From a dialectical critical realist perspective it is worth noting that it is the generative separation of the immediate producers from their labour, i.e. a 2E split, which induces the fivefold alienation noted in Chapter 5.3, i.e. 3L detotalizations, resulting in the reification (4D) and commodification of labour-power, which is the condition of possibility of the 1M illicit fusion or exchange of non-equivalents (based on the analogue of 1M destratification, identification of powers and their exercise) foundational of the capitalist economy that yields the 2E lack (unpaid labour) that drives capitalism on.

Let us now look at the positivist account of science, which pivots on the reduction of theory to autonomized sense-experience, which is held to apprehend reified facts (in the theory of the production of particular facts). These are now naturalistically generalized as constant conjunctions, presupposing the fetishism of closed systems. Figure A.2 illustrates its ideo-logic. Now facts are social products. But at the level of expressive-referential duality in the analysis of truth, given our prior formation by a conceptual scheme and social-theoretical matrix, we do just tend to 'read' the world like a text as we tell the time off a clock, as if it were constituted by facts. But we can easily see that, if we are unreflective of the conditions of possibility of the bipolarity at this level of the analysis of the concept of truth, the fact form can function as an ideology of Kuhnian 'normal science'; and we have the possibility of an analogue of Marx's second-order critique and an analogue of Figure A.1 in Figure A.3. However, the constant conjunction form (which we could nickname constant conjunctivitis), which destratifies reality,

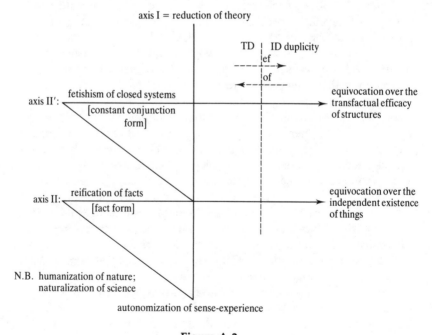

Figure A.2

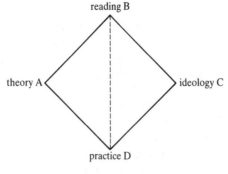

BD = bipolarity of truth

Figure A.3

confounding (like the wage form) powers and their exercise, is wholly false and has to be submitted to a first-order critique. Its ideological effect is to naturalistically eternalize the epistemic, social and ontic status quos, blocking change and dogmatically normalizing (and reinforcing) the status quo ante. In addition, one could note the resonance that the atomism, affected by the autonomization at axis I, has with both the classical corpuscularian scheme in science and bourgeois-individualist 'man'.

This raises a number of more general questions. First, how are philosophical ideologies reproduced and/or transformed? Here, it is equally important to avoid the positivistic illusion, which would imply a sociological reductionism, and the speculative illusion, which would entail total philosophical autonomy. Philosophy is a tradition-imbued disciplinary matrix set in a wider social sphere; and in the reproduction of a philosophical ideology both intra- and extra-philosophical inputs will typically play a role. Let us take 'P' as a philosophical system, generated at level I by intra-discursive operator κ on a pre-product C, so I C—$\overset{\kappa}{\longrightarrow}$P . . . theory production. P is applied and has ideological effects on the components of four-planar social being, but particularly at what I have called the ideological intersect of the discursive, normative and power$_2$ sub-dimensions of the social cube (which embraces the totality of social practices from chemistry to farming). So we have now at level II P $\overset{A}{\longrightarrow}$ S . . . theory application, where A is the axiological operator and S represents the totality of social effects. A general schema can be drawn up if we allow κ and A inter-/intra-dependency or just interpose a third level III S $\overset{O}{\longrightarrow}$ C, where O indicates the social conditioning, condensation and articulation on to a philosophical theory problem-field solution set, e.g. by the analogical grammars to which I have already referred, but also in principle by a range of inputs including the direct exercise of power$_2$ relations. Thus we have I C $\xrightarrow{\kappa}$ P; II P $\xrightarrow{A}$ S; III S $\xrightarrow{O}$ C iteratively, depicted in Figure A.4 in what should be seen as a rhythmic process, mediated by holistic causality and dependent on intentional agency.

This leads on to the second question as to whether we can refine our understanding of philosophical ideological systems as Tina compromise formations. We have seen the role that the quest for an unhypothetical starting-point plays in generating philosophical theory problem-field solution sets, and in particular in the drive to subject−object identity and/or equivalent theory. This may be said to satisfy philosophy's *epistemic* function. But what induces scepticism, or rather the desire that it be satisfied in the first place? It is, I am going to argue, an underlying fear of change, and because change in the geo-historical-social world is inevitable (transformative praxis will always tendentially negate the given), this means the normalization of recent and local changes, which replicates philosophical ideologies. In fact I would go so far as to essay a real definition of philosophy as the unconscious and aporetic normalization of the status quo, and in particular recent and local changes (because the status quo will always be changing). Now this at once gives them a *Janus-faced character* because the recent and local will contain new beginnings as well as dead-ends, the good and the bad, the directionally progressive

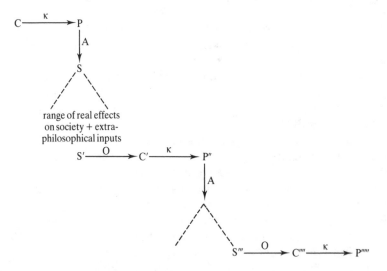

Figure A.4 Theory Production, Use and Reproduction

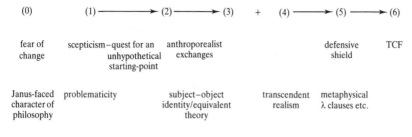

Figure A.5

as well as regressive, changes which are validly naturalistically (or more generally dialectically) grounded or not. So philosophy can be rational or rationalizing; and it can act against as well as for oppressive power$_2$-holders. I have already stressed the aporetic character of philosophy, its *problematicity*, but it is worth emphasizing its *dialogicality*: the fact that, like any tradition, it is constituted by internal antagonistic positions. Thus we have noted how the problem of induction, for example, generates a new transcendent (most typically God or the social structure) — the fideist response to it. But if the new transcendent is not allowed to license an achieved identity theory, it will be as useless (cf. strong actualism) as an achieved one (cf. weak actualism) is untenable. It is important to appreciate that all anthroporealisms, even those of a specifically dualist kind, entail actualism and a fortiori subject—object identity and/or equivalent theory; but that non-anthroporealisms must either fall back (as Plato does) on anthroporealism to adjudicate claims to *doxa* — with the transcendent assuming a mere regulative function, as in a Fichtean *Sollen* — and/or be explicitly projected on to the ethical realm. The only alternative is a partial, fallible achieved subject—object non-identity theory, i.e. commitment to all the dimensions of dialectical critical realist ontology. Thus we have the tacit complicity of contraries within the irrealist problematic. This whole (e.g. any form or combination of actualisms) is liable to immanent, omissive and metacritique and so requires a defensive shield in the form of a metaphysical λ clause. And the whole complex is forced to satisfy a *realist function* or the reality principle, and, as, for instance, S, to adopt a whole series of Tina compromises, constituting a Tina compromise formation. So we have the configuration depicted in Figure A.5. Two other schematisms may be useful — that in Figure A.6 and that in Figure A.7. Figure A.7 depicts philosophy as a theory

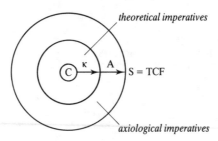

Figure A.6

problem-field solution set, which should be seen as in Figure A.4 and Figure A.5 as a tensed cubic stretch in space-time. These schemata apply not just to positivism, but to any subject–object identity theory (e.g. Hegel's) and, as I have just argued, to any anthroporealism (such as Kant's empirical realism). In fact one can go further and show how these positions presuppose each other. Thus if one accepts Marx's critique of Hegel, he is epistemologically forced to rely for his hyperintuitive methodological claims on unreflected empirical data. Similarly, ontologically, Humean empiricism covertly presupposes hypostatized ideas in the guise of reified facts (see Figure A.8). Moreover, if theory is irreducible, both subjective empiricist and objective idealists are forced within an anthroporealist framework into Kantian epistemological heteronomy. And Kant for his part must

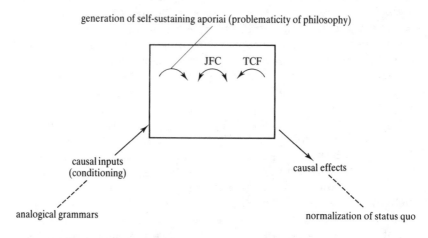

JFC = Janus-faced character
TCF = Tina compromise formation (duplex rationality of philosophy)

Figure A.7

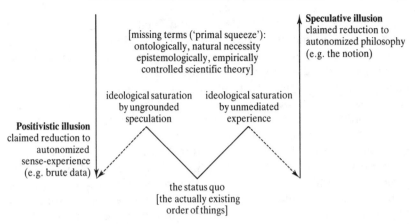

Figure A.8

accept something like an empiricist account of sense-experience and a Hegelian account of the categories!

One other determination and its consequences is worth recording before we move on to look at some other specific figures. The internal structure of positivism, or any subject – object identity or equivalent theory, depends upon *equivocation*. The real meaning of the point of identity in identity theories is the point of duplicity which goes over to a point of great ideological plasticity. Tina compromise forms violate axiological necessities. But within them we can distinguish (α) internal duplicity, generating fissions and splits; (β) external grafting, necessitating such devices as metaphysical λ clauses; and (γ) the mutual presupposition of transcendentally refuted contraries, such as conceptual and empirical realism in (objective) idealism and (subjective) empiricism. Usually a combination of all three. As such they are of course liable to immanent critique, turning on the identification of theory/practice inconsistencies, metacritique$_1$ (omissive critique) and metacritique$_2$ (explanatory critique). Philosophical ideologies, like other ideologies, are always already there, but their persistence and mutations have to be explained by the internal and external effects they generate.

It is the illicit fission implicit in the generative separation of the immediate producers from their labour and the fivefold alienation that it produces that underpins the illicit fusion involved in the exchange of non-equivalents intrinsic to the wage contract definitional of a capitalist economy, based on the commodification and reification of labour-power, and ultimately, on Marx's analysis, on abstract homogenized time. It is worth taking a longer look at the figure of illicit fusion (a 1M category) and illicit fission (a 3L category). Illicit fusion is manifest philosophically in identity theories, the epistemic fallacy, anthroporealism and actualism (reductionism and monism), and reification and fetishism, as it is substantially in the exchange of non-equivalents which is the labour contract. Illicit fission is manifest philosophically in the detotalizations and (e.g. theory/practice) splits which result from ontological actualism, monovalence, extensionalism and disembodiment (in which it is most obviously manifest), but also from reification, fetishism and voluntarism, as it is substantially in the non-parity of equivalents which occur when men and women are paid differently for the same work. As already mentioned, illicit fusion may be used to represent sectional as universal interests, as happened at the outbreak of the First World War, while illicit fission performs the converse operation, as arguably was the case in the British miners' strike of 1984/5. What is characteristic of illicit fusion is the absence of a distinction; what is characteristic of illicit fission is the absence of a connection. Both are susceptible to omissive metacritique₁, but we may want to emphasize the difference between them by saying that whereas the former commits an error, the latter omits the truth. Ideologically, illicit fusion is internally duplicit (and thus generates illicit fissions), while illicit fission requires an external graft (thus generating an illicit fusion).

The categorial errors of the reification of facts and the fetishism of closed systems mirror the reification implicit in the commodification of labour-power and the fetishism of commodities. In the same way as actualism collapses powers to their exercise, the wage form confounds the two. Illicit fusion naturalizes, and so eternalizes and universalizes, localizes, indexicalizes, ego-ethno- rather than anthropo-centrifies. In being indifferent to difference, illicit fusion evokes the (1M) stance of the Stoic; in being explicit, illicit fission evokes that of the Unhappy Consciousness in one or other of its modes.

Is illicit fusion the source of the ideological complex we are investigating? No. At a first level, it would seem that ontological monovalence is only sustained on the basis of a Parmenidean para-panentheist or pervasive token monism (which may be fairly attributed to Parmenides on the basis of the first part of the poem by which we know him), a huge illicit fusion. But the monist must detotalize herself and so Parmenidean monism reduces to the gaping illicit fission of a Cratylan silence. But silence is still a way of saying something. Even in dying we cannot escape the conceptuality of praxis. And so Cratylan silence must pass over to the ultimate fission of punctualist ego-present-centric solipsism. Leaving this aside, at a second level, ontological monovalence generates both 1M illicit fusion, making impossible the concept of alterity (by valid perspectival switch) and yielding the first great problem of philosophy, the problem of one and the other, i.e. of self-diremption; and at 3L illicit fission, rendering the concept of totality untenable and producing the second great problem, the problem of the one and the many, which dominates the analytic mainstream in the guise of the problem of induction of universals just as the first one determines the trajectory of its dialectical cousin. At either level the condition of possibility of ontological monovalence is a sequestration. If we read for this sequestration generative separation, i.e. the separation of the immediate producers from their labour, manifest most starkly in the 1M-ish wage form, and the reification and commodification of labour-power, the subject of Marx's first-order critique, the illicit fission of these producers from their product and the four planes of social being can be aligned with Marx's second-order critique, manifest most starkly in the (totality) of the detotalized, exploited and oppressed that was thematized in Chapter 5.2 in the context of the world-historical problem of agency. Conversely, the figure of the parity of equivalents may be used, in counter-hegenomic fashion, to justify the normative ideal of a core equality, based on our shared species-being, and to motivate the unity or totality (which presupposes a unity-in-diversity) of the differentially oppressed as part of a dialectics of totalizing self-in-solidarity in opposition to the exchange of non-equivalents intrinsic to the wage form, and the generative separation on which it is based.

Before we move on to the metacritique of philosophy and the consideration of the ideological effect irrealism generates, it may be useful to look briefly at some political, moral and scientific ideologies. We saw in Chapter 1 that in Hegel's chapter on 'Self-Consciousness' in the *Phenomenology of Mind*, following the Life-and-Death Struggle, various social attitudes, conventionally associated with historical periods, are described. If we generalize the concept of the master—slave relationship to include all relations of exploitation, domination, subjugation and control, we can treat

(a) Stoicism as indifference to such relations on the part of the oppressed subjects (or slaves);
(b) Scepticism as denial in theory, while affirming in practice, the reality of such relations; and
(c) the Unhappy Consciousness as involving either:
   (i) the internalization of the master's ideology, as in the case of so-called Essex man; or
   (ii) the projective duplication of another world, as in the case of absorption in the fantasy worlds of soap or sport, the Royal family, Madonna or other media stars.

It would not be difficult to apply a similar type of analysis to specifically political ideologies, but I leave this for another occasion. Sticking with the master–slave trope but turning now to moral ideologies, we can see how emotivism functions as an ideology for masters, personalism for slaves and decisionism for those who are the slaves of masters who are themselves masters of slaves. Emotivism is the ideology of the leisured elite to whom a philosopher like Rorty appeals; decisionism is the ideology of the bureaucrat; and personalism that fashioned for those who are at the bottom of the global pile.

If we take the Stoicism–Unhappy Consciousness sequence and apply it to attitudes to reality, we can use it to illuminate the transmutation route that orthodox philosophy of science underwent following the collapse of positivism. We can map conventionalism on to Stoicism, post-structuralism on to Scepticism and the pragmatism of Rorty, who admits that there is 'something out there' but avers that we cannot talk about it (at least in philosophy), to the first phase of the Unhappy Consciousness. Feyerabend's 'Dadaist' vision of an unconstrained science would then correspond to the second (superidealist) phase in which we are free to construct any world we like. One could be much more specific about philosophical ideologies, of course. For instance, we could consider Kuhn's rhetoric as providing the ideology of chemistry students, Popper's that of Nobel Prize-winners. Or treat behaviourism as the ideology par excellence of manipulative instrumental reason, while social constructionism often appears as the self-theory of those who need only referentially detach themselves from discursive acts, whose wider social presuppositions are unquestioned.

But it is time to turn from the zoo to the heart of the ideological jungle.

§ 2 On the Metacritique of Philosophy

My aim in this section and the next is to unify the (explanatory) metacritique$_2$ of philosophy around the critique of ontological monovalence. We have seen in Chapter 3 how irrealism about truth leads to the aporiai of the transdictive complex. Analogously irrealism about society, and more especially the pre-existence of social structure (see Chapter 5), must lead to solipsism. Irrealism about transfactuality (see Chapter 2) must lead to irrealism about causality and ultimately about existence. Irrealism about tense (the A-series) — see Chapter 4 — must lead to irrealism about the past and future, more generally space and time in the tacit complicity of transcendentally refuted contraries, which are dialectical counterparts, ego-

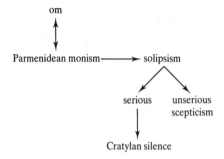

Figure A.9

present-centric punctualist indexicalism (position I) and blockist closure (position II), leading once more to irrealism about causality and thence to irrealism aboiut existence. Irrealism about negativity (see Chapter 6) again leads to irrealism about causality and thence existence, and either position I or position II, that is, to Cratylan solipsism at the subjective pole and/or Parmenidean monism at the objective one. Now Parmenidean monism, which initiated the western philosophical quest, detotalizes the monist. If you cannot say what is not you cannot say anything at all. Even more seriously — this is the real reductio of Parmenidean monism — the absence of the concept of absence, which entails the absence of the concept of alterity, makes referential detachment impossible. So Parmenidean monism must reduce either to an unserious scepticism — like the scepticism of the modern academy — or to serious scepticism and resort to Cratylan solipsism. For an act implies change, hence absenting, hence another. Ontological monovalence entails monism which reduces to solipsism; it is the elimination of absence and hence change and it implies the elimination of alterity and hence diversity and multiplicity alike. It immediately generates the epistemic fallacy, actualism, the absence of alethic truth and hence primal squeeze, together with transfactuality, spatio-temporality, intra-activity and sociality (cf. 1M–4D). This is depicted in Figures A.9 and A.10. We thus have a line representable as in Figure A.11 or more fully and metacritically as in Figure A.12.

The absence of a necessary concept is immediately manifest in a void, which, insofar as it violates an axiological necessity, must be filled or covered by the presence of another, e.g. in a Tina compromise form. The presence of a false or counterfeit concept immediately or mediately induces a split. Thus we saw in Chapter 2.3 how actualism necessarily divides reality into that part which it can 'save', and that part which it cannot, producing a dilemma between the universal and the empirical or conceptual and between philosophy and science; that is to say, the actual, presupposed as self-identical with itself (cf. 1M), must split (cf. 2E), leaving one or more metacritically identifiable absences or voids (cf. 2E), viz. of natural necessity, ontological stratification, transfactual efficacy and alethic truth, and depositing a reification (cf. 4D), viz. in the constant conjunction (closed systemic) analysis of laws. Exactly the same happens in the case of ontological monovalence, extensionalism and at

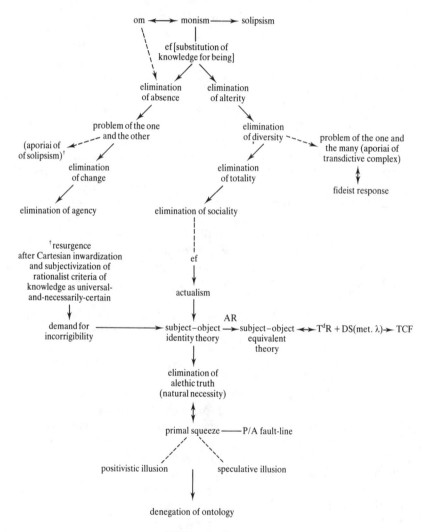

Figure A.10

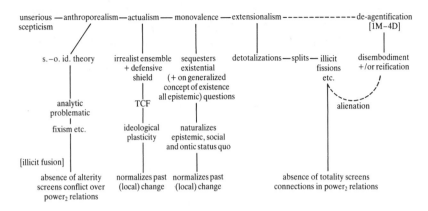

Figure A.11

4D (and the activity-dependent domain of 5C). The void produced by the detotalization of being which is the consequence of the denegation of the absent produces a split between the fully self-present in any present (which can only be a punctualist now) and the extruded remainder of reality. And a split and dilemma between the conjunctive blockist past, present and future, inside and outside, and the disjunctive sequence of indexicalist immediately present presents.[†] These two splits are manifest in Hegel as demi's — demi-actualities and demi-presents, the index of his failure to achieve an absolute absolute.

At 3L ontological extensionalism again divides reality into that part which is merely externally related and that part which is not. For the latter it cannot account. This is manifest in such aporiai as the necessity for an intentionalist analysis of the same to sustain any logical extensionalism, the inability to think intra-activity or even the distinction, let alone the co-incidence or connection, of distinctions and connections. It functions ideologically to screen connection and so dialectical contradiction and social conflicts, on the one hand, and dialectical intradependence or unity and social solidarity, on the other, alike. At 4D the split between reification in the extrinsic aspect

---

[†] If it is, as I have argued, the absence of the concept of absence in the form of ontological monovalence that unifies the problems of philosophy, it is not surprising that it should produce not just a solipsism which is ineffable about itself (as in the *Tractatus*) but also a solipsism which is ineffable *simpliciter* — a position from which nothing can be said or done. This is the heat-death of philosophical rationality and the outcome of its primordial quest. But we can see very clearly how the ideological effect of 2E is to sequester existential questions and mask their epistemological and ontological contingency as at 1M reality is destratified and the epistemic status quo reified, naturalized and eternalized. Both block change.

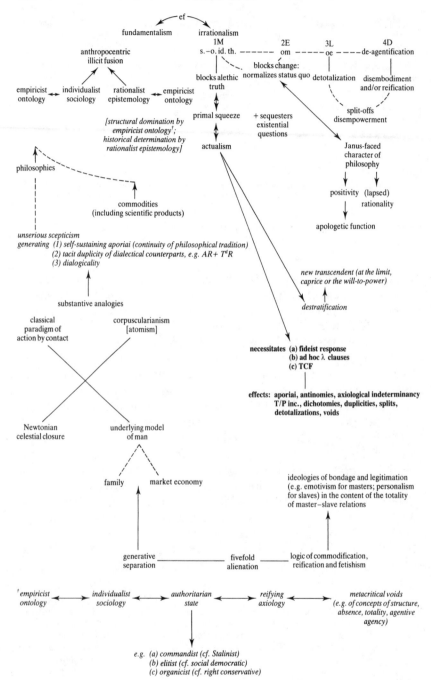

Figure A.12

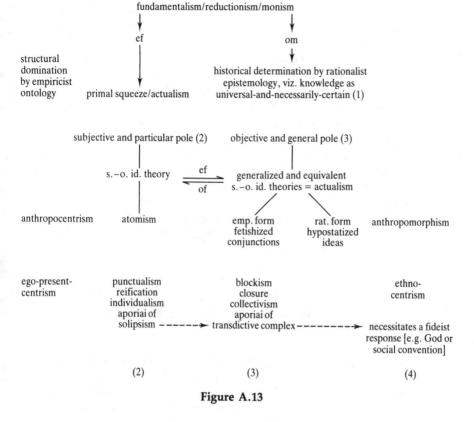

Figure A.13

and dualistic disembodiment (e.g. in a denaturalized hermeneutic) in the intrinsic aspect is explicit. This is easily generalized into a split between 'us' and 'them', as in what has been nicely called 'the syntax of hegemony'.[1] Similarly, at 5C (fifth component) there arises the dichotomy between structure and agency (the reified and the voluntarized) generated by the absence of a transformationalism, as that at 4D is produced by the lack of the concept of intentional causality and more generally of an emergent powers materialism. Or, again, relationism (of a sort) is confined to the family, while individualism reigns supreme in a free market economy fortified by an authoritarian quasi-collectivist state.

I have so far argued that it is the fear of change, or more fully the unconscious and normally aporetic normalization of the status quo ante, that proximately accounts for the intra-discursive reproduction of philosophies. It is their normalization of existing social arrangements, and in particular mediated via their role in the generation of ideologies of bondage and legitimation of existing power$_2$ relations which they thus help to discursively moralize, that explains their extra-discursive reproduction. But, as I have stressed, this is always Janus-faced.

Now I have already set out the $(0) \rightarrow (1) \rightarrow (2) \leftrightarrow (3)$ schema, where (3) is the *proxy-realist dual* of anthroporealism. Anthropomorphism is what corresponds at the objective, general pole of subject—object identity or equivalent theory in response to the subjective, particular pole of subject—object identity theory, united by the intertwining of the epistemic and ontic fallacies. Figure A.13 illustrates its historical genesis and structure. Descartes is the great subjectivizer who by inwardizing rationalist criteria of knowledge ensures the eventual victory of empiricism.

It is now time to pursue a unification of the problems of philosophy around the critique of ontological monovalence and the epistemic fallacy, and the alienations and reifications they entail; and so thematize the problem of the *real* resolution of the problems of philosophy.

§ 3 On the Problems of Philosophy and Their Real Resolution

It is not quite true to say, as Marx did in his celebrated 1859 Preface to *A Contribution to the Critique of Political Economy*, that 'mankind sets itself only such tasks as it is able to solve',[†] since we have seen that it is precisely a characteristic of philosophical 'packages' or theory (underlying generative presupposition) problem-field [aporetic and dialogical character of discourse] solution sets [Tina compromise forms] that they generate self-sustaining aporiai. On the other hand, another set of epigrams from Marx may seem to the point. In the 1844 *Manuscripts* he argues, contra the Young Hegelians and Stirner who believe 'one has only to get a few ideas out of one's head to abolish the conditions which have given rise to those ideas', that 'the resolution of theoretical *oppositions* is possible only in a practical way, and hence is by no means a task of knowledge but a task of *actual* life; which philosophy could not resolve because it grasped the task *only* as a theoretical one'. Hence the famous eleventh thesis on Feuerbach, 'the philosophers have only *interpreted* the world in various ways; the point is to *change* it'. This book seeks to give a critical diagnosis and rational resolution of the

---

[†] The text continues 'since closer examination will always show that the problem itself arises when the material conditions for its solution are already present or at least in the course of its formation'.

problems of philosophy. But it is under no illusion that this will thereby abolish them. That rather requires the transformed transformative praxis that its metacritical₂ explanation indicates.

In the preceding section we established the schema depicted in Figure A.14. Corresponding to (1), (2)−(4), (5) and (6) and (0) we can match antinomial, immanent, omissive and meta₂critiques. It is the job of a metacritique₁ to identify the T in TPF(SS), that is, the *dialectical ground* in, as we saw in Chapter 9, an irrealist problematic of transcendentally refuted contraries (which are also dialectical counterparts or complements), viz. (2) and (3) and (2) + (3) and (4), in an ensemble of categorially significant mistakes. It is a job of a metacritique₂ to explain them. What have we learned from the preceding section? That is to say, how might one set about the first step (metacritique₁) of an explanatory critique of irrealism? *What does irrealism make impossible?* One has to be specific here. At 1M the epistemic fallacy and at 2E ontological monovalence block change (epistemic and ontic alike); they congeal, acting as ideologies of stasis, legitimating the status quo ante (which means normalizing local and recent changes, or, in the lapsed time of philosophy, more distance ones). Inter alia, this doubly dogmatically reinforces current knowledge and, on the generalized concepts of reference and existence, it sequesters existential questions, screening the epistemological contingency of what is held to be and the ontological contingency of what is the case. But 1M actualism undermines the concept of natural necessity and thus prohibits the asking of structural or essential questions, so rendering impossible the kind of concrete utopian exercise which could naturalistically ground hope for oppressed subjects₂. Similarly it blocks the concept of alethic truth, which is required to give a rational resolution of most of the standard textbook problems of philosophy. The point of identity becomes, via the anthroporealist exchanges, a point of duplicity and equivocation and further flexibility is endowed to it by (4), (5) and (6) so that it is a point of ideological plasticity, in virtue of which almost any measure or position can be justified. Metacritically, 2E sets up theory/practice inconsistenies and the Tina compromise formations

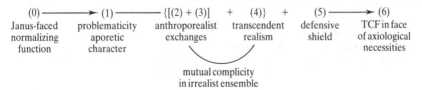

Figure A.14

they generate. The significant question we will have to ask here is *why do philosophical problems typically take the form of an opposition?* It is easy enough to see how they can become real. If one assumes the uniformity of nature and knowledge, then change in either dimension will produce a real problem. 3L detotalizes, fragments, disconnects, alienates, splits and splits off. 4D de-agentifies either by reification and/or by disembodiment at the level of agency. But the 'axiological imperative' will ensure that the given, and its auto-poietic conditions of possibility, are transformatively negated. Demonstration of the illicit fission — and fusion — of past, present and future and the exchange of ethnocentricity and ethnomorphism (paralleling the anthroporealist exchange), which underpins chauvinism, e.g. in war or on the football field, or at the job bureau, will illustrate but not dissolve the problems of philosophy. If the social effects of social ideologies will be, as I have argued, to legitimate the recent past or local custom (the unconscious and aporetic attempt to congeal what has been here), we can see easily enough how spatio-temporal irrealism is of a piece with 1M−4D irrealism; just as alethic realism is entailed by actualism. Moral irrealism, denying that there is a moral truth, makes the world fit for emotivist masters and decisionist-makers to sustain existing power$_2$ structures, as at the level of 5C (fifth component — society) we are offered the tacitly complicit options of voluntarism and reification. At the same time, ethical anti-naturalism, splitting off the realm of values from the realm of facts (a monstrous detotalization), denies any possible moral truth grounds.

We have to distinguish here

(α) real occurrences of the problems of philosophy, i.e. their realization in practice;

(β) the extent to which the problems of philosophy are illusory, that is, to which they can be rationally resolved in theory;

(γ) the conditions under which they can be, more or less rationally, overcome, i.e. abolished or dissolved in practice (both intra- and extra-philosophical).

Clearly there will be overlaps and causal connections between (α)−(γ).

Now underlying the fear of change — or, better, its denegation (lapsed denial in theory, lagged affirmation in practice) — are the following set of phenomena:

(a) Alienation, especially in the form of the acceptance of an Unhappy Consciousness, of a split between philosophy's rational mission and its 'positive', apologetic (normalizing), rationalizing effect. This is manifest superficially in its aporetic character (1), more deeply in duplicities, theory/practice inconsistencies, detotalizations, metaphysical λ clauses and Tina compromise forms (cf. (2)–(6)). It is especially true of its modern period, in which a Hume is as split as a Hegel from reality, as disengaged in his philosophy from materialized practices (a fact perhaps ultimately to be explained by the division of labour which lends to philosophers the character of a [normally] dependent elite).

(b) The reification or naturalization of the status quo ante, either by explicit theory (as in subjective empiricism) or by unconscious reflection or absorption (as in objective idealism), which acts so as to legitimate existing power$_2$ relations.

(c) The exploitation of normally, but not always, lapsed analogical grammars.

Why do philosophical problems typically take the form of an opposition? Problems pose (potentially practical) dilemmas. (I) They are to be explained by the absence of a necessary concept (the non-actual real, absenting process, intra-activity, agentive agency, moral truth, the tacit duplicity of dialectical counterparts) and theoretically remedied by its presence. (II) In its absence, a metacritical void, philosophical aporetics or axiological necessity will produce a false or counterfeit concept. Both (I) and (II) exemplify one oppositional figure, *the dialectics of co-inclusion*,[2] or of absence and presence, more precisely of positive contraries and negative sub-contraries, which, in the mode of succession over distanciated space-time, is the 'rational' core of Hegelian dialectics. Moreover, it is this figure which unifies the problems of philosophy and their resolution (as connected and differentiated by $(\alpha)-(\gamma)$. For it embraces the concepts of generative separation, master–slave relations and the archetypical ideological 'attitudes' to them; the totalizing depth praxis of the oppressed and most of the specifically 'dialectical' categories of dialectical critical realism (the presence of the past, constellationality, Tina formation), without the reduction of externality or difference. This is involved in the metacritique$_2$ of philosophies, as I shall show in *Philosophical Ideologies*, in the dialectics of dialectical and analytical reasoning, in the multifold completion of the traditional table of oppositions, in the explanation of fission, alienation and change. Conversely, denial of the dialectics of co-inclusion renders change unsustainable and fixes the lineaments of the analytic problematic, forming the backbone of an ideology of stasis and repression.

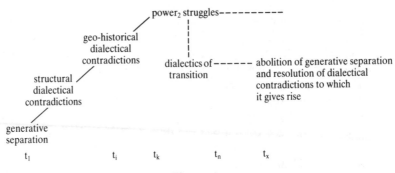

Figure A.15

The most relevant forms of the dialectic of co-inclusion for the understanding of change are:

(a) as dialectical contradictions in the modes of ontological stratification, absence, intra-activity and agentive agency;
(b) as social conflicts in the modes of power$_2$ struggles, constituted by or grounded in dialectical contradictions; and
(c) as dialectical transitions over distanciated space-time.

Starting from a generative separation, initiating a power$_2$ relation, Figure A.15 illustrates a possible schema. Resistance may always be expected in some or other form. But only at time t_k does it take the explicit form of power struggles over the generative separation. And if, to take Marx's epigram seriously, theoretical oppositions are questions of actual life, one should not expect (γ) to pertain without a social dialectic of transition, however enlightened philosophy becomes, or however rationally resolved at level (β) its problems may be. In any event, this schema illustrates the way in which (α)–(γ) are united by the structure of oppositionality.

It should be said in respect of the difference between (β) and (γ) that exposing an illicit fusion, such as involved in subject–object identity theory, actualism or blockism, or an illicit fission, such as involved in atomism, extensionalism or indexicalism, will often show the opposition not to be a real one after all. There are three main ways, each instantiating the dialectics of co-inclusion, in which this can occur — by situating a mediating figure such as constellationality in the problem of the reality of the external world; by showing the common mistaken causal ground(s) of transcendentally refutable dialectical counterparts (or tacitly duplicit contraries); or by repairing a metacritical void, such as the concept of alethic truth in respect of the problem of induction.[†] So it is incumbent upon us to distinguish between illusory and real oppositions. The two come together, of course, in the metacritical$_2$ exploration of the problem-fields of philosophy, such as that schematized in Figure A.12 on p. 235 above.

At this juncture two questions may be posed. (1) Is fear of change really such a potent force as I have made out? (2) How widespread is the structure of oppositionality in philosophy? (1) It is fear of change in the course of nature that generates the problem of induction, the archetypal aporia of the transdictive complex in modern times, as it was a worrying relativism that generated the Platonic self-predicative paradoxes. It was the demand for the universal-and-necessarily-certain that formed the basis of Aristotelian kinetic actualist hylomorphism. It was the drive for incorrigibility, the renaissance of the quest for an unhypothetical starting-point, that produced the Cartesian *cogito* and paved the way for the aporiai of the solipsistic complex. It is the same drive that produces the reification of facts and/or the hypostatization of ideas. Then with the coming of the age of modernity there arises the phenomenon of historicity (the self-reflexive consciousness of history) — the first symptom of which is to be found in the younger Hegel (Mark I) but which is apparent throughout nineteenth-century thought — and the normalization of change follows. Then comes the period of super- or radical historicity, the normalization of the changing of change, only registered much later (Bachelard, Popper, Kuhn) in the lapsed time of philosophy. Various attitudes to this phenomenon, along different dimensionalities, can be mapped (progressive/nostalgic; emancipatory/regressive; universalist/ethnocentric), corresponding to the Janus-faced character of philosophy. Then, when change stops, or appears to stop — in 1973, with the end of the post-war boom and a variety of other phenomena which I have discussed elsewhere[3] — comes the age of 'post-modernity', the repression of time, and the re-emergence of the thematics of the end of history and of ideology.

Change is ontologically oppositional because, as we have seen, at the point of transition the traditional table of opposites is completed by a combination of positive contraries and negative sub-contraries. This is also a real problem for philosophy, which is remedied in

---

[†] Variants of these strategies are situation within metacritical limits (neither fixism nor fluxism); recognition of the identities of ultimata (including those in the processual dynamic of the Achilles' Heel critique; and emergent domains) and/or of the identities of identity and change and identity and difference in their rhythmics or essential constitution or both (as in the case of personal identity where a person's identity is radically constituted by her process of formation and her changing intra-subjective relations).

theory by the concepts of real and transformative negation and in practice by the transformative praxis consisting in the self-emancipation of the oppressed₂. This is perhaps the point to emphasize that the kind of phenomenon of oppositionality which I am theorizing is always grounded in an absence or lapse, typically for the problems of philosophy the absence of alethic truth and transfactuality (at 1M), of unity-in-diversity and other totalizing and/or mediating figures such as intra-activity (including tacit duplicity) hiatus (at 3L), of agentive agency (intentional causality) at 4D and pre-existing ongoing structure at 5C, and at 2E the absence of absence itself and its derivative figures, including real or false oppositionality, whether in the form of change or not. Diagnostically, the alienation, reification and exploitation of lapsed analogical grammars that I have pinpointed as underlying the repression of change is manifest most obviously in the failure to complete the traditional table of opposition in any of the three modes I have distinguished as $(\alpha)-(\gamma)$.

(2) Oppositionality is most starkly manifest in the modes of social struggle, dialectical contradiction and transition, but irrelevance, reductio ad absurdum and incoherence manifest absences and as such constitute illicit fissions, splits or gulfs as general as oppositionality per se. But just consider some of the myriad figures that oppositionality in philosophy takes:

- Co-inclusion — in any of the three modes we have discussed.
- Dilemma — either/or (or rejection of bivalence or excluded middle or both).
- Antinomy — both (or rejection of non-contradiction).
- The presence of the past and outside, especially in the form of existential constitution by geo-historical processes of formation.
- Existential constitution, permeation or connection of one internally related element by another.
- Inversion — reversal of hierarchy.
- Chiasmus — juxtaposition of the terms of a polarity.
- Aporiai — interminably insoluble indeterminacy.
- Ambivalence — tendency to both of two or more incompatible positions.
- Anomaly — incompatibility with an established pattern.
- Ambiguity — vague indeterminacy of positions.
- Denegation — denial in theory, affirmation in practice.
- Unseriousness — the inversion of denegation.
- Split-off — e.g. in the form of extra-jection, pro-jection or retro-jection.

- Duplicity — equivocation between incompatible positions.
- Paradox — incompatibility between established (e.g. epistemological) canons and perceived reality.
- Complicity — acceptance of or dependence upon an incompatible position.
- Domination — in any of a number of modes including suppression, exclusion, and fragmentation.
- Plasticity — susceptibility to a multiplicity of incompatible positions.
- Compromise formation — inconsistent ensemble forced by the reality principle.
- Alienation — estrangement from self.
- Theory/practice inconsistency — e.g. immanent critique.
- Theory/practice incompleteness — e.g. lack of dialectical universalizability.

Or consider the multiplicity of modes of contradiction (including 'inner complicity') or the number of occasions in which the principle of non-contradiction is violated, suspended, bracketed or over-reached. Or consider the alienation involved in the Janus-faced character of philosophy poised between rationality and positivity.[†] It is no wonder that philosophical problems typically take the form of oppositions. They are remedied by repairing the absences which underpin them, constituting their dialectical grounds (the alethic truth of their falsity — irrealism). They are reproduced by their conditioning and efficacy (including their intended consequences). They are abolished by overthrowing their dialectical grounds.

We are then justified in considering the problems of philosophy for their more general diagnostic social value. Thus consider Figure A.16. It will be remembered that negativity is often projected on to the ethical plane, where it functions as a forbidding 'not'; and that, conversely, aesthetics is often roped on to repair the oppositional aporiai of 4D and 5C — of mind and body and intra-/inter-subjectivity, more generally to effect a reconciliation to opposition; and in aesthetic experience a reconciliation to power$_2$ subjugation (or in disguise of or compensation

---

[†] Again consider the class of what I have elsewhere called problematic axiological choice situations, characterized by axiological indeterminacy (the absence of grounds for choice, which is not the same as the axiological underdetermination or openness necessary for freedom of choice), where a non-valent response may complete the table of opposition, as in the co-incidence of identity and change in processes of transformation or identity and differences in processes of structural generation, or in the limit situations of dispositional rhythmic and constellational identities where opposites are co-present.

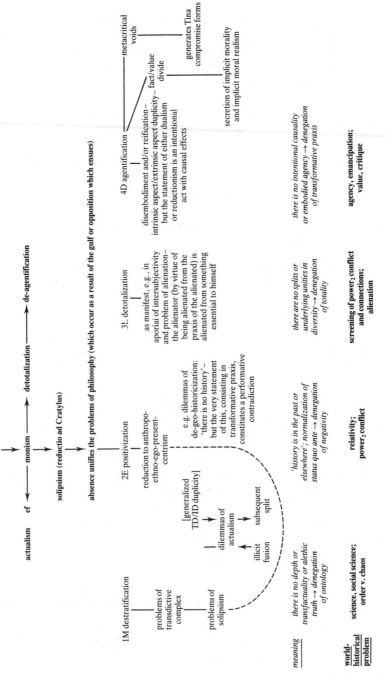

Figure A.16

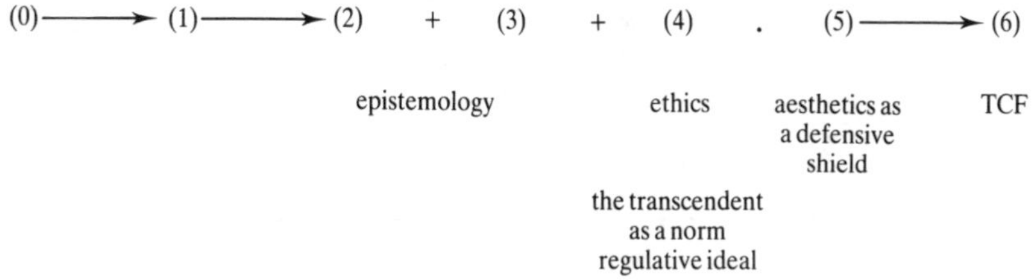

$$(0) \longrightarrow (1) \longrightarrow (2) \quad + \quad (3) \quad + \quad (4) \quad . \quad (5) \longrightarrow (6)$$

| | epistemology | | ethics | aesthetics as a defensive shield | TCF |

the transcendent
as a norm
regulative ideal

Figure A.17

for opposition of interest) in four-planar social being. Thus it is interesting to consider the possibility of the schema in Figure A.17. Alternatively one could shift register and consider part of (5) as ethics (or philosophy?) and (6) as aesthetic experience (or culture?).

I have been engaged in a 2E unification of the problems and problematics of philosophy. Earlier we have seen how the two main problem groups at 2E can be unified by seeing each of (a) the nodal oppositions at points of a changing process of transition, (b) the structural or geo-historical oppositions of transfactually efficacious tendencies and (c) the oppositionality of groups in social conflict around structurally sedimented power$_2$ relations as involving the co-presence of positive absence and negative presence (or of positive contraries and negative sub-contraries). The oppositionality of the third type may exemplify the logical features of either or both nodal processual transitional and structural and/or geo-historical dialectical contradictory paradigms. The real basis for the resolution of the problems of philosophy lies here — in the abolition of structurally sedimented power relations of domination (including relations of exploitation of nature) in the development of the life of four-planar social being (including the unfinished moral evolution of the species informing our response to the intra-social and eco-social contradictions currently confronting humanity); that is to say, in the project of universal human emancipation, which in Chapter 7 I sought to show to be implicit in every act.

Notes

1. Is Philosophy Worth It?

1. See especially *The Philosophical Discourse of Modernity*, Cambridge 1987.
2. See *Conjectures and Refutations*, London 1959.
3. *De Caelo* 1.10.279 b 5.
4. D. Oldroyd, *The Arch of Knowledge*, London 1986.
5. 'On Vagueness', *Australasian Journal of Psychology and Philosophy*, 1 (1923).
6. *Dialectic*, London 1993.
7. Oxford 1980.
8. For the philosophical aporiai to which this gives rise, see my *Philosophy and the Idea of Freedom*, Oxford 1991, Part 2.
9. *Lectures and Conversations*, ed. C.J. Barnet, Oxford 1966, pp. 15–16.
10. Oxford 1962, p. 249. Original emphasis.

2. Explanation and the Laws of Nature

1. See L. Kolakowski, *Positivist Philosophy*, Harmondsworth 1972.
2. *Popular Scientific Lectures*, Chicago 1894, p. 192.
3. See *A Realist Theory of Science*, 2nd edn, Brighton 1978 (Hemel Hempstead 1989), Chapter 2.4.
4. *Objective Knowledge*, Oxford 1972, Chapter 1.
5. *The Structure of Scientific Revolutions*, 2nd edn, Chicago 1970.
6. 'Falsification and the Methodology of Scientific Research Programmes', in I. Lakatos and A. Musgrave, eds, *Criticism and the Growth of Knowledge*, Cambridge 1967.
7. *Against Method*, 3rd edn, London 1993.
8. Cf. M. Hesse, *Models and Analogies in Science*, Indianapolis 1966, and R. Harré, *The Principles of Scientific Thinking*, London 1970, especially Chapter 2.
9. *Science and Hypothesis*, New York 1903, p. 98.
10. See my *Scientific Realism and Human Emancipation*, London 1986, p. 30.
11. See *A History of Philosophy and Social Sciences*, Oxford 1987, p. 10.
12. Cf. my *Possibility of Naturalism*, 2nd edn, Hemel Hempstead 1989, Chapter 4.4.
13. For a discussion, see S. Haack, *Philosophy of Logics*, Cambridge 1977.
14. *Scientific Realism and Socialist Thought*, Hemel Hempstead 1989.
15. Ibid.
16. For which see my entry on 'Knowledge, theory of', in *Dictionary of Twentieth-Century Social Thought*, eds W. Outhwaite and P. Bottomore, Oxford 1992.
17. 'Laws and Explanation in Sociology', in J. Hughes et al., *Classical Disputes in Sociology*, London 1987.
18. See, e.g., A. Donagan, 'The Popper–Hempel Theory Reconsidered', in *Philosophical Analysis in History*, New York 1966. Cf. also W. Outhwaite, *New Philosophies of Social Science*, London 1986; P. Manicas, *A History and Philosophy of Social Science*, Oxford 1967; A Sayer, *Method in Social Science: A Realist Approach*, 2nd edn, London 1992; and A. Collier, *Critical Realism: An Introduction to Roy Bhaskar's Philosophy*, London 1994.

19. For discussion (and criticism) of the reasons why Putnam now rejects this, see *Dialectic*, p. 227.

20. Cf. ibid., Chapter 2.10 and Chapter 3.5.

3. Reference, Truth and Meaning

1. *A System of Logic*, 8th edn, London 1961, Book III,Chapter 3, Section 1.
2. Cf. my *Philosophy and the Idea of Freedom*, Part 2.
3. *The Structure of Scientific Revolutions*, p. 121.
4. See *The Possibility of Naturalism*, p. 47.
5. Harmondsworth 1978.
6. Oxford 1980.
7. Oxford 1986, p. 67.
8. *Individuals*, London 1959, and *The Bounds of Sense*, London 1966.
9. Cf. *A Realist Theory of Science*, p. 87.
10. Cf. J.N. Findlay, *Kant and the Transcendental Object*, Oxford 1981, Chapter VIII.
11. See my entry on 'Truth', in *A Dictionary of Marxist Thought*, ed. T. Bottomore, Oxford 1983.

4. Causality, Change and Emergence

1. Cf. D. Parfitt, *Reasons and Persons*, Oxford 1984.
2. For the feminist critique of this concept, see Chapter 10.2.
3. Cf. J. Berger, *Keeping a Rendez-Vous*, London 1993.
4. London 1991.
5. See *Dialectic*, Chapter 3.6.
6. *Causality and Determination*, Cambridge 1971, p. 21.
7. Cf. D. Dennett, *Consciousness Explained*, London 1991.
8. For an introduction, see W. Outhwaite, *Habermas*, Cambridge 1994.
9. See *Dialectic*, Chapter 1.8.
10. See, e.g., R. Harré, 'Exploring the Human *Umwelt*', in R. Bhaskar, ed., *Harré and His Critics*, Oxford 1990.
11. Cf. 'Falsification and the Methodology of Scientific Research Programmes'.

5. Making It Happen (Social Agency)

1. London 1956.
2. *Critical Hermeneutics*, Cambridge 1980.
3. *The Constitution of Society*, Cambridge 1984.
4. I am here indebted to M. Archer, *Morphogenesis* (forthcoming), Chapter 5.
5. Cf. *Dialectic*, Chapter 2.9, especially pp. 164–7.
6. Cf. M. Rustin, *The Good Society and the Inner World*, London 1991, and J. Shotter, *Conversational Realities*, London 1993.

6. Dialectic

1. *Man of Reason*, London 1984, Chapter 5.
2. 'Shaping Ends: Reflections on Fukuyama', *New Left Review*, 202 (1993).

3. Cf. *Reclaiming Reality*, London 1989, Chapter 7, Section II.
4. Letter to Engels, 14 January 1858.
5. *Capital, Vol. 1*, Harmondsworth 1976, p. 102.
6. See *Dialectic*, especially Chapter 4.8.
7. Cf. ibid., pp. 188ff.

7. Living Well

1. See W. Outhwaite, *Habermas*, Cambridge 1994.
2. See *Dialectic*, Chapter 3.7–3.11.
3. Oxford 1991.
4. Oxford 1990.

8. Dialectical Critical Realism

1. In *Dialectic*, Chapter 2.10, p. 197, Chapter 3.5, p. 247 and Chapter 3.11, p. 303. The argument that all the basic categories of dialectical critical realism can be derived from absence is given at ibid., p. 248.
2. Cf. ibid., p. 248.
3. In ibid., Chapter 2.10.

9. Socrates and So On?

1. J. Locke, *An Essay Concerning Human Understanding*, Book III, Chapter 6, point 9.
2. See, e.g., *Spectres of Marx*, London 1994.

10. Philosophy and the Dialectic of Emancipation

1. *The Critique of Pure Reason*, p. xxxiv. Original emphasis.
2. Cf. Y. Yovel, *Kant and the Philosophy of History*, Princeton, New Jersey 1980.
3. *People and Pronouns*, Oxford 1991.
4. *Dialectic*, Chapter 4.7–4.8.
5. London 1987.
6. On this, see *Dialectic*, Chapter 3.11.
7. See *Scientific Realism and Human Emancipation*, Chapter 1.3

Appendix

1. M. Billig, 'Nationalism and Richard Rorty: The Test as a Flag for *Pax Americana*', *New Left Review*, 202 (1993).
2. On the dialectics of co-inclusion, see my *Dialectic*, Chapter 2.3–2.4.
3. See my 'Critical Realism in Context', in R. Bhaskar, ed., *A Meeting of Minds*, London 1991, Chapter 3.

Glossary

1M = Prime (first) moment. Characterized by non-identity relations, such as those involved in the critique of the epistemic and anthropic fallacies, of identity theory and actualism. Unified by the concept of alterity, it emphasizes existential intransitivity, referential detachment, the reality principle and ontology which it necessitates. More concretely, it fastens on to the transcendentally necessary stratification and differentiation of the world, entailing concepts of causal powers and generative mechanisms, alethic truth and transfactuality, natural necessity and natural kinds. Its dialectics are characteristically of stratification and ground, but also of inversion and virtualization. Its metacritics turn on the isolation of the error of destratification.

2E = Second edge. Unified by the category of absence, from which the whole circuit of 1M−4D links and relations can be derived, its critical cutting edge is aimed at the Parmenidean doctrine of ontological monovalance (q.v.), the Platonic analysis of negation and change in terms of difference and the Kantian analysis of negative into positive predicates. It spans the gamut of categories of negativity, contradiction and critique. It emphasizes the tri-unity of causality, space and time in tensed rhythmic spatializing process, thematizing the presence of the past and existentially constitutive process. Its dialectics are typically of process, transition, frontier and node, but also generally of opposition including reversal. Its metacritics pivot on the isolation of the error of positivization and the oppositional aporiai to which it inevitably gives rise.

3L = Third level. Unified by the category of totality, it pinpoints the error of ontological extensionalism, including the hypostatization of thought. It encompasses such categories and themes as reflexivity, emergence, constellationality, holistic causality, internal relationality and intra-activity, but also detotalization, alienation, split and split-off, illicit fusion and fission. Its dialectics are of centre and periphery, form and content, figure and ground, generative separation and de-alienation, retotalization in a unity-in-diversity. Its metacritics pivot on the identification of detotalization. There is a special affinity with 1M, since totality is a structure.

4D = Fourth dimension. Unified by the category of transformative praxis or agency. In the human sphere it is implicit in the other three. Metacritically, it pinpoints two complementary kinds of ontological de-agentification — (dualistic) disembodiment, typical of (e.g. discourse in) the intrinsic aspect (q.v.), and (reductionist) reification, characteristic of the extrinsic aspect. There is a special affinity with 2E, since agency is (intentional) causality, which is absenting. Agency is sustained philosophically by an emergent powers materialist orientation and substantively by the concept of four-planar social being in nature with the moral evolution of the species, like the future generally, open. Its dialectics are at the site of ideological and material struggles, but also of absolute reason, and it incorporates dialectical critical realism's dialectic of desire to freedom.

5C = Fifth component. Supervenient on 4D, since all the concepts necessary for a philosophical characterization of sociality can be derived from the sole premiss of intentional agency. Positively it asserts a transformationalism, which sees structure as dependent upon but necessary for agency; a relationalism which grasps society as a geo-historically dynamic relational system of positioned practices; and a critical naturalism comprehending society as characterized by sui generis principles but subsumable within a critical realist account of science. See Chapter 5.

A-series. The ordination of events by the explicitly tensed past, present and future as distinct from the B-serial earlier, simultaneous and later or the spatio-temporally indefinite C-series.

Absence. Understood to include non-existence anywhere anywhen. It is systematically bipolar, designating absenting (distanciating and/or trans-forming) process as well as simple absence in a more or less determinate level-/context-specific region of space-time; and in fact reveals a fourfold polysemy: product, process, process-in-product and product-in-process, which may be recursively embedded and systematically intermingled. It includes, but is far from exhausted by, the past and outside. It is the central category of dialectic, whether conceived as argument, change or the augmentation of (or aspiration to) freedom, which depend upon the identification and elimination of mistakes, states of affairs and constraints, or more generally ills — argued to be absences alike.

Absolute reason (or dialectical rationality). The unity — or, better, coherence — of theory and practice in practice.

Actualism. The reduction of the necessary and the possible, constitutive of the domain of the real, to the actual. Actualism is inherently dilemmatic since these reductions cannot be consistently carried out. This is readily witnessed in open systems, where actualism can be saved only by the forfeit of knowledge (i.e. philosophy sustained at the price of science) or, as in the case of the Hegelian demi-actual, by according the non-actual a lower ontological status as irrational existents. In general $D_r > D_a > D_s$, whether D_s is empirical or conceptual.

Alethic truth. A species of ontological truth constituting and following on the truth of, or real reason(s) for, or dialectical ground of, *things*, as distinct from *propositions*, possible in virtue of the ontological stratification of the world and attainable in virtue of the dynamic character of science.

Alienation. The condition of being estranged or separated from what is constitutive of, or essential to, one's nature, causal powers or wellbeing. Its origin is in the Hegelian Beautiful Soul, alienated from her community, which eventually becomes the self-alienation of absolute spirit. In Marx it signifies generative separation or the alienation of the immediate producers from (a) their labour, (b) their product, (c) the means and materials of their production, (d) each other, and the nexus of social relations within which their production takes place, and (e) ultimately themselves. It is the sign of detotalization and split.

Analytic problematic. Constituted by the illicit ontological contra-position of the logical norms of identity and non-contradiction, and underpinned by the mutually endorsing epistemic and ontic fallacies, it entails 'identity-thinking' and, inter alia, 'fixism', i.e. the presupposition of fixed subjects, generating an ideology of stasis and repression.

Anthropism. Incorporates, subjectively, anthropocentrism — literally, taking man as the centre or goal of the cosmos — and, objectively, projective anthropomorphism — painting or interpreting the cosmos in the image of man. The anthropic fallacy is the analysis or definition of being in terms of human being. As such, it underpins anthroporealism in its various guises — empirical, conceptual, Nietzschean (will-to-power) realism. Anthroporealism is implicit in subject — object identity or equivalent theory, where it involves a tacit exchange of epistemic and ontic fallacies.

Autonomy. Self-determination. Rational autonomy entails the capacity (hence the knowledge, power and opportunity) and disposition to act in one's real interests. A theoretico-practical bridge concept linking truth to freedom mediated by wisdom in a two-way dialectic.

Blockism. The postulation of a simultaneous conjunctive totality of all events.

Cause/Causation. A cause is typically either an antecedent condition or a generative mechanism. The causal chain in *Plato Etc.* characteristically consists in the transfactual efficacy of the generative mechanisms of a structure, the rhythmic (spatio-temporal) exercise of their causal powers, possibly multiply mediated by holistic causality, and, in the human sphere, dependent upon intentional human agency, codetermining a conjuncture.

Conjuncture. Events in open systems are multiply determined, hence conjunctures, and things are correspondingly compounds.

Consistency/Inconsistency. No general formula for developmental consistency can be given other than progressive import, which is necessarily dependent upon judgement intrinsic to the (description of the) process concerned. Theory/practice consistency in a praxis in a process should be practical, directional and universalizably accountable such that it is transfactual, concrete, actionable and transformative. Theory/practice inconsistency leads to pathologies of action, from repression through compromise formation to ad hoc grafting.

Constellationality. A figure of containment within an over-reaching term (e.g. epistemology within ontology, reasons within causes), from which the over-reached term may be diachronically or synchronically emergent. It may take the form of identity, unity, fluidity, etc. In Hegel it is invariably teleological and a sign of closure.

Constraint. An absolute or relative prohibition, whether natural or social. If remediable, the concept may be negatively generalized in the social sphere to include any kind of ill.

Contradiction. This concept ranges from constraints to conflicts. External should be distinguished from internal contradictions, which include the 'inner complicity' arguably necessary for change; and dialectical from logical contradictions, which intersect (when grounded in a common mistake) but are not coterminous. Dialectical contradictions are mutually inclusive internally related oppositions, conveying tendencies to change.

Critique. Paradigmatically distinguished from criticism in that it includes the source or ground of the imputed error. As such an explanatory critique may license a negative evaluation on the causes of the error concerned. An immanent critique isolates a theory/practice inconsistency; a metacritique$_1$ an absence or incompleteness in the theory of the practice which a metacritique$_2$ additionally explains.

De-agentification. This may take the philosophical forms of (dualistic) disembodiment or (reductionist) reification, manifesting itself sociologically in the enervation or fragmentation of agents or groups, impotent empty selves, fissiparousness and alienating retrojective, introjective, projective, etc. modes of identification (e.g. in a fantasy world).

Detotalization. A split, e.g. a dualistic dichotomy or split-off, which may manifest itself in a projected exteriorization or some other guise. Detotalization may be induced by an absence, separation, illicit fission or gulf.

Dialectic. Anything from any relation between differential elements to the absenting of constraints on the absenting of absences, or ills.

Dialectical argument. A form of transcendental argument in which the ontological necessity of false (or limited) premisses, categories or results is established.

Dialectical universalizability. All four aspects of the judgement form are universalizable although in different ways. Action and its groundings should both be universalizable, in the sense of transfactual, concrete, actionable (i.e. agent-specific) and transformatively directional.

Duality. Necessary co-relatives, such as theoretical and practical reasoning, so that typically, but not always, one may be seen under the aspect of the other. In dialectical critical realism dualities are punctuated by a hiatus, which stops a reductionist collapse and signifies a difference in orientation or spatio-temporal lag.

Ego-present-centrism. See Indexicalism.

Emancipation. Characteristically the transition from an unwanted, unnecessary and oppressive situation to a wanted and/or needed and empowering or more flourishing situation.

Emergence. A relationship between two terms such that one term diachronically or perhaps synchronically arises out of the other, but is capable of reacting back on the first and is in any event causally and taxonomically irreducible to it.

Epistemic fallacy. The analysis or definition of statements about being in terms of statements about our knowledge (of being). In subject—object identity or equivalent theory it entails the converse ontic fallacy, viz. the definition or assumption of the compulsive determination of knowledge by being. It nowadays most usually takes the form of the linguistic fallacy, and underpinning it lies the deep-rooted anthropic fallacy.

Explanation. Theoretical explanation consists in description, retroduction, elimination, identification and correction: DREI(C). Applied explanation in resolution, redescription, retroduction, elimination, identification and correction: RRREI(C). Practical problem resolution in diagnosis, explanation and action: DEA. Normative change in description, explanation and transformation: DET.

[Ontological] extensionalism. The division of a totality into discrete, separable, externally related parts, manifest as in, for example, the extrusion of thought, or contradiction, or morality, from reality — for instance, in the fact/value divide.

Four-planar social being. Defined by the planes of (a) material transactions with nature, (b) inter-/intra-subjective relations, e.g. along the power, communicative and moral sub-dimensions of the social cube, (c) social relations sui generis, defining the level of social institutions, and (d) the stratification of the personality. The moral evolution of the species is to be regarded as unfinished.

Freedom. Degrees of freedom consist of agentive freedom, formal legal freedom, negative freedom from, positive freedom to, emancipation from specific constraints, autonomy, rational autonomy, universal human autonomy, wellbeing, flourishing, progressively dependent on the positive generalization of the concept of freedom to include needs and possibilities for development as rights.

Holistic causality. May be said to operate when a complex coheres in such a way that (a) the totality, i.e. the form or structure of the combination, causally codetermines the elements; and (b) the form and structure of the elements causally codetermine each other, and so causally codetermine the whole.

Identities. Constellational identity is the containment or co-inclusion of one thing within or by another. Dispositional identity is the identity of a thing with its changing causal powers. Rhythmic identity is the identity of a thing with the exercise of its changing causal powers. These identities constitute three kinds of ultimata.

Indexicalism. The assumption that only the present (and by extension, the here) exists. It inevitably leads back to irrealism about causality and existence, and thence to a punctualist solipsistic ego-present-centrism.

Internal relationality. An element A is internally related to B if B is a necessary condition for the existence of A, whether this relation is reciprocal/symmetrical or not.

Intra-action. Occurs among internally related elements in three basic modes: (1) existential constitution, in which one element is essential and intrinsic to another; (2) permeation, in which one element contains another; and (3) connection, in which one element is merely causally efficacious on the other.

Intransitive/transitive dimensions. The intransitive dimension is initially the domain of the objects of scientific knowledge; but the concept can be extended to take in anything existentially intransitive, whether known, knowable or not. The transfactuality of laws and socialization into science implies the distinction between the intransitive or ontological and the transitive or epistemological dimensions of science. This latter must logically be extended to include the whole material and cultural infrastructure of society.

Intrinsic/extrinsic aspect. The intrinsic aspect is the normative aspect of science, or, more generally, the intentional aspect of agency. It is constellationally contained, in the case of science, within the transitive dimension; more macroscopically, within the extrinsic or causal aspect of agency. So the category of causality, for instance, constellationally includes, but is not exhausted by, that of rationality.

Judgement form. Has four aspects — expressive veracious; fiduciary; descriptive; and evidential — all of which are universalizable, and has a theoretico-practical duality built into it.

[Metaphysical] λ clause. An escape clause that every axiologically, transcendentally and/or dialectically refutable metaphysical system requires as a safety net, reflecting the posture of weak actualism.

Levels. A key concept for distinguishing strata of ontological depth, levels of discursive analysis (e.g. talking about from talking within), layers of emergence and superstructuration.

Materialism. Epistemological materialism asserts the independent existence and transfactual activity of at least some of the objects of scientific thought. That is to say, it is equivalent to transcendental realism. Ontological materialism asserts the unilateral dependence of social upon biological (and more generally physical) being and the emergence of the former from the latter. It is thus consistent with the emergent powers materialist orientation defended here, which is in turn consistent with the possibility of dual and multiple control. Practical materialism asserts the constitutive role of human transformative agency in the reproduction and transformation of social forms. This makes it congruent with the transformational model of social activity — providing we understand both in the negatively generalized way of Chapter 5.

Mediation. If A achieves C via B, then B may be said to mediate their relation.

[Ontological] monovalence. A purely positive account of reality. Fatally flawed by the transcendental deduction of the necessity for real negation or absence, it acts ideologically to screen the epistemological and ontological contingency of being and to sequester existential questions generally, as ontological actualism sequesters 'essential' ones. The result is the doubly dogmatically reinforced positivization of knowledge, and eternalization of the status quo.

Negation. Has a process/product homonomy and a fourfold polysemy (see Absence). Real negation is consistent with distanciation without transformation; transformative negation is consistent with exogenous sources of change; and radical negation is consistent with multiple determination within a totality. Therefore we have the theorem; real negation ≥ transformative negation ≥ radical negation ≥ linear negation. I argue that negation is a condition for positive being and hence knowledge.

Negativity. Conveys better than negation simpliciter the processual aspect of absence. It also incorporates the other primary sense of negativity in dialectic besides absent being: ill-being. These are united in the dialectic of freedom outlined in Chapter 7.

Open systems. Systems in which constant conjunctions of events do not occur, so laws cannot be regarded as empirical regularities or actual qua universal-and-necessarily-certain generalizations of instances. If the openness of systems entails the falsity of actualism, the openness of the future entails the falsity of endism, blockism and historicism (in Popper's sense); while the depth openness of nature entails the falsity of cognitive triumphalism.

Perspectival switch. The switch from one transcendentally or dialectically necessary condition or aspect of a phenomenon, thing or totality to another which is also transcendentally or dialectically necessary for it.

Power$_1$ – Power$_2$. Power$_1$ is the transformative capacity intrinsic to the concept of action as such, whereas power$_2$ is the capacity to get one's way against either the overt wishes and/or the real interests of others in virtue of structures of exploitation, domination, subjugation and control, i.e. generalized master – slave-type relations. Around such relations hermeneutic and other more material (but still conceptualized) hegemonic/counter-hegemonic struggles may be waged.

Primal squeeze. The squeeze between the domains of metaphysics (cf. the speculative illusion) and the a priori, and those of experience (cf. the positivistic illusion) and the a posteriori ruling out empirically controlled scientific theory and natural necessity alike.

Primary polyadization. Necessary for individuation, and hence self-identity. It operates as transcendental refutations of any monism, including solipsism, and of straightforward dialectics of a Schillerian type, presupposing a unitary origin prior to the moment of diremption and self-alienation.

Punctualism. An atomistic concept of space-time, refuted by the distanciated spatio-temporality necessary for time-consciousness and more generally any non-contiguous (or even contiguous) causality.

Realism/Irrealism. Realism in philosophy asserts the existence of some disputed entity; irrealism denies it. Thus one can be a realist about causal laws and an irrealist about God. Generally in *Plato Etc.* irrealism is taken to include anthropism, actualism, monovalence, extensionalism, de-agentification and spatio-temporal and moral irrealism. Most hitherto existing dialectics, like analytics, have been irrealist (under the dominance of analytic irrealism). I argue that realism, like ontology, is inexorable.

Referential detachment. The detachment of the act of reference from that to which it refers. This establishes at once its existential intransitivity and the possibility of another reference to it, a condition of any intelligible discourse at all. Referential detachment is implicit in all language-use and conceptualized praxis, e.g. playing football. There are no a priori limits on what can be referred to — this is the generalized concept of reference and referent.

Reflexivity. The inwardized form of totality. It is necessary for accountability and the monitoring of intentional causal agency. The concept of a meta-reflexively totalizing situation can explain how knowledge is possible without erasure.

Reification. To be turned into a thing, as in the commodification of labour-power, closely connected with fetishism, to be invested with magical powers, as in the animation of the commodity, especially in the form of money. In philosophy, it occurs in physicalistic reductionism, where it is often accompanied by — in the tacit complicity of contraries — dualistic disembodiment (e.g. in discourse theory, denaturalized hermeneutics). In epistemology the reification of facts, accompanied by the fetishism of conjunctions, implies and is implied by the hypostatization of ideas.

Relativism. Epistemic, like spatio-temporal, relativity must be accepted and foundationalism rejected. It is quite consistent with judgemental rationalism in the intrinsic aspect and ontological realism in the intransitive dimension of science. Epistemic relativism must be distinguished from judgemental relativism, into which non-foundationalist irrealism tends to fall.

Rhythmic. Tensed spatializing process consisting in the exercise of the causal efficacy of a structure or a thing; which, as such, may have supervenient causal powers of its own. Symbolic of the tri-unity of space, time and causality in dialectics.

Scepticism. In Hegel, the denial or denegation of reality, including, as I generalize it, power$_2$ relations. Its real basis is alienation or generative separation. It is the archetypal figure for theory/practice inconsistency — e.g. in Hegel's case between those who make and those who understand history. Generally philosophy is inherently aporetic and, as a disciplinary matrix, typically takes the form of a theory problem-field solution set.

Social cube. Highlights the differentiation and dislocation within four-planar social being.

Spatio-temporality. Spatio-temporality has a fivefold character as (a) a referential grid, (b) a measure, (c) a set of prima facie mutual exclusion relations, (d) a potentially emergent property, perhaps with causal powers of its own, and (e) a generally entropic process. Spatio-temporalities may be emergent either as new relata of an existing system of material things or as relata of a new system of material things. Spatio-temporalities may be multiple, elongated, disjoint, intersecting, overlapping, contradictory, etc. As a process, causality is typically intrinsically both spatialized and tensed. But both the disembedding and emergence of space from time and vice versa are possible and instantiated in our world.

Structure. Science reveals levels of structure which are knowable in the dialectic described in Chapter 2. Its essential movement is given by that from manifest phenomena to generative explanatory structure, which may eventually be empirically identified or otherwise detected, e.g. via its causal powers to effect perceivable phenomena. The structure of a thing is constituted by its causal powers, which, when exercised, manifest themselves as tendencies. A structure will typically be instantiated in a multiplicity of structurata.

Tendency. In open systems laws must be analysed as tendencies, which may be possessed without being exercised, and exercised without being actualized. Corresponding to the distinction between intrinsic and extrinsic and between stimulus and releasing conditions, a variety of different concepts of tendency can be built up. And the same exercise can be repeated in respect of the other moments of the causal chain.

Tina formation. Theories and practices which violate axiological necessities require defence mechanisms, including λ escape clauses, supporting connections which may function as Derridean supplements, and assume the form of a compromise — a Tina formation — as a necessary accommodation to reality.

Totality. Totalities are systems of internal relations (q.v.), which may assume various forms of intra-activity (q.v.) and operate via holistic causality. Sub-totalities are separated by blocks, but most totalities of concern to science, at least macroscopically, are *partial* as well, displaying external in addition to internal and contingent besides necessary connections. Absenting an essential element or component of a thing effects detotalization.

Transcendental. Transcendental realism asserts the independent existence and transfactual efficacy of structures and efficacious things. Transcendental arguments are species of retroductive-explanatory arguments (familiar to science), in which the premises embody some categorical necessity. Transcendental detachment is from the premises of a transcendental argument to a focus on the implications of its conclusion(s), or, dialectically, of its metacritical presuppositions.

Transdiction. Transdiction is inference from the observed to the unobserved. It includes induction and transduction, retroduction and retrodiction. The aporiai of the transdictive complex are generated by the absence of a concept of natural necessity and, more especially, that of alethic truth.

Transfactuality. The exercise of the causal powers of structure, that is, the working of a generative mechanism, e.g. as manifest in the operation of all the natural laws known to science, must be interpreted as applying transfactually, that is to say, in closed and open systems alike. Other critical realists have used concepts such as transphenomenality and trans-situationality to highlight this necessity. The result of not interpreting laws transfactually is that the normic statements with which they are expressed are immediately falsified in open systems, and practical science is left without any epistemic credentials.

Transformational model of social activity (TMSA). Articulates relationships between social structure and human agency. Dialectic requires its negative generalization so that structures can persist in virtue of our present inaction, having been generated in virtue of the practices of the dead. Process here appears as the mediator between structure and agency. The generalization of TMSA situates the tensed dislocated dialectics of structure and agency, as well as correcting a one-sided emphasis on particular kinds of transformation/work/care/forbearance, while still avoiding the errors of reification and voluntarism.

Unhappy Consciousness. Scepticism, or theory/practice inconsistency, or more generally categorial error aware of itself, seeking refuge, in the case of reality, in asceticism or other-worldliness and, in respect of power$_2$ relations, in, for example, introjective identification with the master's ideology or projective absorption in a fantasy world made for slaves. If Stoicism typically corresponds to 1M, and Scepticism to 2E, the Unhappy Consciousness reflects detotalization at 3L, and may further manifest itself in dualistic disembodiment and/or reductionist reification at 4D. In this book philosophy is argued to be a veritable citadel of the Unhappy Consciousness.

Unholy trinity. The trio constituted by the epistemic fallacy, ontological monovalence and primal squeeze. As the epistemic fallacy, mediated by actualism, determines primal squeeze, the trinity can be seen as a function of a couple. Moreover as ontological monovalence, taken literally, entails the exclusion of alterity (primeval monism) as a perspectival switch on absence, it must be regarded as the primordial failing of western philosophy.

Unity-in-diversity. For a human totality to be genuine it must represent the concrete singularity, and particular differentiations of each individual. The ultimate basis of unity is given by our shared species-being or common humanity and social relationality; and in practice, by our subjugation to the effects of the same or similar sets of oppressive power$_2$ relations.

Index